ElasticSearch Server

Create a fast, scalable, and flexible search solution with the emerging open source search server, ElasticSearch

Rafał Kuć

Marek Rogoziński

BIRMINGHAM - MUMBAI

ElasticSearch Server

First published: February 2013

Production Reference: 1110213

Published by Packt Publishing Ltd.
Livery Place
35 Livery Street
Birmingham B3 2PB, UK.

ISBN 978-1-84951-844-4

www.packtpub.com

Cover Image by Neha Rajappan (neha.rajappan1@gmail.com)

Credits

About the Authors

Rafał Kuć is a born team leader and software developer. He currently works as a consultant and a software engineer at Sematext Group, Inc., where he concentrates on open source technologies such as Apache Lucene and Solr, ElasticSearch, and Hadoop stack. He has more than 11 years of experience in various software branches, from banking software to e-commerce products. He focuses mainly on Java but is open to every tool and programming language that will make the achievement of his goal easier and faster. Rafał is also one of the founders of the `solr.pl` site where he tries to share his knowledge and help people with their problems with Solr and Lucene. He is also a speaker for various conferences around the world, such as Lucene Eurocon, Berlin Buzzwords, and ApacheCon.

Rafał began his journey with Lucene in 2002, and it wasn't exactly love at first sight. When he came back to Lucene in late 2003, he revised his thoughts about the framework and saw the potential in search technologies. Then Solr came along and that was it. He started working with ElasticSearch in the middle of 2010. Currently, Lucene, Solr, ElasticSearch, and information retrieval are his main points of interest.

Rafał is also the author of *Apache Solr 3.1 Cookbook* and the update to it — *Apache Solr 4 Cookbook* — published by *Packt Publishing*.

Acknowledgement

The book you are holding was a new experience for me although it is not the first book I've written. When we started working on it, we thought that we would be able to write about all the functionalities we wanted, but we couldn't have imagined how big ElasticSearch is and how much time it would take to write about it. Finally, we had to choose the topics and hopefully we've chosen wisely and you'll find this book helpful in your work. When I described a single functionality, I tried to write about it like I would like to read about it myself, so I hope that you'll find those descriptions helpful and interesting.

Although I would go the same way if I went back in time, the time of writing this book was not easy for my family, especially because this was not the only book I was working on at the time. *Apache Solr 4 Cookbook* was also being updated at the same time. The ones that suffered from this the most were my wife, Agnes, and our two lovely kids—our son, Philip, and daughter, Susanna. Without their patience and understanding, writing this book wouldn't have been possible. I would also like to thank my parents and Agnes' parents for their support and help.

I would like to thank all the people involved in creating, developing, and maintaining the ElasticSearch and Lucene projects for their work and passion. Without them this book couldn't have been written.

Finally, a big thanks to all the reviewers on this book. Their in-depth comments and insights have made this book better, at least from my point of view.

Once again, thank you all!

Marek Rogoziński is a software architect and consultant with more than 10 years of experience. His specialization concerns solutions based on open source projects such as Solr and ElasticSearch.

He is also the co-funder of the `solr.pl` site, publishing information and tutorials about the Solr and Lucene library.

He currently holds the position of Chief Technology Officer in Smartupz, the vendor of the Discourse™ social collaboration software.

Acknowledgement

Writing this book was hard work but also a great opportunity to try something new. Looking at more and more pages being created with time, I realized how rich ElasticSearch is and how difficult it is to fit the description of its features within the page limit. I hope that topics that finally made it to the book are the most important and interesting ones.

The biggest thank-you goes to all the people involved in the development of Lucene and ElasticSearch. Great work!

I would like to thank also the team working on this book. I am impressed how smoothly and quickly we passed through all the organizational stuff. Special thanks to the reviewers for a long list of comments and suggestions.

Last but not the least, thanks to all my friends, both those who persuaded me to write a book and those to whom it will be a complete surprise.

About the Reviewers

Ravindra Bharathi has worked in the software industry for over a decade in various domains such as education, digital media marketing/advertising, enterprise search, and energy management systems. He has a keen interest in search-based applications that involve data visualization, mashups, and dashboards. He blogs at http://ravindrabharathi.blogspot.com.

Matthew Lee Hinman currently develops distributed archiving software for high availability and cloud-based systems written in both Clojure and Java. He enjoys contributing to open source software and spending time hiking outdoors.

Marcelo Ochoa works at the System Laboratory of Facultad de Ciencias Exactas of the Universidad Nacional del Centro de la Provincia de Buenos Aires, and is the CTO at Scotas.com, a company specialized in near real-time search solutions using Apache Solr and Oracle. He divides his time between University jobs and external projects related to Oracle and big data technologies. He has worked in several Oracle-related projects such as translation of Oracle manuals and multimedia CBTs. His background is in database, network, web, and Java technologies. In the XML world, he is known as the developer of the DB Generator for the Apache Cocoon project, the open source projects DBPrism and DBPrism CMS, the Lucene-Oracle integration using Oracle JVM Directory implementation, and in the Restlet.org project, the Oracle XDB Restlet Adapter (an alternative to writing native REST web services inside the database-resident JVM).

Since 2006, he has been part of the Oracle ACE program. Oracle ACEs are known for their strong credentials as Oracle community enthusiasts and advocates, with candidates nominated by ACEs in the Oracle Technology and Applications communities.

He is the author of *Chapter 17* of the book *Oracle Database Programming using Java and Web Services*, *Kuassi Mensah*, *Digital Press* and *Chapter 21* of the book *Professional XML Databases*, *Kevin Williams*, *Wrox Press*.

www.PacktPub.com

Support files, eBooks, discount offers and more

You might want to visit www.PacktPub.com for support files and downloads related to your book.

Did you know that Packt offers eBook versions of every book published, with PDF and ePub files available? You can upgrade to the eBook version at www.PacktPub.com and as a print book customer, you are entitled to a discount on the eBook copy. Get in touch with us at service@packtpub.com for more details.

At www.PacktPub.com, you can also read a collection of free technical articles, sign up for a range of free newsletters and receive exclusive discounts and offers on Packt books and eBooks.

http://PacktLib.PacktPub.com

Do you need instant solutions to your IT questions? PacktLib is Packt's online digital book library. Here, you can access, read, and search across Packt's entire library of books.

Why Subscribe?

- Fully searchable across every book published by Packt
- Copy and paste, print and bookmark content
- On demand and accessible via web browser

Free Access for Packt account holders

If you have an account with Packt at www.PacktPub.com, you can use this to access PacktLib today and view nine entirely free books. Simply use your login credentials for immediate access.

Table of Contents

Preface

Welcome to the *ElasticSearch Server* book. While reading this book, you will be taken on a journey to the wonderful world of full-text search provided by ElasticSearch enterprise search server. We will start with a general introduction to ElasticSearch, which covers how to start and run ElasticSearch and how to configure it using both configuration files and the REST API. You will also learn how to create your index structure and tell ElasticSearch about it, how to configure different analyses for fields, and how to use the built-in data types.

This book will also discuss the query language, the so-called Query DSL, that allows you to create complicated queries and filter returned results. In addition to all that, you'll see how you can use faceting to calculate aggregated data based on the results returned by your queries. We will implement the autocomplete functionality together and will learn how to use ElasticSearch's spatial capabilities and how to use prospective search.

Finally, this book will show you some capabilities of the ElasticSearch administration API, with features such as shard placement control, cluster handling, and more. In addition to all that, you'll learn how to overcome some common problems that can come up on your journey with ElasticSearch server.

What this book covers

Chapter 1, Getting Started with ElasticSearch Cluster, covers ElasticSearch installation and configuration, REST API usage, mapping configuration, routing, and index aliasing.

Chapter 2, Searching Your Data, discusses Query DSL—basic and compound queries, filtering, result sorting, and using scripts.

Chapter 3, Extending Your Structure and Search, explains how to index data that is not flat, how to handle highlighting and autocomplete, and how to extend your index with things such as time to live, source, and so on.

Chapter 4, Make Your Search Better, covers how to influence your scoring, how to use synonyms, and how to handle multilingual data. In addition to that, it describes how to use position-aware queries and check why your document was matched.

Chapter 5, Combining Indexing, Analysis, and Search, shows you how to index tree-like structures, use nested objects, handle parent-child relationships, modify your live index structure, fetch data from external systems, and speed up your indexing by using batch processing.

Chapter 6, Beyond Searching, is dedicated to faceting, "more like this", and the prospective search functionality.

Chapter 7, Administrating Your Cluster, is concentrated on the cluster administration API and cluster monitoring. In this chapter you'll also find information about external plugin installation.

Chapter 8, Dealing with Problems, will guide you through fetching large results sets efficiently, controlling cluster rebalancing, validating your queries, and using warm-up queries.

What you need for this book

This book was written using ElasticSearch server 0.20.0, and all the examples and functions should work with it. In addition to that, you'll need a command that allows sending HTTP requests such as `curl`, which is available for most operating systems. Please note that all examples in this book use the mentioned `curl` tool. If you want to use another tool, please remember to format the request in an appropriate way that is understood by the tool of your choice.

In addition to that, some chapters may require additional software, such as ElasticSearch plugins or MongoDB NoSQL database, but when needed this is explicitly mentioned.

Who this book is for

If you are a beginner to the work of full-text search and ElasticSearch server, this book is especially for you. You will be guided through the basics of ElasticSearch, and you will learn how to use some of the advanced functionalities.

If you know ElasticSearch and have worked with it, you may find this book interesting as it provides a good overview of all the functionalities with examples and descriptions. However, you may encounter sections that you already know about.

If you know the Apache Solr search engine, this book can also be used to compare some functionalities of Apache Solr and ElasticSearch. This may help you judge which tool is more appropriate for your use case.

If you know all the details about ElasticSearch and know how each of the configuration parameters works, this is definitely not the book you are looking for!

Conventions

In this book, you will find a number of styles of text that distinguish between different kinds of information. Here are some examples of these styles, and an explanation of their meaning.

Code words in text are shown as follows: "The `indices` object contains information about `library` and `map` indices. The `primaries` object contains information about all primary shards allocated on the current node."

A block of code is set as follows:

```
"store" : {
 "size" : "7.6kb",
 "size_in_bytes" : 7867,
 "throttle_time" : "0s",
 "throttle_time_in_millis" : 0
}
```

When we wish to draw your attention to a particular part of a code block, the relevant lines or items are set in bold:

```
public class HashCodeSortScript extends AbstractSearchScript {
   private String field = "name";

   public HashCodeSortScript(Map<String, Object> params)
```

Any command-line input or output is written as follows:

```
curl -XPOST 'localhost:9200/_cluster/reroute' -d '{
 "commands" : [
 {"move" : {"index" : "shop", "shard" : 1, "from_node" : "es_node_one",
"to_node" : "es_node_two"}},
 {"cancel" : {"index" : "shop", "shard" : 0, "node" : "es_node_one"}}
```

New terms and **important words** are shown in bold.

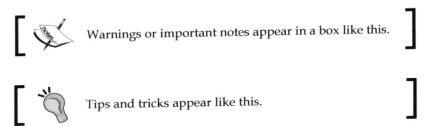

[Warnings or important notes appear in a box like this.]

[Tips and tricks appear like this.]

Reader feedback

Feedback from our readers is always welcome. Let us know what you think about this book—what you liked or may have disliked. Reader feedback is important for us to develop titles that you really get the most out of.

To send us general feedback, simply send an e-mail to feedback@packtpub.com, and mention the book title through the subject of your message.

If there is a topic that you have expertise in and you are interested in either writing or contributing to a book, see our author guide on www.packtpub.com/authors.

Customer support

Now that you are the proud owner of a Packt book, we have a number of things to help you to get the most from your purchase.

Downloading the example code

You can download the example code files for all Packt books you have purchased from your account at http://www.packtpub.com. If you purchased this book elsewhere, you can visit http://www.packtpub.com/support and register to have the files e-mailed directly to you.

Errata

Although we have taken every care to ensure the accuracy of our content, mistakes do happen. If you find a mistake in one of our books—maybe a mistake in the text or the code—we would be grateful if you would report this to us. By doing so, you can save other readers from frustration and help us improve subsequent versions of this book. If you find any errata, please report them by visiting http://www.packtpub.com/submit-errata, selecting your book, clicking on the **errata submission form** link, and entering the details of your errata. Once your errata are verified, your submission will be accepted and the errata will be uploaded to our website, or added to any list of existing errata, under the Errata section of that title.

Piracy

Piracy of copyright material on the Internet is an ongoing problem across all media. At Packt, we take the protection of our copyright and licenses very seriously. If you come across any illegal copies of our works, in any form, on the Internet, please provide us with the location address or website name immediately so that we can pursue a remedy.

Please contact us at copyright@packtpub.com with a link to the suspected pirated material.

We appreciate your help in protecting our authors, and our ability to bring you valuable content.

Questions

You can contact us at questions@packtpub.com if you are having a problem with any aspect of the book, and we will do our best to address it.

1
Getting Started with ElasticSearch Cluster

The first thing we need to do with ElasticSearch is install it. As with many applications, you start with the installation and configuration, usually forgetting about the importance of those steps until something bad happens. In this chapter we will focus quite extensively on this part of ElasticSearch. Be advised that this chapter is not a definitive guide to every configuration option and parameter. Of course, we would like to describe them all, but if we did that we would have to write a book that is twice (or even more) the size of the one you are holding in your hands! In addition to that, ElasticSearch is like all the other software applications available today — it evolves every day and keeps changing. We will cover only what we feel is commonly required, as well as specific functionalities that are sometimes hard to understand or those that are so wide that having them described in a single place would save you some time. By the end of this chapter, you will have learned the following:

- The basic concepts of ElasticSearch
- How to install and configure your Cluster
- Using the ElasticSearch REST API
- How to create an index
- How to configure your mappings
- How to use dynamic mappings
- What a template is and how to use it
- What routing is and how to use it
- How to use index aliasing

What is ElasticSearch?

ElasticSearch is an open source search server project started by Shay Banon and published in February 2010. The project grew into a major player in the field of search solutions. Additionally, due to its distributed nature and real-time abilities, many people use it as a document database. Let's go through the basic concepts of ElasticSearch.

Index

An **index** is the place where ElasticSearch stores data. If you come from the relational database world, you can think of an index like a table. But in contrast to a relational database, the table values stored in an index are prepared for fast and efficient full-text searching and in particular, do not have to store the original values. If you know MongoDB, you can think of the ElasticSearch index as being like a collection in MongoDB; and if you are familiar with CouchDB you can think about an index as you would about the CouchDB database.

Document

The main entity stored in ElasticSearch is a document. In an analogy to relational databases, a **document** is a row of data in a database table. Comparing an ElasticSearch document to a MongoDB one, both can have different structures, but the one in ElasticSearch needs to have the same types for common fields.

Documents consist of fields (row columns), but each field may occur several times and such a field is called **multivalued**. Each field has a type (text, number, date, and so on). Field types can also be complex—a field can contain other subdocuments or arrays. The field type is important for ElasticSearch—it gives the search engine information about how various operations such as comparison or sorting should be performed. Fortunately, this can be determined automatically. Unlike relational databases, documents don't need to have a fixed structure; every document may have a different set of fields and in addition to that, the fields don't have to be known during application development. Of course, one can force a document structure with the use of schema.

Document type

In ElasticSearch, one index can store many objects with different purposes. For example, a blog application can store articles and comments. Document type lets us easily differentiate these objects. It is worth noting that practically every document can have a different structure; but in real operations, dividing it into types significantly helps in data manipulation. Of course, one needs to keep the limitations in mind. One such limitation is that the different document types can't set different types for the same property.

Node and cluster

ElasticSearch can work as a standalone, single-search server. Nevertheless, to be able to process large sets of data and to achieve fault tolerance, ElasticSearch can be run on many cooperating servers. Collectively, these servers are called a **cluster** and each of them is called a **node**. Large amounts of data can be split across many nodes via index sharding (splitting it into smaller individual parts). Better availability and performance are achieved through the replicas (copies of index parts).

Shard

When we have a large number of documents, we can come to a point where a single node is not enough because of the RAM limitations, hard disk capacity, and so on. The other problem is that the desired functionality is so complicated that the server computing power is not sufficient. In such cases, the data can be divided into smaller parts called **shards**, where each shard is a separate Apache Lucene index. Each shard can be placed on a different server and thus your data can be spread among the clusters. When you query an index that is built from multiple shards, ElasticSearch sends the query to each relevant shard and merges the result in a transparent way so that your application doesn't need to know about shards.

Replica

In order to increase query throughput or achieve high availability, shard replicas can be used. The primary shard is used as the place where operations that change the index are directed. A replica is just an exact copy of the primary shard and each shard can have zero or more replicas. When the primary shard is lost (for example, the server holding the shard data is unavailable), a cluster can promote a replica to be the new primary shard.

Installing and configuring your cluster

The first step is to make sure that a Java SE environment is installed properly. ElasticSearch requires Version 6 or later, which can be downloaded from the following location: `http://www.oracle.com/technetwork/java/javase/downloads/index.html`. You can also use OpenJDK if you wish.

To install ElasticSearch, just download it from `http://www.elasticsearch.org/download/` and unpack it. Choose the lastest stable version. That's it! The installation is complete.

 During the writing of this book we used Version 0.20.0.

The main interface to communicate with ElasticSearch is based on an HTTP protocol and REST. This means that you can even use a web browser for some basic queries and requests; but for anything more sophisticated, you'll need to use additional software, such as the cURL command. If you use the Linux or OS X command, the `curl` package should already be available. In case you're using Windows, you can download it from `http://curl.haxx.se/download.html`.

Directory structure

Let's now go to the newly created directory. We can see the following directory structure:

Directory	Description
bin	The scripts needed for running ElasticSearch instances and for plugin management
config	The directory where the configuration files are located
lib	The libraries used by ElasticSearch

After ElasticSearch starts, it will create the following directories (if they don't exist):

Directory	Description
data	Where all the data used by ElasticSearch is stored
logs	Files with information about events and errors that occur during the running of an instance
plugins	The location for storing the installed plugins
work	Temporary files

Configuring ElasticSearch

One of the reasons—but of course, not the only one—that ElasticSearch is gaining more and more attention is because getting started with ElasticSearch is quite easy. Because of the reasonable default values and automatics for simple environments, we can skip the configuration and go straight to the next chapter without changing a single line in our configuration files. However, in order to truly understand ElasticSearch, it is worth understanding some of the available settings.

The whole configuration is located in the `config` directory. We can see two files there: `elasticsearch.yml` (or `elasticsearch.json`, which will be used if present) and `logging.yml`. The first file is responsible for setting the default configuration values for the server. This is important because some of these values can be changed at runtime and be kept as a part of the cluster state, so the values in this file may not be accurate. We will show you how to check the accurate configuration in *Chapter 8, Dealing with Problems*. The two values that we cannot change at runtime are `cluster.name` and `node.name`.

The `cluster.name` property is responsible for holding the name of our cluster. The cluster name separates different clusters from each other. Nodes configured with the same name will try to form a cluster.

The second value is the instance name. We can leave this parameter undefined. In this case, ElasticSearch automatically chooses a unique name for itself. Note that this name is chosen during every startup, so the name can be different on each restart. Defining the name can help when referring to concrete instances by API or when using monitoring tools to see what is happening to a node during long periods of time and between restarts. If you don't provide a name, ElasticSearch will automatically choose one randomly—so you can have different names given to the same node on each restart. Think about giving descriptive names to your nodes. Other parameters are well commented in the file, so we advise you to look through it; do not worry if you do not understand the explanation. We hope that everything will become clear after reading the next few chapters.

The second file (`logging.yml`) defines how much information is written to the system logs, defines the log files, and creates new files periodically. Changes in this file are necessary only when you need to adapt to monitoring or back up solutions, or during system debugging.

Let's leave the configuration files for now. An important part of configuration is tuning your operating system. During the indexing, especially when you have many shards and replicas, ElasticSearch will create several files; so the system cannot limit the open file descriptors to less than 32,000. For Linux servers, this can usually be changed in `/etc/security/limits.conf` and the current value can be displayed using the `ulimit` command.

The next settings are connected to the memory limit for a single instance. The default values (`1024MB`) may not be sufficient. If you spot entries with `OutOfMemoryError` in a log file, set the environment variable `ES_HEAP_SIZE` to a value greater than `1024`. Note that this value shouldn't be set to more than 50 percent of the total physical memory available—the rest can be used as disk cache and it greatly increases the search performance.

Running ElasticSearch

Let's run our first instance. Go to the `bin` directory and run the following command from the command line:

```
./elasticsearch -f (Linux or OS X)
elasticsearch.bat -f (Windows)
```

The `-f` option tells ElasticSearch that the program should not be detached from the console and should be run in the foreground. This allows us to see the diagnostic messages generated by the program and stop it by pressing *Ctrl + C*. The other option is `-p`, which tells ElasticSearch that the identifier of the process should be written to the file pointed by this parameter. This can be executed by using additional monitoring software or admin scripts.

Congratulations, we now have our ElasticSearch instance up and running! During its work, a server usually uses two port numbers: one for communication with the REST API by using the HTTP protocol and the second one for the transport module used for communication in a cluster. The default port for the HTTP API is 9200, so we can check the search readiness by pointing a web browser at `http://127.0.0.1:9200/`. The browser should show a code snippet similar to the following:

Downloading the example code

You can download the example code files for all Packt books you have purchased from your account at `http://www.packtpub.com`. If you purchased this book elsewhere, you can visit `http://www.packtpub.com/support` and register to have the files e-mailed directly to you.

```
{
    "ok" : true,
    "status" : 200,
    "name" : "Donald Pierce",
    "version" : {
        "number" : "0.20.0"
    },
    "tagline" : "You Know, for Search"
}
```

The output is structured as a **JSON (JavaScript Object Notation)** object. We will use this notation in more complex requests too. If you are not familiar with JSON, please take a minute and read the article available at http://en.wikipedia.org/wiki/JSON.

>
> Note that ElasticSearch is smart. If the default port is not available, the engine binds to the next free port. You can find information about this on the console, during booting:
>
> ```
> [2012-09-02 22:45:17,101][INFO ][http] [Red Lotus] bound_
> address {inet[/0:0:0:0:0:0:0:0%0:9200]}, publish_address
> {inet[/192.168.1.101:9200]}
> ```
>
> Note the fragment with [http]. ElasticSearch uses a few ports for various tasks. The interface that we are using is handled by the HTTP module.

Now we will use the cURL program. For example, our query can be executed as follows:

```
curl -XGET http://127.0.0.1:9200/_cluster/health?pretty
```

The -X parameter is a request method. The default value is GET (so, in this example, we can omit this parameter). Do not worry about the GET value for now, we will describe it in more detail later in this chapter.

Note the ?pretty parameter. As a standard, the API returns information in a JSON object in which the new line signs are omitted. This parameter forces ElasticSearch to add a new line character to the response, making the response more human-friendly. You can try running the preceding query with and without the ?pretty parameter to see the difference.

ElasticSearch is useful in small and medium-sized applications, but it is built with large installations in mind. So now we will set up our big, two-node cluster. Unpack the ElasticSearch archive in a different directory and run the second instance. If we look into the log, we see something similar to the following:

```
[2012-09-09 11:23:05,604][INFO ][cluster.service          ]
[Orbit] detected_master [Bova][fo2dHTS3TlWKlJiDnQOKAg]
[inet[/192.168.1.101:9300]], added {[Bova][fo2dHTS3TlWKlJiDnQOKAg]
[inet[/192.168.1.101:9300]],}, reason: zen-disco-receive(from master
[[Bova][fo2dHTS3TlWKlJiDnQOKAg][inet[/192.168.1.101:9300]]])
```

This means that our second instance (named `Orbit`) found the previously running instance (named `Bova`). ElasticSearch automatically formed a new, two-node cluster.

Shutting down ElasticSearch

Even though we expect our cluster (or node) to run flawlessly for a lifetime, we may end up needing to restart it or shut it down properly (for example, for maintenance). There are three ways in which we can shut down ElasticSearch:

- If your node is attached to the console (run with the `-f` option), just press *Ctrl + C*
- The second option is to kill the server process by sending the TERM signal (see the kill command on the Linux boxes and program manager on Windows)
- The third method is to use a REST API

We will focus on the last method now. It allows us to shut down the whole cluster by executing the following command:

```
curl -XPOST http://localhost:9200/_cluster/nodes/_shutdown
```

To shut down just a single node, execute the following command:

```
curl -XPOST http://localhost:9200/_cluster/nodes/BlrmMvBdSKiCeYGsiHijdg/_shutdown
```

In the previous command line, `BlrmMvBdSKiCeYGsiHijdg` is the identifier for a given node. The former may be read from ElasticSearch logs or from another API call:

```
curl -XGET http://localhost:9200/_cluster/nodes/
```

Running ElasticSearch as a system service

Running an instance in the foreground using the -f option is comfortable for testing or development. In the real world, an instance should be managed by the operating system tools; it should start automatically during system boot and close correctly when the system is shut down. This is simple when using a system like Linux Debian. ElasticSearch has the deb archive available with all the necessary scripts. If you don't use the deb archive, you can always use the ElasticSearch service wrapper (https://github.com/elasticsearch/elasticsearch-servicewrapper), which provides all the needed startup scripts.

Data manipulation with REST API

ElasticSearch REST API can be used for various tasks. Thanks to it, we can manage indexes, change instance parameters, check nodes and cluster status, index data, and search it. But for now, we will concentrate on using the **CRUD (create-retrieve-update-delete)** part of the API, which allows us to use ElasticSearch in a similar way to how you would use a NoSQL database.

What is REST?

Before moving on to a description of various operations, a few words about REST itself. In a REST-like architecture, every request is directed to a concrete object indicated by the path part of the address. For example, if /books/ is a reference to a list of books in our library, /books/1 is a reference to the book with the identifier 1. Note that these objects can be nested. /books/1/chapter/6 is the sixth chapter in the first book in the library, and so on. We have the subject of our API call. What about an operation that we would like to execute, such as GET or POST? To indicate that, request types are used. An HTTP protocol gives us quite a long list of request types to use as verbs in the API calls. Logical choices are GET in order to obtain the current state of the requested object, POST for changing the object state, PUT for object creation, and DELETE for destroying an object. There is also a HEAD request that is only used for fetching the base information about an object.

If we look at the examples of the operations discussed in the Shutting down ElasticSearch section, everything should make more sense:

- `GET http://localhost:9000/`: Retrieves information about an instance as a whole
- `GET http://localhost:9200/_cluster/nodes/`: Retrieves information about the nodes in an ElasticSearch cluster
- `POST http://localhost:9200/_cluster/nodes/_shutdown`: Sends information to shut down an object in the nodes in a cluster of ElasticSearch

Now we will check how these operations can be used to store, fetch, alter, and delete data from ElasticSearch.

Storing data in ElasticSearch

In ElasticSearch, every piece of data has a defined index and type. You can think about an index as a collection of documents or a table in a database. In contrast to database records, documents added to an index have no defined structure and field types. More precisely, a single field has its type defined, but ElasticSearch can do some magic and guess the corresponding type.

Creating a new document

Now we will try to index some documents. For our example, let's imagine that we are building some kind of CMS for our blog. One of the entities in this blog is (surprise!) articles. Using the JSON notation, a document can be presented as shown in the following example:

```
{
  "id": "1",
  "title": "New version of Elastic Search released!",
  "content": "…",
  "priority": 10,
  "tags": ["announce", "elasticsearch", "release"]
}
```

As we can see, the JSON document contains a set of fields, where each field can have a different form. In our example, we have a number (`priority`), text (`title`), and an array of strings (`tags`). In the next examples, we will show you the other types. As mentioned earlier in this chapter, ElasticSearch can guess these type (because JSON is semi-typed; that is, the numbers are not in quotation marks) and automatically customize the way of storing this data in its internal structures.

Now we want to store this record in the index and make it available for searching. Choosing the index name as `blog` and type as `article`, we can do this by executing the following command:

```
curl -XPUT http://localhost:9200/blog/article/1 -d '{"title": "New
version of Elastic Search released!", "content": "...", "tags":
["announce", "elasticsearch", "release"] }'
```

You can notice a new option to cURL, `-d`. The parameter value of this option is the text that should be used as a request payload—a request body. This way we can send additional information such as a document definition.

Note that the unique identifier is placed in the URL, not in the body. If you omit this identifier, the search returns an error, similar to the following:

```
No handler found for uri [/blog/article/] and method [PUT]
```

If everything is correct, the server will answer with a JSON response similar to this:

```
{
  "ok":true,
  "_index":"blog",
  "_type":"article",
  "_id":"1",
  "_version":1
}
```

In the preceding reply, ElasticSearch includes information about the status of the operation and shows where the new document was placed. There is information about the document's unique identifier and current version, which will be incremented automatically by ElasticSearch every time the document changes.

In the above example, we've specified the document identifier ourselves. But ElasticSearch can generate this automatically. This seems very handy, but only when an index is the only source of data. If we use a database for storing data and ElasticSearch for full text searching, synchronization of this data will be hindered unless the generated identifier is stored in the database as well. Generation of a unique key can be achieved by using the following command:

```
curl -XPOST http://localhost:9200/blog/article/ -d '{"title": "New
version of Elastic Search released!", "content": "...", "tags":
["announce", "elasticsearch", "release"] }'
```

Notice POST instead of PUT. Referring to the previous description of the REST verbs, we wanted to change the list of documents in an index rather than create a new entity, and that's why we used POST instead of PUT. The server should respond with a response similar to the following:

```
{
  "ok" : true,
  "_index" : "blog",
  "_type" : "article",
  "_id" : "XQmdeSe_RVamFgRHMqcZQg",
  "_version" : 1
}
```

Note the highlighted line, which has an automatically generated unique identifier.

Retrieving documents

We already have documents stored in our instance. Now let's try to retrieve them:

```
curl -XGET http://localhost:9200/blog/article/1
```

Then the server returns the following response:

```
{
  "_index" : "blog",
  "_type" : "article",
  "_id" : "1",
  "_version" : 1,
  "exists" : true,
  "_source" : {
  "title": "New version of Elastic Search released!",
  "content": "...",
  "tags": ["announce", "elasticsearch", "release"]
}
```

In the response, besides index, type, identifier, and version, we also see the information saying that the document was found and the source of this document. If the document is not found, we get a reply as follows:

```
{
  "_index" : "blog",
  "_type" : "article",
  "_id" : "9999",
  "exists" : false
}
```

Of course, there is no information about the version and source.

Updating documents

Updating documents in an index is a more complicated task. Internally, ElasticSearch must fetch the document, take its data from the _source field, remove the old document, apply changes, and index it as a new document. ElasticSearch implements this through a script given as a parameter. This allows us to do more sophisticated document transformation than simple field changes. Let's see how it works in a simple case.

After executing the following command:

```
curl -XPOST http://localhost:9200/blog/article/1/_update -d '{
  "script": "ctx._source.content = \"new content\""
}'
```

The server replies with the following:

```
{"ok":true,"_index":"blog","_type":"article","_id":"1","_version":2}
```

It works! To be sure, let's retrieve the current document:

```
curl -XGET http://localhost:9200/blog/article/1


{
   "_index" : "blog",
   "_type" : "article",
   "_id" : "1",
   "_version" : 2,
   "exists" : true,
   "_source" : {
   "title":"New version of Elastic Search released!",
   "content":"new content",
   "tags":["announce","elasticsearch","release"]}
}
```

The server changed the contents of our article and the version number for this document. Notice that we didn't have to send the whole document, only the changed parts. But remember that to use the update functionality, we need to use the _source field—we will describe how to use the _source field in the *Extending your index structure with additional internal information* section in *Chapter 3, Extending Your Structure and Search*.

There is one more thing about document updates—if your script uses a field value from a document that is to be updated, you can set a value that will be used if the document doesn't have that value present. For example, if you would like to increment the counter field of the document and it is not present, you can use the upsert section in your request to provide the default value that is going to be used. For example:

```
curl -XPOST http://localhost:9200/blog/article/1/_update -d '{
  "script": "ctx._source.counter += 1",
  "upsert": {
    "counter" : 0
  }
}'
```

In the preceding example, if the document we are updating doesn't have a value in the counter field, the value of 0 will be used.

Deleting documents

We have already seen how to create (PUT) and retrieve (GET) documents. A document can be removed in the similar way but the only difference is in the verb used. Let's execute the following delete command:

```
curl -XDELETE http://localhost:9200/blog/article/1
{"ok":true,"found":true,"_index":"blog","_type":"article","_id":"1","_version":3}
```

Now we are able to use the CRUD operations. This lets us create applications using ElasticSearch as a simple key-value store. But this is only the beginning!

Manual index creation and mappings configuration

So, we have our ElasticSearch cluster up and running and we also know how to use ElasticSearch REST API to index our data, delete it, and retrieve it, although we still don't know the specifics. If you are used to SQL databases, you might know that before you can start putting the data there, you need to create a structure, which will describe what your data looks like. Although ElasticSearch is a schema-less search engine and can figure out the data structure on the fly, we think that controlling the structure and thus defining it ourselves is a better way. In the following few pages, you'll see how to create new indexes (and how to delete them) and how to create mappings that suit your needs and match your data structure.

Please note that we didn't include all the information about the available types in this chapter and some features of ElasticSearch (such as nested type, parent-child handling, geographical points storing, and search) are described in the following chapters of this book.

Index

An index is a logical structure in ElasticSearch that holds your data. You can imagine it as a database table that has rows and columns. A row is a document we index and a column is a single field in the index. Your ElasticSearch cluster can have many indexes inside it running at the same time. But that's not all. Because a single index is made of shards, it can be scattered across multiple nodes in a single cluster. In addition to that, each shard can have a replica — which is an exact copy of a shard — and is used to throttle search performance as well as for data duplication in case of failures.

All the shards that an index is made up of are, in fact, Apache Lucene indexes, which are divided into types.

Types

In ElasticSearch, a single index can have multiple types of documents indexed — for example, you can store blog posts and blog users inside the same index, but with completely different structures using types.

Index manipulation

As we mentioned earlier, although ElasticSearch can do some operations for us, we would like to create the index ourselves. For the purpose of this chapter, we'll use the index named posts to index the blog posts from our blogging platform. Without any more hesitation, we will send the following command to create an index:

```
curl -XPOST 'http://localhost:9200/posts'
```

We just told ElasticSearch that is installed on our local machine that we want to create the posts index. If everything goes right, you should see the following response from ElasticSearch:

```
{"ok":true,"acknowledged":true}
```

But there is a problem; we forgot to provide the mappings, which are responsible for describing the index structure. What can we do? Because we have no data at all, we'll go for the simplest approach — we will just delete the index. To do that, we run a command similar to the preceding one, but instead of using the POST HTTP method, we use DELETE. So the actual command is as follows:

```
curl -XDELETE 'http://localhost:9200/posts'
```

And the response is very similar to what we got earlier:

```
{"ok":true,"acknowledged":true}
```

So now that we know what an index is, how to create it, and how to delete it, let's define the index structure.

Schema mapping

The schema mapping — or in short mappings — are used to define the index structure. As you recall, each index can have multiple types; but we will concentrate on a single type for now. We want to index blog posts that can have the following structure:

- Unique identifier
- Name
- Publication date
- Contents

So far, so good right? We decided that we want to store our posts in the posts index and so we we'll define the post type to do that. In ElasticSearch, mappings are sent as JSON objects in a file. So, let's create a mappings file that will match the previously mentioned needs — we will call it posts.json. Its contents are as follows:

```
{
  "mappings": {
    "post": {
      "properties": {
        "id": {"type":"long", "store":"yes",
        "precision_step":"0" },
        "name": {"type":"string", "store":"yes",
        "index":"analyzed" },
        "published": {"type":"date", "store":"yes",
        "precision_step":"0" },
```

```
        "contents": {"type":"string", "store":"no",
        "index":"analyzed" }
      }
    }
  }
}
```

And now to create our `posts` index with the preceding file, we need to run the following command:

```
curl -XPOST 'http://localhost:9200/posts' -d @posts.json
```

`@posts.json` allows us to tell the cURL command that we want to send the contents of the `posts.json` file.

 Please note that you can store your mappings and use a file named however you want.

And again, if everything goes well, we see the following response:

```
{"ok":true,"acknowledged":true}
```

We have our index structure and we can index our data, but we will take a pause now; we don't really know what the contents of the `posts.json` file mean. So let's discuss some details about this file.

Type definition

As you can see, the contents of the `posts.json` file are JSON objects and because of that, it starts and ends with curly brackets (if you want to learn more about JSON, please visit `http://www.json.org/`). All the type definitions inside the mentioned file are nested in the `mappings` object. Inside the `mappings` JSON object there can be multiple types defined. In our example, we have a single `post` type. But for example, if you would also like to include the `user` type, the file would look as follows:

```
{
  "mappings": {
    "post": {
      "properties": {
        "id": { "type":"long", "store":"yes",
        "precision_step":"0" },
        "name": { "type":"string", "store":"yes",
        "index":"analyzed" },
        "published": { "type":"date", "store":"yes",
        "precision_step":"0" },
```

```
      "contents": { "type":"string", "store":"no",
      "index":"analyzed" }
    }
  },
  "user": {
    "properties": {
      "id": { "type":"long", "store":"yes",
      "precision_step":"0" },
      "name": { "type":"string", "store":"yes",
      "index":"analyzed" }
    }
  }
}
}
```

You can see that each type is a JSON object and those are separated from each other by a comma character—like typical JSON structured data.

Fields

Each type is defined by a set of properties—fields that are nested inside the `properties` object. So let's concentrate on a single field now, for example, the `name` field, whose definition is as follows:

```
"contents": { "type":"string", "store":"yes", "index":"analyzed" }
```

So it starts with the name of the field, which is `contents` in the preceding case. After the name of the field, we have an object defining the behavior of the field. Attributes are specific to the types of fields we are using and we will discuss them in the next section. Of course, if you have multiple fields for a single type (which is what we usually have), remember to separate them with a comma character.

Core types

Each field type can be specified to a specific core type provided by ElasticSearch. The core types in ElasticSearch are as follows:

- String
- Number
- Date
- Boolean
- Binary

So now, let's discuss each of the core types available in ElasticSearch and the attributes it provides to define their behavior.

Common attributes

Before continuing with all the core type descriptions I would like to discuss some common attributes that you can use to describe all the types (except for the binary one).

- index_name: This is the name of the field that will be stored in the index. If this is not defined, the name will be set to the name of the object that the field is defined with. You'll usually omit this property.

- index: This can take the values analyzed and no. For the string-based fields, it can also be set to not_analyzed. If set to analyzed, the field will be indexed and thus searchable. If set to no, you won't be able to search such a field. The default value is analyzed. In the case of the string-based fields, there is an additional option—not_analyzed, which says that the field should be indexed but not processed by the analyzer. So, it is written in the index as it was sent to ElasticSearch and only the perfect match will be counted during a search.

- store: This can take the values yes and no, and it specifies if the original value of the field should be written into the index. The default value is no, which means that you can't return that field in the results (although if you use the _source field, you can return the value even if it is not stored), but if you have it indexed you still can search on it.

- boost: The default value of this attribute is 1. Basically, it defines how important the field is inside the document; the higher the boost, the more important are the values in the field.

- null_value: This attribute specifies a value that should be written into the index if that field is not a part of an indexed document. The default behavior will just omit that field.

- include_in_all: This attribute specifies if the field should be included in the _all field. By default, if the _all field is used, all the fields will be included in it. The _all field will be described in more detail in *Chapter 3, Extending Your Structure and Search*.

String

String is the most basic text type, which allows us to store one or more characters inside it. A sample definition of such a field can be as follows:

```
"contents" : { "type" : "string", "store" : "no", "index" : "analyzed" }
```

In addition to the common attributes, the following ones can also be set for string-based fields:

- `term_vector`: This can take the values `no` (the default one), `yes`, `with_offsets`, `with_positions`, or `with_positions_offsets`. It defines whether the Lucene term vectors should be calculated for that field or not. If you are using highlighting, you will need to calculate term vectors.

- `omit_norms`: This can take the value `true` or `false`. The default value is `false`. When this attribute is set to `true`, it disables the Lucene norms calculation for that field (and thus you can't use index-time boosting).

- `omit_term_freq_and_positions`: This can take the value `true` or `false`. The default value is `false`. Set this attribute to `true`, if you want to omit term frequency and position calculation during indexing. (Deprecated since ElasticSearch 0.20).

- `index_options`: This allows to set indexing options. The possible values are `docs` which affects in number of documents for terms to be indexed, freqs which results in indexing number of documents for terms and term frequencies and positions which results in the previously mentioned two and term positions. The default value is `freqs`. (Available since ElasticSearch 0.20.)

- `analyzer`: This is the name of the analyzer used for indexing and searching. It defaults to the globally defined analyzer name.

- `index_analyzer`: This is the name of the analyzer used for indexing.

- `search_analyzer`: This is the name of the analyzer used for processing the part of the query string that is sent to that field.

- `ignore_above`: This is the maximum size of the field. The rest of the fields beyond the specified value characters will be ignored. This attribute is useful if we are only interested in the first N characters of the field.

Number

This is the core type that gathers all the numeric field types available to be used. The following types are available in ElasticSearch:

- `byte`: A byte value; for example, 1
- `short`: A short value; for example, 12
- `integer`: An integer value; for example, 134
- `long`: A long value; for example, 12345
- `float`: A float value; for example, 12.23
- `double`: A double value, for example, 12.23

A sample definition of a field based on one of the numeric types can be as follows:

```
"price" : { "type" : "float", "store" : "yes", "precision_step" : "4"
}
```

In addition to the common attributes, the following ones can also be set for the numeric fields:

- `precision_step`: This is the number of terms generated for each value in a field. The lower the value, the higher the number of terms generated, resulting in faster range queries (but a higher index size). The default value is 4.

- `ignore_malformed`: This can take the value `true` or `false`. The default value is `false`. It should be set to `true` in order to omit badly formatted values.

Date

This core type is designed to be used for date indexing. It follows a specific format that can be changed and is stored in UTC by default.

The default date format understood by ElasticSearch is quite universal and allows us to specify the date and optionally the time; for example, `2012-12-24T12:10:22`. A sample definition of a field based on the date type can be as follows:

```
"published" : { "type" : "date", "store" : "yes", "format" : "YYYY-mm-
dd" }
```

A sample document that uses the preceding field can be as follows:

```
{
   "name" : "Sample document",
   "published" : "2012-12-22"
}
```

In addition to the common attributes, the following ones can also be set for the date type- based fields:

- `format`: This specifies the format of the date. The default value is `dateOptionalTime`. For a full list of formats, please visit `http://www.elasticsearch.org/guide/reference/mapping/date-format.html`.

- `precision_step`: This specifies the number of terms generated for each value in that field. The lower the value, the higher is the number of terms generated, resulting in faster range queries (but a higher index size). The default value is 4.

- `ignore_malformed`: This can can take the value `true` or `false`. The default value is `false`. It should be set to `true` in order to omit badly formatted values.

Boolean

This is the core type that is designed to be used for indexing. The Boolean values can be `true` or `false`. A sample definition of a field based on the Boolean type can be as follows:

```
"allowed" : { "type" : "boolean" }
```

Binary

The binary field is a BASE64 representation of the binary data stored in the index. You can use it to store data that is normally written in binary form, like images. Fields based on this type are, by default, stored and not indexed. The binary type only supports the `index_name` property. A sample field definition based on the binary field looks like the following:

```
"image" : { "type" : "binary" }
```

Multi fields

Sometimes you would like to have the same field values in two fields—for example, one for searching and one for faceting. There is a special type in ElasticSearch—`multi_field`—that allows us to map several core types into a single field and have them analyzed differently. For example, if we would like to calculate faceting and search on our name field, we could define the following `multi_field`:

```
"name": {
  "type": "multi_field",
  "fields": {
    "name": { "type" : "string", "index": "analyzed" },
    "facet": { "type" : "string", "index": "not_analyzed" }
  }
}
```

The preceding definition will create two fields, one that we could just refer to as `name` and the second one that we would use as `name.facet`. Of course, you don't have to specify two separate fields during indexing, a single one named `name` is enough and ElasticSearch will do the rest.

Using analyzers

As we mentioned during the mappings for the fields based on the string type, we can specify the analyzer used. But what is an analyzer? It's a functionality that is used to analyze data or queries in a way we want them to be indexed or searched — for example, when we divide words on the basis of whitespaces and lowercase characters, we don't have to worry about users sending words in lower- or uppercases. ElasticSearch allows us to use different analyzers for index time and during query time, so we can choose how we want our data to be processed in each stage of the search. To use one of the analyzers, we just need to specify its name to the correct property of the field and that's all!

Out-of-the-box analyzers

ElasticSearch allows us to use one of the many analyzers defined by default. The following analyzers are available out of the box:

- `standard`: A standard analyzer that is convenient for most European languages (please refer to `http://www.elasticsearch.org/guide/reference/index-modules/analysis/standard-analyzer.html` for the full list of parameters).

- `simple`: An analyzer that splits the provided value on non-letter characters and converts letters to lowercase.

- `whitespace`: An analyzer that splits the provided value on the basis of whitespace characters.

- `stop`: This is similar to a simple analyzer; but in addition to the simple analyzer functionality, it filters the data on the provided stop words set (please refer to `http://www.elasticsearch.org/guide/reference/index-modules/analysis/stop-analyzer.html` for the full list of parameters).

- `keyword`: This is a very simple analyzer that just passes the provided value. You'll achieve the same by specifying that field as `not_analyzed`.

- `pattern`: This is an analyzer that allows flexible text separation by the use of regular expressions (please refer to `http://www.elasticsearch.org/guide/reference/index-modules/analysis/pattern-analyzer.html` for the full list of parameters).

- `language`: This is an analyzer that is designed to work with a specific language. The full list of languages supported by this analyzer can be found at `http://www.elasticsearch.org/guide/reference/index-modules/analysis/lang-analyzer.html`.

- `snowball`: Ths is an analyzer similar to the standard one, but in addition, it provides a stemming algorithm (please refer to `http://www.elasticsearch.org/guide/reference/index-modules/analysis/snowball-analyzer.html` for the full list of parameters).

Defining your own analyzers

In addition to the analyzers mentioned previously, ElasticSearch allows us to define new ones. In order to do that, we need to add an additional section to our mappings file, the `settings` section, which holds the required information for ElasticSearch during index creation. This is how we define our custom `settings` section:

```
"settings" : {
  "index" : {
    "analysis": {
      "analyzer": {
        "en": {
          "tokenizer": "standard",
          "filter": [
            "asciifolding",
            "lowercase",
            "ourEnglishFilter"
          ]
        }
      },
      "filter": {
        "ourEnglishFilter": {
          "type": "kstem"
        }
      }
    }
  }
}
```

As you can see, we specified that we want a new analyzer named `en` to be present. Each analyzer is built from a single tokenizer and multiple filters. A complete list of default filters and tokenizers can be found at http://www.elasticsearch.org/guide/reference/index-modules/analysis/. As you can see, our `en` analyzer includes the standard tokenizer and three filters: `asciifolding` and `lowercase`—which are available by default—and the `ourEnglishFilter`, which is a filter that we have defined.

To define a filter, we need to provide its name, its type (the `type` property), and a number of additional parameters required by that filter type. The full list of filter types available in ElasticSearch can be found at http://www.elasticsearch.org/guide/reference/index-modules/analysis/. That list is changing constantly, so I'll skip commenting on it.

So, the mappings with the analyzer defined would be as follows:

```
{
  "settings" : {
    "index" : {
      "analysis": {
        "analyzer": {
          "en": {
            "tokenizer": "standard",
            "filter": [
             "asciifolding",
             "lowercase",
             "ourEnglishFilter"
            ]
          }
        },
        "filter": {
          "ourEnglishFilter": {
            "type": "kstem"
          }
        }
      }
    }
  },
  "mappings" : {
    "post" : {
      "properties" : {
        "id": { "type" : "long", "store" : "yes",
        "precision_step" : "0" },
        "name": { "type" : "string", "store" : "yes", "index" :
        "analyzed", "analyzer": "en" }
      }
    }
  }
}
```

Analyzer fields

An analyzer field (_analyzer) allows us to specify a field value that will be used as the analyzer name for the document to which the field belongs. Imagine that you have some software running that detects the language the document is written in and you store that information in the language field in the document. Additionally, you would like to use that information to choose the right analyzer. To do that, just add the following to your mappings file:

```
  "_analyzer" : {
    "path" : "language"
}
```

So the whole mappings file could be as follows:

```
{
  "mappings" : {
    "post" : {
      "_analyzer" : {
        "path" : "language"
      },
      "properties" : {
        "id": { "type" : "long", "store" : "yes",
        "precision_step" : "0" },
        "name": { "type" : "string", "store" : "yes",
        "index" : "analyzed" },
        "language": { "type" : "string", "store" : "yes",
        "index" : "not_analyzed"}
      }
    }
  }
}
```

However, please be advised that there has to be an analyzer defined with the same name as the value provided in the language field.

Default analyzers

There is one more thing we should say about analyzers — the ability to specify the one that should be used by default if no analyzer is defined. This is done in the same way as configuring a custom analyzer in the settings section of the mappings file, but instead of specifying a custom name for the analyzer, the default keyword should be used. So to make our previously defined analyzer default, we can change the en analyzer to the following:

```
{
  "settings" : {
    "index" : {
      "analysis": {
        "analyzer": {
          "default": {
            "tokenizer": "standard",
            "filter": [
              "asciifolding",
              "lowercase",
              "ourEnglishFilter"
```

```
        ]
      }
    },
    "filter": {
      "ourEnglishFilter": {
        "type": "kstem"
      }
    }

  }
}
```

Storing a document source

Sometimes, you may not want to store separate fields; instead, you may want to store the whole input JSON document. In fact, ElasticSearch does that by default. If you want to change that behavior and do not want to include the source of the document, you need to disable the _source field. This is as easy as adding the following part to our type definition:

```
"_source" : {
  "enabled" : false
}
```

So the whole mappings file would be as follows:

```
{
  "mappings": {
    "post": {
      "_source": {
        "enabled": false
      },
      "properties": {
        "id": {"type":"long", "store":"yes",
        "precision_step":"0" },
        "name": {"type":"string", "store":"yes",
        "index":"analyzed" },
        "published": {"type":"date", "store":"yes",
        "precision_step":"0" },
        "contents": {"type":"string", "store":"no",
        "index":"analyzed" }
      }
    }
  }
}
```

All field

Sometimes, it's handy to have some of the fields copied into one; instead of searching multiple fields, a general purpose field will be used for searching—for example, when you don't know which fields to search on. By default, ElasticSearch will include the values from all the text fields into the _all field. On the other hand, you may want to disable such behavior. To do that we should add the following part to our type definition:

```
"_all" : {
  "enabled" : false
}
```

So the whole mappings file would look like the following:

```
{
  "mappings": {
    "post": {
      "_all": {
        "enabled": false
      },
      "properties": {
        "id": {"type":"long", "store":"yes",
        "precision_step":"0" },
        "name": {"type":"string", "store":"yes",
        "index":"analyzed" },
        "published": {"type":"date", "store":"yes",
        "precision_step":"0" },
        "contents": {"type":"string", "store":"no",
        "index":"analyzed" }
      }
    }
  }
}
```

However, please remember that the _all field will increase the size of the index, so it should be disabled if not needed.

Dynamic mappings and templates

The previous topic described how we can define type mapping if the mapping generated automatically by ElasticSearch is not sufficient. Now let's go one step back and see how automatic mapping works. Knowledge about this prevents surprises during development of your applications and let's you build more flexible software. In this second case, if sometimes our application grows and automatically generates new indexes (for example, for storing a massive number of time-based events), it is more convenient to adjust the mechanism of determining the data types. Also, if an application has many indexes, the possibility of defining the mapping templates is very handy.

Type determining mechanism

ElasticSearch can guess the document structure by looking at the JSON, which defines the document. In JSON, strings are surrounded by quotation marks, Booleans are defined using specific words and numbers are just a few digits. This is a simple trick, but it usually works. For the following document:

```
{
  "field1": 10,
  "field2": "10"
}
```

field1 will be guessed as a long type, but field2 will be determined as a string. The other numeric types are guessed similarly. Of course, this can be a desired behavior, but sometimes the data source may omit the type information and everything may be presented as strings. The solution to this is enabling more aggressive text checking in the mapping definition. For example, we may do the following during index creation:

```
curl -XPUT http://localhost:9200/blog/?pretty -d '{
  "mappings" : {
    "article": {
      "numeric_detection" : true
    }
  }
}'
```

Unfortunately, this problem is also true for the Boolean type and there is no option to force guessing Boolean types from the text. In such cases, when a change of source format is impossible, we can only define the field directly in the mappings definition.

Another type that causes trouble is date. ElasticSearch tries to guess the dates given as timestamps or strings that match the date format. Fortunately, a list of recognized formats can be defined as follows:

```
curl -XPUT http://localhost:9200/blog/?pretty -d '{
  "mappings" : {
    "article" : {
      "dynamic_date_formats" : ["yyyy-MM-dd hh:mm"]
    }
  }
}
```

As in the previous example, the preceding command shows the mappings definition during index creation. Analogically, this works in the PUT mapping API call of ElasticSearch. The format of the data definition is determined by the ones used in the joda-time library (visit http://joda-time.sourceforge.net/api-release/ org/joda/time/format/DateTimeFormat.html). As you can see, this allows you to adapt to almost any format that can be used in the input document. Note that dynamic_date_format is an array. This means that we can handle several date formats simultaneously.

Now we know how ElasticSearch guesses what is in our document. The important information is that a server can guess that for any new document. Let's check this simple case of how it can deal with changes:

```
curl -XPUT localhost:9200/objects/obj1/1?pretty -d '{ "field1" : 254}'
```

Now we have a new index called objects with a single document in it—a document with only a single field. This is obviously a number, isn't it? So let's query ElasticSearch and retrieve the automatically generated mappings:

```
curl -XGET localhost:9200/objects/_mapping?pretty
```

And the reply is as follows:

```
{
  "objects" : {
    "obj1" : {
      "properties" : {
        "field1" : {
          "type" : "long",
          "ignore_malformed" : false
        }
      }
    }
  }
}
```

No surprise here, we got what we expected (more or less). Now let's try something different—the second document with the same field name, but another value:

```
curl -XPUT localhost:9200/objects/obj1/2?pretty -d '{
  "field1" : "one hundred and seven"
}'
```

And the reply is as follows:

```
{
    "error" : "MapperParsingException[Failed to parse [field1]];
    nested: NumberFormatException[For input string:
    \"one hundred and seven\"]; ",
    "status" : 400
}
```

It doesn't work. ElasticSearch assumes the `field1` field as a number, and successive documents must fit into this assumption. To be sure, let's have one more try:

```
curl -XPUT localhost:9200/objects/obj1/2?pretty -d '{
  "field1" : 12.2
}'
```

Now that we have tried to index a document with a number, but a number of a different type, it succeeded. If we query for the mappings, we will notice that the type hasn't been changed. ElasticSearch silently changed our value and truncated the fractional part. It's not good, but this can happen when the input data is not so good (it usually isn't) and this is why we sometimes want to turn off automatic mapping generation. Another reason for turning it off is a situation when we don't want to add new fields to an existing index—fields that were not known during application development. To turn off automatic field adding, we can set the `dynamic` property to `false`, as follows:

```
{
    "objects" : {
      "obj1" : {
        "dynamic" : "false",
        "properties" : {
          ...
        }
      }
    }
}
```

Dynamic mappings

Sometimes we want to have the possibility of different type determination dependent on situations such as the field name and type defined in JSON. This is the situation in which dynamic templates can help. Dynamic templates are similar to the usual mappings. Each template has its pattern defined, which is applied to the document's field names. If a field matches the pattern, the template is used. The pattern can be defined in a few ways:

- `match`: The template is used if the name of the field matches the pattern.

- `unmatch`: The template is used if the name of the field doesn't match the pattern.

By default, the pattern is very simple and allows us to use the asterisk character. This can be changed by using `match_pattern=regexp`. After using this option, we can use all the magic provided by regular expressions.

There are variations such as `path_match` and `path_unmatch` that can be used to match the names in nested documents.

When writing a target field definition, the following variables can be used:

- `{name}`: The name of the original field found in the input document

- `{dynamic_type}`: The type determined from the original document

The last important bit of information is that ElasticSearch checks templates in order of their definitions and the first matching template is applied. This means that the most generic templates (for example, with `"match"`: `"*"`) should be defined at the end. Let's have a look at the following example:

```
{
  "mappings" : {
    "article" : {
      "dynamic_templates" : [
        {
          "template_test": {
            "match" : "*",
            "mapping" : {
              "type" : "multi_field",
              "fields" : {
                "{name}": { "type" : "{dynamic_type}"},
```

```
                    "str": {"type" : "string"}
                }
            }
        }
    }
  ]
}
}
}
```

In the preceding example, we defined a mapping for the `article` type. In this mapping, we have only one dynamic template named `template_test`. This template is applied for every field in the input document because of the single asterisk pattern. Each field will be treated as a `multi_field`, consisting of a field named as the original field (for example, `title`) and the second field with the same name as the original field, suffixed with `str` (for example, `title.str`). The first of the created fields will have its type determined by ElasticSearch (with the `{dynamic_type}` type) and the second field will be a string (because of the `string` type).

Templates

As we have seen earlier in this chapter, the index configuration, and mappings in particular, can be complicated beasts. It would be very nice if there was a possibility of defining one or more mappings once and then using them in every newly created index, without the need to send them every time. ElasticSearch's creators predicted this and included a feature called index templates. Each template defines a pattern, which is compared to the newly created index name. When both match, the values defined in the template are copied to the index structure definition. When multiple templates match with the newly created index name, all of them are applied and values from the later applied templates override those defined in the previously applied templates. This is very convenient, because we can define a few common settings in the more general templates and change them into more specialized ones. Additionally, there is an `order` parameter, which lets us force desired template ordering. You can think of templates as dynamic mappings, which can be applied not to the types in documents, but to the indexes.

Let's see a real example of a template. Imagine that we want to create several indexes where we don't want to store the source of the documents so that the indexes will be smaller. We also don't need any replicas. The templates can be created by calling ElasticSearch REST API and an example cURL command would be similar to the following:

```
curl -XPUT http://localhost:9200/_template/main_template?pretty -d '
{
  "template" : "*",
  "order" : 1,
  "settings" : {
    "index.number_of_replicas" : 0
  },
  "mappings" : {
    "_default_" : {
      "_source" : {
        "enabled" : false
      }
    }
  }
}'
```

From now on, all created indexes will have no replicas and no source stored. Note the _default_ type name in our example. This is a special type name indicating that the current rule should be applied to every document type. The second interesting thing is the order parameter. Lets define the next template with the following command:

```
curl -XPUT http://localhost:9200/_template/ha_template?pretty -d '
{
  "template" : "ha_*",
  "order" : 10,
  "settings" : {
    "index.number_of_replicas" : 5
  }
}'
```

All new indexes will behave as before except the ones with the names beginning with ha_. In this case, both the templates are applied. First, the template with the lower order is used and then, the next template overwrites the replicas setting. So, these indexes will have five replicas and disabled source storage.

There is one more important thing about this example. If we try to create a document with five replicas and we have only a single node in the cluster, it will probably fail after some time and display a message similar to the following:

```
{
  "error" : "UnavailableShardsException[[ha_blog][2] [6] shardIt,
  [1] active : Timeout waiting for [1m], request: index
  {[ha_blog][article][1], source[\n{\n  \"priority\" : 1,\n
  \"title\" : \"Test\"\n}]}]",
  "status" : 503
}
```

This is because ElasticSearch tries to create multiple copies of each of the shards of which the index is built, but this only makes sense when each of these copies can be placed on different server instances.

Storing templates in files

Templates can also be stored in files. By default, the files should be placed in the config/templates directory. For example, our ha_template should be placed in the config/templates/ha_template.json file and have the following contents:

```
{
  "ha_template" : {
    "template" : "ha_*",
    "order" : 10,
    "settings" : {
      "index.number_of_replicas" : 5
    }
  }
}
```

Note that the structure of the JSON is a little bit different and has the template name as the main object key. The second important thing is that the templates must be placed in every instance of ElasticSearch. Also, the templates defined in the files are not available with the REST API calls.

When routing does matter

In this section, we will discuss one of the most powerful control mechanisms that we have in our hands—routing. To be concise, it allows us to choose a shard that will be used to index or search data. It doesn't sound interesting, right? So, before continuing with some use cases I'll try to show you how the standard, distributed search and indexing works in ElasticSearch.

How does indexing work?

During an index operation, when you send a document for indexing, ElasticSearch looks at its identifier to choose the shard in which the document should be indexed. By default, ElasticSearch calculates the hash value of the document's identifier and on the basis of that, puts the document in one of the available primary shards. Then those documents are redistributed to replicas. The following diagram shows a simple illustration of how indexing works by default:

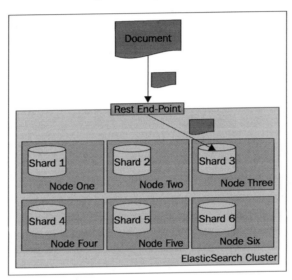

How does searching work?

Searching is a bit different from indexing, because in most situations you need to ask all the shards to get the data you are interested in. Imagine the situation when you have the following mappings describing your index:

```
{
  "mappings" : {
    "post" : {
      "properties" : {
        "id" : { "type" : "long", "store" : "yes",
        "precision_step" : "0" },
        "name" : { "type" : "string", "store" : "yes",
        "index" : "analyzed" },
```

```
        "contents" : { "type" : "string", "store" : "no",
        "index" : "analyzed" },
        "userId" : { "type" : "long", "store" : "yes",
        "precision_step" : "0" }
      }
    }
  }
}
```

As you can see, our index consists of four fields — the identifier (the id field), the name of the document (the name field), the contents of the document (the contents field), and the identifier of the user to which the documents belong (the userId field). To get all the documents for a particular user — one with userId equal to 12 — you can run the following query:

```
curl -XGET 'http://localhost:9200/posts/_search?q=userId:12'
```

The preceding request is run against the _search endpoint, which allows us to send queries to ElasticSearch. All the queries we send to ElasticSearch will be sent to that endpoint. The following diagram shows a simple illustration of how searching works by default:

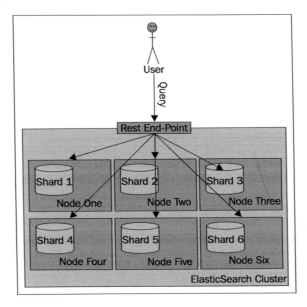

What if we could put all the documents for a single user into a single shard and query on that shard? Wouldn't that be performance wise? Yes, that is handy, and that is what routing allows you do to.

Routing

Routing can be used to control to which shard your documents and queries will be forwarded. As we have already mentioned, by default, ElasticSearch uses the value of the document's identifier to calculate the hash value, which is then used to place the document in a given shard. With such behavior, all the shards get a similar amount of data indexed and during search all those shards are queried. By now you would probably have guessed that in ElasticSearch you can specify the routing value both at index-time and during querying, and in fact if you decide to specify explicit routing values, you'll probably do that during both indexing and searching.

In our case, we would use the `userId` value to set routing during indexing and the same value during searching. You can imagine that for the same `userId` value, the same hash value will be calculated and thus all the documents for that particular user will be placed in the same shard. Using the same value during searching will result in searching a single shard instead of the whole index.

Please remember that when using routing, you should still add a filter for the same value as the routing one. This is because you'll probably have more distinct routing values than the number of shards of which your index will be built. Because of that, a few distinct values can point to the same shard; if you were to omit the filtering, you would get data not for a single value you route on, but for all those that reside in a particular shard. The following diagram shows a simple illustration of how searching works with a custom routing value provided:

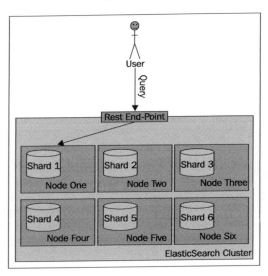

Now let's look at how we can specify the routing values.

Routing parameters

The simplest way (but not always the most convenient one) to provide routing values is to use the `routing` parameter. When indexing or querying, you should just add the `routing` parameter to your HTTP or set it by using the client library of your choice.

So, to index a sample document to the previously shown index, we would use the following command:

```
curl -XPUT 'http://localhost:9200/posts/post/1?routing=12' -d '{
  "id": "1",
  "name": "Test document",
  "contents": "Test document",
  "userId": "12"
}'
```

This is what our previous query would look like, if we were to add the `routing` parameter:

```
curl -XGET 'http://localhost:9200/posts/_search?routing=12&q=userId:12'
```

As you can see, the same routing value was used during indexing and querying. We did that because we knew that during indexing we have used the value `12`. We wanted to point our query to the same shard, therefore we used exactly the same value.

Please note that you can specify multiple routing values, which should be separated by comma characters. For example, if we want the preceding query to be additionally routed with the use of the `section` parameter (if such existed) and we also want to filter by this parameter, our query will look like the following:

```
curl -XGET 'http://localhost:9200/posts/_search?routing=12,6654&q=userId:
12+AND+section:6654'
```

Routing fields

Specifying the routing value with each request that we send to ElasticSearch works, but it is not convenient. In fact, ElasticSearch allows us to define a field whose value will be used as the routing value during indexing, so we only need to provide the `routing` parameter during querying. To do that, we need to add the following section to our type definition:

```
"_routing" : {
  "required" : true,
  "path" : "userId"
}
```

The preceding definition means that the routing value needs to be provided (the `"required":` `true` property); without it, an index request will fail. In addition to that we specified the `path` attribute, which decides which field value of the document will be used as the routing value. In our case, the `userId` field value will be used. These two parameters mean that each document we send for indexing needs to have the `userId` field defined. This is convenient, because we can now use batch indexing without the limitation of having all the documents from a single branch using the same routing value (which would be the case with the `routing` parameter). However, please remember that when using the routing field, ElasticSearch needs to do some additional parsing. Therefore, it's a bit slower than the use of the `routing` parameter.

After adding the routing part, the whole updated mappings file will be as follows:

```
{
  "mappings" : {
    "post" : {
      "_routing" : {
        "required" : true,
        "path" : "userId"
      },
      "properties" : {
        "id" : { "type" : "long", "store" : "yes",
        "precision_step" : "0" },
        "name" : { "type" : "string", "store" : "yes",
        "index" : "analyzed" },
        "contents" : { "type" : "string", "store" : "no",
        "index" : "analyzed" },
        "userId" : { "type" : "long", "store" : "yes",
        "precision_step" : "0" }
      }
    }
  }
}
```

Index aliasing and simplifying your everyday work using it

When working with multiple indexes in ElasticSearch, you can sometimes lose track of them. Imagine a situation where you store logs in your indexes. Usually, the number of log messages is quite large; therefore, it is a good solution to have the data divided somehow. A quite logical division of such data is obtained by creating a single index for a single day of logs (if you are interested in an open source solution for managing logs, look at Logstash—`http://logstash.net`). After a while, if we keep all the indexes, we start having problems in understanding which are the newest indexes, which ones should be used, which ones are from the last month, and maybe which data belongs to which client. With the help of aliases, we can change that to work with a single name, just as we would use a single index, but instead work with multiple indexes.

An alias

What is an index alias? It's an additional name for one or more indexes that allow(s) us to query indexes with the use of that name. A single alias can have multiple indexes as well as the other way around, a single index can be a part of multiple aliases.

However, please remember that you can't use an alias that has multiple indexes for indexing or real-time GET operations—ElasticSearch will throw an exception if you do that. We can still use an alias that links to only one single index for indexing though. This is because ElasticSearch doesn't know in which index the data should be indexed, or from which index the document should be fetched.

Creating an alias

To create an index alias, we need to run an HTTP POST method to the `_aliases` REST endpoint with an action defined. For example, the following request will create a new alias called `week12` that will have indexes named `day10`, `day11`, and `day12`:

```
curl -XPOST 'http://localhost:9200/_aliases' -d '{
  "actions" : [
    { "add" : { "index" : "day10", "alias" : "week12" } },
    { "add" : { "index" : "day11", "alias" : "week12" } },
    { "add" : { "index" : "day12", "alias" : "week12" } }
  ]
}'
```

If the alias `week12` isn't present in our ElasticSearch cluster, the preceding command will create it. If it is present, the command will just add the specified indexes to it.

If everything goes well, instead of running a search across three indexes as follows:

```
curl -XGET 'http://localhost:9200/day10,day11,day12/_search?q=test'
```

We can run it as follows:

```
curl -XGET 'http://localhost:9200/week12/_search?q=test'
```

Isn't that better?

Modifying aliases

Of course, you can also remove indexes from an alias. Doing that is similar to how we add indexes to an alias, but instead of the `add` command, we use the `remove` one. For example, to remove the index named `day9` from the `week12` index, we would run the following command:

```
curl -XPOST 'http://localhost:9200/_aliases' -d '{
 "actions" : [
    { "remove" : { "index" : "day9", "alias" : "week12" } }
 ]
}'
```

Combining commands

The `add` and `remove` commands can be sent as a single request. For example, if you want to combine all the previously sent commands into a single request, you will have to send the following command:

```
curl -XPOST 'http://localhost:9200/_aliases' -d '{
  "actions" : [
    { "add" : { "index" : "day10", "alias" : "week12" } },
    { "add" : { "index" : "day11", "alias" : "week12" } },
    { "add" : { "index" : "day12", "alias" : "week12" } },
    { "remove" : { "index" : "day9", "alias" : "week12" } }
  ]
}'
```

Retrieving all aliases

In addition to adding or removing indexes to or from aliases, the applications that use ElasticSearch may need to retrieve all the aliases available in the cluster or all the aliases an index is connected to. To retrieve these aliases, we send a request using an HTTP GET command. For example, the following command gets all the aliases for the day10 index and the second one will get all the available aliases:

```
curl -XGET 'localhost:9200/day10/_aliases'
curl -XGET 'localhost:9200/_aliases'
```

The response from the second command is as follows:

```
{
    "day10" : {
      "aliases" : {
        "week12" : { }
      }
    },
    "day11" : {
      "aliases" : {
        "week12" : { }
      }
    },
    "day12" : {
      "aliases" : {
        "week12" : { }
      }
    }
}
```

Filtering aliases

Aliases can be used in a similar way to how views are used in SQL databases. You can use full Query DSL (discussed in detail in the *Querying ElasticSearch* section in the next chapter) and have your query applied to all the count, search, delete by query, and more such operations. Let's look at an example. Imagine that we want to have aliases that return data for a certain client, so we can use it in our application. Let's say that the client identifier we are interested in is stored in the clientId field and we are interested in client 12345. So, let's create an alias named client with our data index, which will apply a filter for the clientId automatically:

```
curl -XPOST 'http://localhost:9200/_aliases' -d '{
  "actions" : [
  {
    "add" : {
      "index" : "data",
      "alias" : "client",
      "filter" : { "term" : { "clientId" : "12345" } }
    }
  } ]
}'
```

So, when using the preceding alias, you will always get your queries, counts, deletes by query, and more such queries filtered by a term query that ensures that all the documents have the 12345 value in the clientId field.

Aliases and routing

Similar to the aliases that use filtering, we can add routing values to the aliases. Imagine that we are using routing on the basis of user identifier and we want to use the same routing values with our aliases. For the alias named client, we will use the routing value of 12345,12346,12347 for indexing, and only 12345 for querying. So, we create an alias with the following command:

```
curl -XPOST 'http://localhost:9200/_aliases' -d '{
  "actions" : [
  {
    "add" : {
      "index" : "data",
      "alias" : "client",
      "index_routing" : "12345,12346,12347"
      "search_routing" : "12345"
    }
  } ]
}'
```

This way, when we index our data by using the client alias, the values specified by the index_routing property will be used, and during query time, the one specified by the search_routing property will be used.

If you run the following query with the preceding alias:

```
curl -XGET 'http://localhost:9200/client/_search?q=test&routi
ng=99999,12345'
```

The value used as a routing value will be 12345. This is because ElasticSearch will take the common values of the search_routing attribute and the query routing parameter, which in our case is 12345.

Summary

In this chapter, we've looked at how to install, configure, and start using the ElasticSearch server. We've also learned how to make use of the default mappings and templates feature of ElasticSearch. We also looked at some of the more advanced topics such as index aliasing and index- and query-time routing.

In the upcoming chapters, we will learn how to query ElasticSearch, what types of queries we can use, and how to filter the results of our queries.

2
Searching Your Data

In the previous chapter we installed and configured our cluster. We also prepared our mappings and indexed our data. We can now do the thing you first had in mind when you chose ElasticSearch, searching! In this chapter you will learn how to query ElasticSearch. Of course, you could say, "Hey, I can just run `curl -XGET 'http://localhost:9200/_search?q=first+query'` and get all the data I am interested in", and you would be right. However, ElasticSearch supports a wide variety of queries both simple and complicated. In this chapter we will start to get used to some of the search capabilities that ElasticSearch exposes. By the end of this chapter you will have learned:

- How to query ElasticSearch using its Query DSL
- How to use basic queries
- How to use compound queries
- How to filter your results and why it is important
- How to change the sorting of your results
- How to use scripts in ElasticSearch

Understanding the querying and indexing process

Before we see how to search for data, it would be good to understand how the documents and queries sent to ElasticSearch are processed. If you already know that, you can skip this part of the chapter.

In order to understand the querying and indexing process, you should understand the following concepts:

- **Indexing**: This is the process of preparing the document sent to ElasticSearch and storing it in the index.

- **Searching**: This is the process of matching the documents that satisfy the query requirements.

- **Analysis**: This is the process of preparing the content of a field and converting the content to terms that can be written into the Lucene index. During indexing, the data in the fields is divided into a stream of tokens (words) that are written into the index as terms (tokens with additional information such as position in the input text). The analysis process can consist of the following steps:

  - **Tokenization**: During this stage, the input text is turned into a token stream by the tokenizer.

  - **Filtering**: During this stage, zero or more filters can process tokens in the token stream. For example, the stopwords filter can remove irrelevant tokens from the stream, the synonyms filter can add new tokens or change existing ones, and the lowercase filter will make all tokens lowercase.

- **Analyzer**: This is a single tokenizer with zero or more filters. We can specify analyzers when working with fields, types, and queries.

It is worth mentioning that the analysis process we've just discussed is used during searching and indexing and both index-time analysis and query-time analysis can be configured differently. However, it is very important that the terms produced during index and query time match because, if they don't, you'll want to find your documents manually. For example, if you use stemming during indexing and you don't use stemming while searching, you'll have to pass the stemmed words in order to find your documents.

Mappings

If not stated otherwise, the following mappings will be used for the rest of the chapter:

```
{
  "book" : {
    "_index" : {
      "enabled" : true
    },
```

```
    "_id" : {
      "index": "not_analyzed",
      "store" : "yes"
    },
    "properties" : {
      "author" : {
        "type" : "string"
      },
      "characters" : {
        "type" : "string"
      },
      "copies" : {
        "type" : "long",
        "ignore_malformed" : false
      },
      "otitle" : {
        "type" : "string"
      },
      "tags" : {
        "type" : "string"
      },
      "title" : {
        "type" : "string"
      },
      "year" : {
        "type" : "long",
        "ignore_malformed" : false,
        "index" : "analyzed"
      },
      "available" : {
        "type" : "boolean",
        "index" : "analyzed"
      }
    }
  }
}
```

 Please note that the string-based fields will be analyzed if not stated otherwise.

The preceding mappings were used to create the library index. In order to run that, use the following commands (mappings were written into the mapping.json file):

```
curl -XPOST 'localhost:9200/library'
curl -XPUT 'localhost:9200/library/book/_mapping' -d @mapping.json
```

Data

If not stated otherwise, the following data will be used for the rest of the chapter:

```
{ "index": {"_index": "library", "_type": "book", "_id": "1"}}
{ "title": "All Quiet on the Western Front","otitle": "Im
Westen nichts Neues","author": "Erich Maria Remarque","year":
1929,"characters": ["Paul Bäumer", "Albert Kropp", "Haie Westhus",
"Fredrich Müller", "Stanislaus Katczinsky", "Tjaden"],"tags":
["novel"],"copies": 1, "available": true, "section" : 3}
{ "index": {"_index": "library", "_type": "book", "_id": "2"}}
{ "title": "Catch-22","author": "Joseph Heller","year":
1961,"characters": ["John Yossarian", "Captain Aardvark",
"Chaplain Tappman", "Colonel Cathcart", "Doctor Daneeka"],"tags":
["novel"],"copies": 6, "available" : false, "section" : 1}
{ "index": {"_index": "library", "_type": "book", "_id": "3"}}
{ "title": "The Complete Sherlock Holmes","author": "Arthur Conan
Doyle","year": 1936,"characters": ["Sherlock Holmes","Dr. Watson", "G.
Lestrade"],"tags": [],"copies": 0, "available" : false, "section" :
12}
{ "index": {"_index": "library", "_type": "book", "_id": "4"}}
{ "title": "Crime and Punishment","otitle": "Преступлéние и
наказáние","author": "Fyodor Dostoevsky","year": 1886,"characters":
["Raskolnikov", "Sofia Semyonovna Marmeladova"],"tags": [],"copies":
0, "available" : true}
```

We stored our data in the `documents.json` file, and we used the following command to index it:

```
curl -s -XPOST 'localhost:9200/_bulk' --data-binary @documents.json
```

This command runs bulk indexing. You can find more about it in the *Batch indexing to speed up your indexing process* section in *Chapter 5, Combining Indexing, Analysis, and Search.*

Querying ElasticSearch

Up to now, most of the times we talked to ElasticSearch with the REST API using an HTTP request, we were using JSON-structured data to do that, regardless of whether it was a mappings change, alias creation, or document indexation. A similar situation arises when we want to send more than a simple query to ElasticSearch—we structure it using JSON objects and send it to ElasticSearch. This is called **Query DSL**. In a broader view, ElasticSearch supports two kinds of queries, basic ones and compound ones. Basic queries such as the term query are used just for querying. We will cover these in the *Basic queries* section in this chapter. The second type of query is the compound query, such as the `bool` query, which can combine multiple queries. We will cover these in the *Compound queries* section in this chapter.

However, this is not the entirety of the picture. In addition to these two types of queries, your query can have **filter queries**, which are used to narrow your results with certain criteria.

To make it even more complicated, queries can contain other queries (don't worry, we will try to explain most of it!). Furthermore, some queries can contain filters, and others can contain both queries and filters. Although this is not everything, we will stick with this working explanation for now. We will go over this in detail in the *Compound queries* and *Filtering your results* sections in this chapter.

Simple query

The simplest way to query ElasticSearch is to use the URI request query. For example, if we wanted to search for the word "crime" in the title field, we would send a query like this one:

```
curl -XGET 'localhost:9200/library/book/_search?q=title:crime&pretty=true'
```

If we look from the ElasticSearch Query DSL point of view, the simplest query is the term query, which searches for the documents that have a given term (a word) in a given field. For example, if we wanted to search for the term "crime" (please remember that the term query is not analyzed, and thus, you need to provide the exact term you are searching for) in the title field, we would send the following query to ElasticSearch:

```
{
  "query" : {
   "term" : { "title" : "crime" }
  }
}
```

But, how do we query our data? We send the GET HTTP request to the _search REST end point, pointing to the index/type we want to search (of course, we can omit type, index, or both at the same time). So, if we wanted to search our example library index, we would use the following command:

```
curl -XGET 'localhost:9200/library/book/_search?pretty=true' -d '{
  "query" : {
   "term" : { "title" : "crime" }
  }
}'
```

As you can see, we used the request body (the -d switch) to send the whole JSON-structured query to ElasticSearch. The pretty=true request parameter tells ElasticSearch to structure the response in a way such that we humans can read it more easily. In response, we got the following text:

```
{
  "took" : 1,
  "timed_out" : false,
  "_shards" : {
    "total" : 5,
    "successful" : 5,
    "failed" : 0
  },
  "hits" : {
    "total" : 1,
    "max_score" : 0.19178301,
    "hits" : [ {
      "_index" : "library",
      "_type" : "book",
      "_id" : "4",
      "_score" : 0.19178301, "_source" : { "title": "Crime and
Punishment","otitle": "Преступлёние и наказáние","author": "Fyodor
Dostoevsky","year": 1886,"characters": ["Raskolnikov", "Sofia Semyonovna
Marmeladova"],"tags": [],"copies": 0, "available" : true}
    } ]
  }
}
```

As we said earlier, a query can be directed to a particular index and type, but this is not the only possibility. We can query several indices in parallel or query one index regardless of the type. Let's sum up the possible call types and see what the addressing looks like:

1. Request to index and type:

   ```
   curl -XGET 'localhost:9200/library/book/_search' -d @query.json
   ```

2. Request to index and all types in it:

   ```
   curl -XGET 'localhost:9200/library/_search' -d @query.json
   ```

3. Request to all indices:

   ```
   curl -XGET 'localhost:9200/_search' -d @query.json
   ```

4. Request to few indices:

```
curl -XGET 'localhost:9200/library,bookstore/_search' -d @query.
json
```

5. Request to multiple indices and multiple types in them:

```
curl -XGET 'localhost:9200/library,bookstore/book,recipes/_search'
-d @query.json
```

Neat! We got our first search results!

Paging and results size

As we would expect, ElasticSearch allows us to control how many results we want to get (at most) and from which result we want to start. There are two additional properties that can be set in the request body:

- `from`: This specifies from which document we want to have our results and defaults to `0`, which means we want our results from the first document
- `size`: This specifies the maximum number of documents we want as a result of a single query (defaults to `10`)

So, if we wanted our query to get documents starting from the tenth on the list and get 20 of them, we would send the following query:

```
{
 "from" :   9,
 "size" : 20,
 "query" : {
  "term" : { "title" : "crime" }
 }
}
```

Returning the version

In addition to all the information returned, ElasticSearch can return the version of the document. To do that, we need to add the `version` property with the value `true` to our JSON object (to its top level) so it looks like the following mapping:

```
{
 "version" : true,
 "query" : {
 "term" : { "title" : "crime" }
 }
}
```

After running it, we get the following results:

```
{
  "took" : 2,
  "timed_out" : false,
  "_shards" : {
    "total" : 5,
    "successful" : 5,
    "failed" : 0
  },
  "hits" : {
    "total" : 1,
    "max_score" : 0.19178301,
    "hits" : [ {
      "_index" : "library",
      "_type" : "book",
      "_id" : "4",
      "_version" : 1,
      "_score" : 0.19178301, "_source" : { "title": "Crime and
Punishment","otitle": "Преступление и наказание","author": "Fyodor
Dostoevsky","year": 1886,"characters": ["Raskolnikov", "Sofia Semyonovna
Marmeladova"],"tags": [],"copies": 0, "available" : true}
    } ]
  }
}
```

As you can see, the _version section is present for the single hit we got.

Limiting the score

For nonstandard use cases, ElasticSearch provides a feature that lets one filter the results on the basis of the minimum score value that the document must have to be considered a match. In order to use it, we must provide the min_score property on the top level of our JSON object with the value of the minimum score. For example, if we wanted our query to only return documents with scores higher than 0.75, we would send the following query:

```
{
  "min_score" : 0.75,
  "query" : {
   "term" : { "title" : "crime" }
  .}
}
```

We get the following response after running the preceding query:

```
{
  "took" : 1,
  "timed_out" : false,
  "_shards" : {
    "total" : 5,
    "successful" : 5,
    "failed" : 0
  },
  "hits" : {
    "total" : 0,
    "max_score" : null,
    "hits" : [ ]
  }
}
```

Look at the previous examples; the score of our document was 0.19178301, which is lower than 0.75, and thus, we didn't get any document in response.

Limiting the score doesn't make much sense, usually, because comparing scores between queries is quite hard. However, maybe in your case this functionality will be needed.

Choosing the fields we want to return

With the use of the `fields` array in the request body, ElasticSearch allows us to define which fields should be included in the response. Please remember that you can only return fields that are marked as stored in the mappings used to create the index or if the _source field was used (ElasticSearch will use the _source field to provide the stored values). So, for example, if we want to return only the title and year fields in the results (for each document), we would send the following query to ElasticSearch:

```
    {
      "fields" : [ "title", "year" ],
      "query" : {
        "term" : { "title" : "crime" }
      }
    }
```

And, in response, we would get the following result:

```
{
    "took" : 2,
    "timed_out" : false,
    "_shards" : {
        "total" : 5,
        "successful" : 5,
        "failed" : 0
    },
    "hits" : {
        "total" : 1,
        "max_score" : 0.19178301,
        "hits" : [ {
            "_index" : "library",
            "_type" : "book",
            "_id" : "4",
            "_score" : 0.19178301,
            "fields" : {
                "title" : "Crime and Punishment",
                "year" : 1886
            }
        } ]
    }
}
```

As you can see, everything worked as we wanted it to behave.

There are three things I would like to share with you:

- If we don't define the fields array, it will use the default value and return the _source field if available

- If we use the _source field and request a field that is not stored, that field will be extracted from the _source field (however, please remember that it requires additional processing)
- If you want to return all stored fields just pass ∗ as the field name

 Please note that if you use the _source field, from the performance point of view, it's better to return the _source field instead of multiple stored fields.

Partial fields

In addition to choosing what fields are returned, ElasticSearch allows the use of the so-called **partial fields**. Partial fields allow us to control how fields are loaded from the _source field. ElasticSearch exposes the include and exclude properties of the partial_fields object, so we can include and exclude fields on the basis of those properties. For example, for our query to include fields that start with titl and exclude the ones that start with chara, we would send the following query:

```
{
  "partial_fields" : {
   "partial1" : {
    "include" : [ "titl*" ],
    "exclude" : [ "chara*" ]
   }
  },
  "query" : {
   "term" : { "title" : "crime" }
  }
}
```

Using script fields

ElasticSearch allows us to use script evaluated values to be returned with result documents. In order to use script fields, we need to add the script_fields section to our JSON query object and an object with the name we choose for each scripted value we want to return. For example, to return a value named correctYear that is calculated as the *year* field minus *1800*, we would run the following query:

```
{
 "script_fields" : {
  "correctYear" : {
   "script" : "doc['year'].value - 1800"
  }
 },
 "query" : {
  "term" : { "title" : "crime" }
 }
}
```

However, if you run the preceding query against our sample data, you get an exception in the response as we don't store the year field. Yes, that's right. Only stored fields or the ones available in _source can be used. So, we will modify our query to use the _source field. After modifications, it should look like the following code:

```
{
 "script_fields" : {
  "correctYear" : {
   "script" : "_source.year - 1800"
  }
 },
 "query" : {
  "term" : { "title" : "crime" }
 }
}
```

Notice that we didn't use the value part of the equation. The following response will be returned by ElasticSearch for this query:

```
{
  "took" : 1,
  "timed_out" : false,
  "_shards" : {
    "total" : 5,
    "successful" : 5,
    "failed" : 0
  },
  "hits" : {
    "total" : 1,
    "max_score" : 0.19178301,
    "hits" : [ {
```

```
      "_index" : "library",
      "_type" : "book",
      "_id" : "4",
      "_score" : 0.19178301,
      "fields" : {
        "correctYear" : 86
      }
    } ]
  }
}
```

As you can see, the correctYear field is in the response.

Passing parameters to script fields

Let's look at one more feature of script fields, passing parameters. Instead of having the value 1800 in the equation, we can use a variable name and pass its value in the parameters section. If we did that, our query would look as follows:

```
{
  "script_fields" : {
    "correctYear" : {
      "script" : "_source.year - paramYear",
      "params" : {
        "paramYear" : 1800
      }
    }
  },
  "query" : {
    "term" : { "title" : "crime" }
  }
}
```

As you can see, we added the paramYear variable as a part of the scripted equation and we provided its value in the params section.

You can find more about script usage at the end of this chapter in the *Using scripts* section.

Choosing the right search type (advanced)

ElasticSearch allows us to choose how we want our query to be processed internally. This is exposed to the end user because there are different situations where different search types are appropriate. To control how queries are executed, we can pass the search_type request parameter and set it to one of the following values:

- query_and_fetch: This is usually the fastest and the simplest search type implementation. The query is executed against all the needed shards in parallel, and all the shards return results equal in number to the value of the size parameter. The maximum number of returned documents will be equal to the value of the *size* parameter times the number of shards.

- query_then_fetch: In the first step, the query is executed to get the information needed to sort and rank documents. Only then are the relevant shards for the actual content of the documents fetched. Different from the query_and_fetch value, the maximum number of results returned by this query type will be equal to the size parameter.

- dfs_query_and_fetch: This is similar to the query_and_fetch search type, but in addition to what query_and_fetch does, the initial query phase is executed and calculates the distributed term frequencies to allow more precise scoring of returned documents.

- dfs_query_then_fetch: This is similar to the query_then_fetch search type, but in addition to what query_then_fetch does, the initial query phase is executed and calculates the distributed term frequencies to allow more precise scoring of returned documents.

- count: This is a special search type that only returns the number of documents that matched the query.

- scan: This is another special search type. The scan type should be only used if you expect your query to return a large number of results. It differs a bit from the usual queries because, after sending the first request, ElasticSearch responds with the scroll identifier and all the other queries need to be run against the _search/scroll REST end point and need to send the returned scroll identifier in the request body. You can find more about this functionality in the *Why is the result on the later pages slow* section in *Chapter 8, Dealing with Problems*.

So, if we wanted to use the simplest search type, we would run the following command:

```
curl -XGET 'localhost:9200/library/book/_search?pretty=true&search_
type=query_and_fetch' -d '{
 "query" : {
  "term" : { "title" : "crime" }
 }
}'
```

Search execution preference (advanced)

In addition to all the previous possibilities of controlling your search, you have one more; you can control what types of shards the search will be executed on. By default, ElasticSearch uses both shards and replicas, available both on the node we've sent the request on and on the other nodes in the cluster. And the default behavior is mostly the proper method of shard preference for queries. But there may be times when we would want to change the default behavior. To do that, we can set the preference request parameter to one of the following values:

- _primary: This specifies that the operation will be only executed on primary shards, so replicas won't be used.
- _primary_first: This specifies that the operation will be executed on primary shards if they are available. If not, it will be executed on other shards.
- _local: This specifies the operation will only be executed on the shards available on the node we are sending the request to (if possible).
- _only_node:node_id: This specifies that the operation will be executed on the node with the provided node identifier.
- **A custom value**: This can be any custom string value that may be passed. Requests with the same values provided will be executed on the same shards.

  For example, if we wanted to execute a query only on local shards, we would run the following command:

  ```
  curl -XGET 'localhost:9200/library/_search?preference=_local' -d
  '{
   "query" : {
    "term" : { "title" : "crime" }
   }
  }'
  ```

Basic queries

So, we now know what an ElasticSearch query is, how to construct it, and finally, how to send it using an HTTP request. What we don't know yet is what kind of queries ElasticSearch exposes, and thus, what we can use in order to achieve the desired results. In the next few pages of this chapter, we will try to learn which basic queries ElasticSearch allows us to use and what we can do with them.

The term query

The term query is one of the simplest queries in ElasticSearch and just matches any document that has a term in a given field. You are familiar with this query type because we used it already, but just to have all the query types in one place. The simplest term query is as follows:

```
{
  "query" : {
   "term" : {
    "title" : "crime"
   }
  }
}
```

It will match the documents that have the term "crime" in the `title` field. Please remember that the term query is not analyzed, so you need to provide the exact term that will match the term in the indexed document. However, you can also include the `boost` attribute in your term query; this will affect the importance of the given term. For example, if we wanted to change our previous query and give our term query a boost of `10.0`, we would send the following query:

```
{
  "query" : {
   "term" : {
    "title" : {
     "value" : "crime",
     "boost" : 10.0
    }
   }
  }
}
```

As you can see, the query changes a bit. Instead of a simple term value we nest a new JSON object, which contains the `value` property and the `boost` property. The value of the `value` property should contain the term we are interested in and the `boost` property is the boost value we want to use.

The terms query

This is a query that allows us to match documents that have certain terms in their contents. For example, let's say that we want to get all the documents that have the terms "novel" or "book" in the `tags` field. To achieve that, we could run the following query:

```
{
  "query" : {
   "terms" : {
    "tags" : [ "novel", "book" ],
    "minimum_match" : 1
   }
  }
}
```

The preceding query returns all the documents that have one or both of the searched terms in the `tags` field. Why is that? Because we set the `minimum_match` property to 1, which basically means that one term should be matched. If we wanted the query to match only a document with both the provided terms, we would set the `minimum_match` property to 2.

The match query

The match query takes the values given in the query parameter, analyzes them, and constructs the appropriate query out of them. When using a match query, ElasticSearch will choose the proper analyzer for a field we've chosen, so you can be sure that the terms passed to the match query will be processed by the same analyzer that was used during indexing. Please remember that the match query (and as further explained, the multi match query) doesn't support Lucene query syntax (discussed in the *The query string query* section, later in this chapter); however, it fits perfectly as a query handler for your search box. The simplest (and the default) match query can look like this:

```
{
  "query" : {
   "match" : {
    "title" : "crime and punishment"
   }
  }
}
```

The preceding query would match all the documents that have the terms "crime" or "and" or "punishment" in the `title` field. However, the preceding query is only the simplest one; there are multiple types of match query. They are covered in the following sections.

The Boolean match query

The Boolean match query is a query that analyzes the provided text and makes a Boolean query out of it. There are a few parameters that allow us to control the behavior of Boolean match queries:

- `operator`: This can take the value of `or` or `and` and control what Boolean operator is used to connect the created Boolean clauses. The default value is `or`.

- `analyzer`: This specifies the name of the analyzer that will be used to analyze the query text and defaults to the default analyzer.

- `fuzziness`: Providing the value of this parameter allows one to construct fuzzy queries. It should take values from `0.0` to `1.0` for a `string` object. While constructing fuzzy queries, this parameter will be used to set the similarity.

- `prefix_length`: This allows one to control the behavior of the fuzzy query. For more information on the value of this parameter, please see the *The fuzzy like this query* section in this chapter.

- `max_expansions`: This allows one to control the behavior of the fuzzy query. For more information on the value of this parameter, please see the *The fuzzy like this query* section in this chapter.

- The parameters should be wrapped in the name of the field we are running the query against. So, if we wanted to run a sample Boolean match query against the `title` field, we could send a query like so:

```
{
  "query" : {
   "match" : {
    "title" : {
     "query" : "crime and punishment",
     "operator" : "and"
    }
   }
  }
}
```

The phrase match query

A phrase match query is similar to the Boolean query, but instead of constructing the Boolean clauses from the analyzed text, it constructs a phrase query. The following parameters are available:

- `slop`: This is an integer value that defines how many unknown words can be put between terms in the text query for a match to be considered a phrase.

- `analyzer`: This specifies the name of the analyzer that will be used to analyze the query text and defaults to the default analyzer.

A sample phrase match query against the `title` field could look like the following code:

```
{
 "query" : {
  "match_phrase" : {
   "title" : {
    "query" : "crime and punishment",
    "slop" : 1
   }
  }
 }
}
```

The match phrase prefix query

The last type of the match query is the match phrase prefix query. This query is almost the same as the prefix match query, but in addition, it allows prefix matches on the last term in the query text. Also, in addition to the parameters exposed by the match phrase query, it exposes an additional one, the `max_expansions` parameter, which controls how many prefixes the last terms will be rewritten to. Our sample query changed to the match phrase prefix query could look like this:

```
{
 "query" : {
  "match_phrase_prefix" : {
   "title" : {
    "query" : "crime and punishment",
    "slop" : 1,
    "max_expansions" : 20
   }
  }
 }
}
```

The multi match query

This is the same as the match query, but instead of running against a single field, it can be run against multiple fields with the use of the `fields` parameter. Of course, all the parameters you use with the match query can be used with the multi match query. So, if we want to modify our match query to be run against the `title` and `otitle` fields, we could run the following query:

```
{
 "query" : {
  "multi_match" : {
   "query" : "crime punishment",
   "fields" : [ "title", "otitle" ]
  }
 }
}
```

The query string query

In comparison with the other queries available, the query string query supports full Apache Lucene query syntax, so it uses a query parser to construct an actual query using the provided text. A sample query string query can look like this:

```
{
 "query" : {
  "query_string" : {
   "query" : "title:crime^10 +title:punishment -otitle:cat
+author:(+Fyodor +dostoevsky)",
   "default_field" : "title"
  }
 }
}
```

You may wonder what that weird syntax in the `query` parameter is; we will get to it in the *Lucene query syntax* part of the query string query description.

As with most of the queries in ElasticSearch, the query string query provides a few parameters that allow us to control query behavior:

- `query`: This specifies the query text.
- `default_field`: This specifies the default field the query will be executed against. It defaults to the `index.query.default_field` property, which is by default set to `_all`.

- `default_operator`: This specifies the default logical operator (or/and) used when no operator is specified. The default value of this parameter is or.

- `analyzer`: This specifies the name of the analyzer used to analyze the query provided in the query parameter.

- `allow_leading_wildcard`: This specifies whether a wildcard allowed as the first character of a term; it defaults to true.

- `lowercase_expand_terms`: This specifies whether terms rewritten by the query are lowercased. It defaults to true.

- `enable_position_increments`: This specifies whether position increments are turned on in the result query. It defaults to true.

- `fuzzy_prefix_length`: This is the prefix length for generated fuzzy queries, and it defaults to 0. To learn more about it, please look at the *The fuzzy query* section.

- `fizzy_min_sim`: This specifies the minimum similarity for fuzzy queries and defaults to 0.5. To learn more about it, please look at the *The fuzzy query* section.

- `phrase_slop`: This specifies the phrase slop and defaults to 0. To learn more about it, please look at the *The phrase match query* section.

- `boost`: This is the boost value used and defaults to 1.0.

- `analyze_wildcard`: This specifies whether the wildcard characters should be analyzed. It defaults to true.

- `auto_generate_phrase_queries`: This specifies whether phrase queries should be automatically generated. It defaults to false.

- `minimum_should_match`: This controls how many of the generated Boolean clauses should match to consider a hit for a given document. The value should be provided as a percentage, for example 50%, which would mean that at least 50 percent of the given terms should match.

- `lenient`: This parameter can take the value of true or false. If it is set to true, format-based failures will be ignored.

Please note that the query string query can be rewritten by ElasticSearch, and because of that, ElasticSearch allows us to pass additional parameters that control the rewrite method. However, for more details about that process, see the *Query rewrite* section later in this chapter.

Lucene query syntax

As we have already discussed, Apache Lucene is the full text search library on top of which ElasticSearch is built. Because of that, some of the queries in ElasticSearch (such as the one currently discussed) support Lucene query parsers syntax—the language that allows you to construct queries. Let's take a look at it and discuss some basic features of it. To read about full Lucene query syntax, please visit `http://lucene.apache.org/core/3_6_1/queryparsersyntax.html`.

A query we pass to Lucene is divided into terms and operators by the query parser. Let's start with the terms; you can distinguish them into two types, single terms and phrases. For example, to query the term "book" in the `title` field, we would pass the following query:

```
title:book
```

To query the phrase "elasticsearch book" in the `title` field, we would pass the following query:

```
title:"elasticsearch book"
```

You may have noticed the name of the field in the beginning and the term or phrase later.

As we have already said, Lucene query syntax supports operators. For example, the + operator tells Lucene that the given part must be matched against the document to consider that document a match, while the - operator is the opposite, which means that such a part of the query can't be present in the document. A part of the query without the + or - operator will be treated as part of the query that can be matched, but it is not mandatory. So, if we wanted to find a document with the term "book" in the `title` field and without the term "cat" in the `description` field, we would pass the following query:

```
+title:book -description:cat
```

We can also group multiple terms with parentheses, for example, the following query:

```
title:(crime punishment)
```

We can also boost parts of the query with the ^ operator and the boost value after it. For example, the following query:

```
title:book^4
```

Explaining the query string

So now that we know the basics of the Lucene query syntax, let's get back to the query we sent using the `query_string` query. As you can see, we wanted to get the documents that may have the term "crime" in the `title` field, and such documents should be boosted with the value of `10`. Next, we want only the documents that have the term "punishment" in the `title` field, and we don't want documents with the term "cat" in the `otitle` field. Finally, we tell Lucene that we only want the documents that have the terms "fyodor" and "dostoevsky" in the `author` field.

Running query string query against multiple fields

It is possible to run the query string query against multiple fields. In order to do that, one needs to provide the `fields` parameter in the query body, which should hold an array of field names. There are two methods of running the query string query against multiple fields; the default method will use the Boolean query to make queries, and the other method can use the DisMax query.

 DisMax is an abbreviation of Disjunction Max. The "Disjunction" part refers to the fact that the search is executed across multiple fields and the fields can be given different boost weights. The "Max" part means that only the maximum score for a given term will be included in a final document score, not the sum of all the scores from all fields that have the matched term (which is what the a simple Boolean query would do).

In order to use the DisMax query, one should add the `use_dis_max` property in the query body and set it to `true`. A sample query can look like this:

```
{
  "query" : {
  "query_string" : {
   "query" : "crime punishment",
   "fields" : [ "title", "otitle" ],
   "use_dis_max" : true
  }
 }
}
```

The field query

The field query is a simplified version of the query string query that we just discussed. I would only like to find all the documents that have the term "crime" in the `title` field, that may have the term "nothing" and that don't have the term "let" in the same field. For that, we could run the following query:

```
{
  "query" : {
   "field" : {
    "title" : "+crime nothing -let"
   }
  }
}
```

You can also apply all the properties that apply to the query string query. To do that, we should wrap all the parameters in the field name and pass the actual query in the `query` parameter. So, the preceding query with the `boost` parameter added would look like this:

```
{
  "query" : {
   "field" : {
    "title" : {
     "query" : "+crime nothing -let",
     "boost" : 20.0
    }
   }
  }
}
```

The identifiers query

This is a simple query that filters the returned documents to only those with the provided identifiers. It works on the internal _uid field, so it doesn't require the _id field to be enabled. The simplest version of such a query could look like the following query:

```
{
  "query" : {
   "ids" : {
    "values" : [ "10", "11", "12", "13" ]
   }
  }
}
```

This query would only return documents that have one of the identifiers present in the `values` array. We can complicate the identifiers query a bit and also limit the documents on the basis of their type. For example, if we want to only include documents from the `book` type, we could send the following query:

```
{
 "query" : {
  "ids" : {
   "type" : "book",
   "values" : [ "10", "11", "12", "13" ]
  }
 }
}
```

The prefix query

The prefix query is similar to the term query in terms of configuration and to the multi term query when looking into its logic. The prefix query allows us to match documents that have a value in a certain field that starts with a given prefix. For example, if we want to find all the documents that have values starting with `cri` in the `title` field, we could run the following query:

```
{
 "query" : {
  "prefix" : {
   "title" : "cri"
  }
 }
}
```

As with the term query, you can also include the `boost` attribute with your prefix query; this will affect the importance of the given prefix. For example, if we wanted to change our previous query and give it a boost of `3.0`, we would send the following query:

```
{
 "query" : {
  "prefix" : {
   "title" : {
    "value" : "cri",
    "boost" : 3.0
   }
  }
 }
}
```

Please note that the prefix query is rewritten by ElasticSearch, and because of that, ElasticSearch allows us to pass an additional parameter, controlling the rewrite method. However, for more details about that process please see the *Query rewrite* section later in this chapter.

The fuzzy like this query

The fuzzy like this query is similar to the more like this query. It finds all the documents that are similar to the provided text but works a bit differently from the more like this query because it makes use of fuzzy strings and picks the best differencing terms produced. For example, if we want to run a fuzzy like this query against the title and otitle fields and find all the documents similar to the crime punishment query, we could run the following query:

```
{
 "query" : {
  "fuzzy_like_this" : {
   "fields" : ["title", "otitle"],
   "like_text" : "crime punishment"
  }
 }
}
```

The following query parameters are supported:

- fields: This is an array of fields that the query should be run against. It defaults to the _all field.

- like_text: This is a required parameter that holds the text we compare the documents to.

- ignore_tf: This specifies whether term frequencies be ignored; this parameter defaults to false.

- max_query_terms: This specifies the maximum number of query terms that will be included in a generated query. It defaults to 25.

- min_similarity: This specifies the minimum similarity that differencing terms should have. It defaults to 0.5.

- prefix_length: This specifies the length of the common prefix of the differencing terms. It defaults to 0.

- boost: This is the boost value that will be used when boosting queries. It defaults to 1.

- analyzer: This specifies the name of the analyzer that will be used to analyze the text we provided.

The fuzzy like this field query

The fuzzy like this field query is similar to the fuzzy like this query but works only against a single field, and because of that, it doesn't support the `fields` property. Instead of specifying the fields that should be used for query analysis, we should wrap the query parameters into the field name. Our sample query to a `title` field should look like the following code:

```
{
 "query" : {
  "fuzzy_like_this_field" : {
   "title" : {
    "like_text" : "crime and punishment"
   }
  }
 }
}
```

All the other parameters from the fuzzy like this query work the same for this type of query.

The fuzzy query

The third type of fuzzy query matches documents on the basis of the edit distance algorithm that is calculated on the terms we provide against the searched documents. This query can be expensive when it comes to CPU resources but can help us when we need fuzzy matching, for example, when users make spelling mistakes. In our example, let's assume that, instead of `crime`, our user enters `cirme` into the search box and we would like to run the simplest form of fuzzy query. Such a query could look like this:

```
{
 "query" : {
  "fuzzy" : {
   "title" : "cirme"
  }
 }
}
```

And the response for this query would be as follows:

```
{
  "took" : 2,
  "timed_out" : false,
  "_shards" : {
    "total" : 5,
    "successful" : 5,
    "failed" : 0
  },
  "hits" : {
    "total" : 1,
    "max_score" : 0.625,
    "hits" : [ {
      "_index" : "library",
      "_type" : "book",
      "_id" : "4",
      "_score" : 0.625, "_source" : { "title": "Crime and
Punishment","otitle": "Преступлéние и наказáние","author": "Fyodor
Dostoevsky","year": 1886,"characters": ["Raskolnikov", "Sofia Semyonovna
Marmeladova"],"tags": [],"copies": 0, "available" : true}
    } ]
  }
}
```

As you can see, even though we made a typo, ElasticSearch managed to find the document we were interested in.

You can control the fuzzy query behavior by using the following parameters:

- value: This specifies the actual query (in case we want to pass more parameters).

- boost: This specifies the boost value for the query. It defaults to 1.0.

- min_similarity: This specifies the minimum similarity for a term to be counted as a match. In the case of string fields, this value should be between 0 and 1, both inclusive. For numeric fields, this value can be greater than one, for example, for a query with value equal to 20 and min_similarity set to 3, we would get values from 17 to 23. For date fields, we can have min_similarity values that include 1d, 2d, and 1m. These values correspond to one day, two days, and one month, and so on.

- `prefix_length`: This is the length of the common prefix of the differencing terms, which defaults to 0.

- `max_expansions`: This specifies the number of terms the query will be expanded to. The default value is unbounded.

The parameters should be wrapped in the name of the field we are running the query against. So, if we would like to modify the previous query and add additional parameters, the query could look like the following code:

```
{
  "query" : {
   "fuzzy" : {
    "title" : {
     "value" : "cirme",
     "min_similarity" : 0.2
    }
   }
  }
}
```

The match all query

The match all query is a simple query that matches all documents in the index. So, to match all the documents, we would run the following query:

```
{
  "query" : {
   "match_all" : {}
  }
}
```

If we want to use index-time boosting for some field and want the match all query to take the index-time boosts into consideration during query execution, we can add the `norms_field` property with the value of the boosted field. For example, if we boost the `title` field during indexing and want the match all query to influence the score of the documents with it, the following query will have to be run:

```
{
  "query" : {
   "match_all" : {
    "norms_field" : "title"
   }
  }
}
```

The wildcard query

The wildcard query is a query that allows us to use the * and ? wildcards in the
values we search for. Apart from that, the wildcard query is very similar to the term
query in its body. To send a query that will match all the documents with the value
of the term cr?me, with ? meaning any character, we will use:

```
{
  "query" : {
   "wildcard" : {
    "title" : "cr?me"
   }
  }
}
```

It will match the documents that have any of the terms matching cr?me in the title
field. However, you can also include the boost attribute with your wildcard query,
which will affect the importance of each term that matches the given value. For
example, if we want to change our previous query and give our term query a boost
of 20.0, we will send the following query:

```
{
  "query" : {
   "wildcard" : {
    "title" : {
     "value" : "cr?me",
     "boost" : 20.0
    }
   }
  }
}
```

> Please note that wildcard queries are not very performance oriented
> and should be avoided if possible; leading wildcards (terms starting
> with wildcards) should especially be avoided.
>
> Please note that the wildcard query is rewritten by ElasticSearch, and
> because of that, ElasticSearch allows us to pass an additional parameter,
> controlling the rewrite method. However, for more details about that
> process, please go to the *Query rewrite* section later in this chapter.

The more like this query

The more like this query allows us to get documents that are similar to the provided text. ElasticSearch support a few parameters to define how more like this queries should work:

- `fields`: This is an array of fields that the query should be run against. It defaults to the `_all` field.

- `like_text`: This specifies a required parameter that holds the text to which we compare the documents.

- `percent_terms_to_match`: This specifies the percentage of terms that must match for a document to be considered similar. It defaults to `0.30`, which translates to 30 percent.

- `min_term_freq`: This is the minimum term frequency (for the terms in the documents) below which terms will be ignored. It defaults to `2`.

- `max_query_terms`: This is the maximum number of terms that will be included in a generated query; it defaults to `25`.

- `stop_words`: This specifies an array of words that will be ignored.

- `min_doc_freq`: This specifies the minimum number of documents in which terms have to be present in order not to be ignored. It defaults to `5`.

- `max_doc_freq`: This specifies the maximum number of documents in which terms may be present in order not to be ignored, but the default is for it to be unbounded.

- `min_word_len`: This specifies the minimum length of a single word below which it will be ignored. It defaults to `0`.

- `max_word_len`: This specifies the maximum length of a single word above which it will be ignored. It defaults to being unbounded.

- `boost_terms`: This specifies the boost value that will be used when boosting each term; it defaults to `1`.

- `boost`: This specifies the boost value that will be used when boosting a query. It defaults to `1`.

- `analyzer`: This is the name of the analyzer that will be used to analyze the text we provided.

An example more like this query could look like this:

```
{
  "query" : {
   "more_like_this" : {
    "fields" : [ "title", "otitle" ],
    "like_text" : "crime and punishment",
    "min_term_freq" : 1,
    "min_doc_freq" : 1
   }
  }
}
```

The more like this field query

The more like this field query is similar to the more like this query but works only against a single field, and because of that, it doesn't support the `fields` property. Instead of specifying fields that should be used for query analysis, we should wrap query parameters into the field name. So, our example query to a `title` field would look like the following code:

```
{
  "query" : {
   "more_like_this_field" : {
    "title" : {
     "like_text" : "crime and punishment",
     "min_term_freq" : 1,
     "min_doc_freq" : 1
    }
   }
  }
}
```

All the other parameters from the more like this query work the same for this type of query.

The range query

This is a query that allows us to find documents within a certain range and works for numerical fields as well as for string-based fields (it just maps to a different Apache Lucene query). The range query should be run against a single field, and the query parameters should be wrapped in the field name. The following parameters are supported:

- `from`: This is the lower bound of the range and defaults to the first value.

- `to`: This is the upper bound of the range and defaults to unbounded.

- `include_lower`: This specifies if the left side of the range must be inclusive or not. It defaults to `true`.

- `include_upper`: This specifies whether the right side of the range should be inclusive or not. It defaults to `true`.

- `boost`: This specifies the boost that will be given for the query.

So, for example, if we would like to find all the books that have values ranging from `1700` to `1900` in the `year` field, we could run the following query:

```
{
  "query" : {
   "range" : {
    "year" : {
     "from" : 1700,
     "to" : 1900
    }
   }
  }
}
```

Query rewrite

In some cases, ElasticSearch must rewrite your query into another query to allow efficient query execution. This happens, for example, with the prefix query; behind the scenes, ElasticSearch changes the prefix query to a logical disjunction of all possible tokens with this prefix. Because of the rewriting process, ElasticSearch will set a static score equal to the query boost for each of the documents returned by such queries, but we can change that.

In order to control query rewriting, we need to add the `rewrite` property to our query with one of the following values:

- `scoring_boolean`: This rewrite method translates each generated term into a Boolean **should** clause. This method may be CPU-intensive (because the score for each term is calculated and kept), and for queries that have many terms, it may exceed the Boolean query limit.

- `constant_score_boolean`: This is similar to `scoring_boolean`, but less CPU-intensive because scoring is not computed, and instead, each term receives a score equal to the query boost.

- `constant_score_filter`: This method rewrites the query using a filter for each generated term and marks all the documents for that filter. Matching documents are given a constant score equal to the query boost.

- `top_terms_N`: This rewrite method translates each generated term into a Boolean should clause, but keeps only the N number of top scoring terms. Scoring is calculated and maintained for each query.

- `top_terms_boost_N`: This rewrite method translates each generated term into a Boolean should clause, but keeps only the N number of top scoring terms. Scoring is calculated as the boost given for the query.

When the `rewrite` property is not set, it defaults to either `constant_score_boolean` or `constant_score_filter` depending on the query.

So our example prefix query with the `rewrite` property could look like the following code:

```
{
  "query" : {
   "prefix" : {
    "title" : {
     "value" : "cri",
     "boost" : 3.0,
     "rewrite" : "top_terms_10"
    }
   }
  }
}
```

Filtering your results

We already know how to build queries and searches by using different criteria. We know how scoring works, which document is more important for a given query, and how input text can affect ordering. But sometimes, we want to choose only a subset of our index, and the chosen criterion should not have an influence on scoring. This is the place where filters should be used.

Frankly enough, we should use filters whenever possible. If a given part of the query does not affect scoring, it is a good candidate to turn into a filter. Score calculation complicates things, and filtering is a relatively simple operation like a simple match-don't match calculation. Due to the fact that filtering is done on all index contents, the result of filtering is independent of the found documents and relationship between them. Filters can easily be cached, further increasing the overall performance of filtered queries.

Using filters

To use a filter in any search, just add `filter` to the `query` attribute. Let's take a sample query and add a filter to it:

```
{
 "query" : {
  "field" : { "title" : "Catch-22" }
 },
 "filter" : {
  "term" : { "year" : 1961 }
 }
}
```

This would return all the documents with the given title, but that result would be narrowed down to only books published in 1961. This query can be rewritten as follows:

```
{
 "query": {
  "filtered" : {
   "query" : {
    "field" : { "title" : "Catch-22" }
   },
    "filter" : {
    "term" : { "year" : 1961 }
   }
  }
 }
}
```

If you run both queries by sending the `curl -XGET localhost:9200/library/book/_search?pretty -d @query.json` command, you will see that both responses are exactly the same (except perhaps the response time):

```
{
 "took" : 1,
 "timed_out" : false,
 "_shards" : {
   "total" : 5,
   "successful" : 5,
   "failed" : 0
 },
```

```
"hits" : {
  "total" : 1,
  "max_score" : 0.2712221,
  "hits" : [ {
    "_index" : "library",
    "_type" : "book",
    "_id" : "2",
    "_score" : 0.2712221, "_source" : { "title": "Catch-22","author":
"Joseph Heller","year": 1961,"characters": ["John Yossarian",
"Captain Aardvark", "Chaplain Tappman", "Colonel Cathcart", "Doctor
Daneeka"],"tags": ["novel"],"copies": 6, "available" : false}
  } ]
}
```

This suggests that both forms are equivalent. This is not true because of the different orders of applying the filters and searching. In the first case, filters are applied to all documents found by the query. In the second case, the documents are filtered *before* the query runs. This yields better performance. As we said earlier, filters are fast, so a filtered query is more efficient. We will return to this in the *Faceting* section in *Chapter 6, Beyond Searching*.

Range filters

A range filter allows us to limit searching to only documents where the value of a field is between the given boundaries. For example, to construct a filter that allows only books published between 1930 and 1990, we would use the following query part:

```
{
  "filter" : {
    "range" : {
      "year" : {
        "from": 1930,
        "to": 1990
        }
      }
    }
  }
```

By default, the left and right boundaries of the field are inclusive. If you want to exclude one or both the bounds, you can use the include_lower and/or include_ upper parameters set to false. For example, if we would like to have documents from 1930 (including the ones with that value) to 1990 (excluding that value), we would construct the following filter:

```
{
  "filter" : {
   "range" : {
    "year" : {
     "from": 1930,
     "to": 1990,
     "include_lower" : true,
     "include_upper" : false
    }
   }
  }
}
```

The other option is to use gt (greater than), lt (lower than), gte (greater than or equal to), and lte (lower than or equal to) in place of the to and from parameters. So, the preceding example may be rewritten as follows:

```
{
  "filter" : {
   "range" : {
    "year" : {
     "gte": 1930,
     "lt": 1990
    }
   }
  }
}
```

There is also a second variant of this filter, numeric_filter. It is a specialized version designed for filtering ranges where field values are numerical. This filter is faster but comes at the cost of the additional memory used by field values. Note that sometimes these values should be loaded independently of the range filter. In those cases, there is no reason not to use this filter. This happens, for example, where this data is used in faceting or sorting (we'll discuss it in greater detail in the coming chapters).

Exists

This filter is very simple. It takes only those documents that have the given field defined, for example:

```
{
 "filter" : {
    "exists" : { "field": "year" }
 }
}
```

Missing

The missing filter is the opposite of the exists filter. However, it has a few additional features. Besides selecting the documents where the specified fields are missing, we have the possibility of defining what ElasticSearch should treat as empty. This helps in situations where input data contains tokens such as null, EMPTY, and not-defined. Let's change the preceding example to find all documents without the year field defined (or the ones that have 0 as the value of the year field. The modified filter would look like the following code:

```
{
 "filter" : {
 "missing" : {
  "field": "year",
  "null_value": 0,
  "existence": true
 }
 }
}
```

In the preceding example, you see two parameters in addition to the previous ones: existence,which tells ElasticSearch that it should check the documents with a value existing in the specified field, and the null_value key, which defines the additional value to be treated as empty. If you don't define null_value, existence is set by default, so you can omit existence in this case.

Script

Sometimes, we want to filter our documents by a computed value. A good example for our case can be filtering out all the books that were published more than a century ago. In order to do that, our filter must look like the following code:

```
{
  "filter" : {
   "script" : {
    "script" : "now - doc['year'].value > 100",
     "params" : {
      "now" : 2013
     }
    }
   }
 }
```

Type

A type filter is a simple filter that returns all the documents of a given type. This filter is useful when a query is directed to several indices or an index with a large number of types. The following is an example of such filters that would limit the type of the documents to the book type:

```
{
  "filter" : {
   "type": {
    "value" : "book"
   }
  }
 }
```

Limit

This filter limits the number of documents returned by a shard for a given query. This should not be confused with the `size` parameter. Let's look at the following filter:

```
{
  "filter" : {
    "limit" : {
      "value" : 1
    }
  }
}
```

When using the default settings for a number of shards, the preceding filter will return up to five documents. Why? This is connected with a number of shards (the `index.number_of_shards` setting). Each shard is queried separately, and each shard may return at most one document.

IDs

The IDs filter helps in cases when we have to filter out several, concrete documents. For example, if we need to exclude a document that has 1 as the identifier, the filter would look like this:

```
{
  "filter": {
    "ids" : {
      "type": ["book"],
      "values": [1]
    }
  }
}
```

Note that the `type` parameter is not required. It is only useful when we search among several indices to specify a type we are interested in.

If this is not enough

We have shown several examples for filters. But this is only the tip of the iceberg.
You can wrap any query into a filter. For example, check out the following query:

```
{
 "query" : {
  "multi_match" : {
   "query" : "novel erich",
   "fields" : [ "tags", "author" ]
  }
 }
}
```

This query can be rewritten as a filter, thus:

```
{
"filter" : {
 "query" : {
  "multi_match" : {
   "query" : "novel erich",
   "fields" : [ "tags", "author" ]
  }
 }
}
}
```

Of course, the only difference in the result will be in the scoring. Every document
returned by a filter will have a score of 1.0. Note that ElasticSearch has a few
dedicated filters that act this way (for example, the term query and the term filter).
So, you don't always have to use a wrapped query syntax. In fact, you should
always use a dedicated version wherever possible.

bool, and, or, not filters

Now it's time to combine some filters together. The first option is to use the bool filter, which can group filters on the same basis as described previously for the bool query. The second option is to use the and, or, and not filters. The first two take an array of filters and return every document that matches all of them, in the case of the and filter (or *at least* one filter in the case of the or filter). In the case of the not filter, returned documents are the ones that were not matched by the enclosed filter. Of course, all these filters may be nested as shown in the following example:

```json
{
  "filter": {
    "not": {
      "and": [
        {
          "term": {
            "title": "Catch-22"
          }
        },
        {
          "or": [
            {
              "range": {
                "year": {
                  "from": 1930,
                  "to": 1990
                }
              }
            },
            {
              "term": {
                "available": true
              }
            }
          ]
        }
      ]
    }
  }
}
```

Named filters

Looking at how complicated setting filters may be, sometimes it would be useful to know which filters were used to determine that a document should be returned by a query. Fortunately, it is possible to give every filter a name. This name will be returned with any document matched during the query. Let's check how that works. The following query will return every book that is available and tagged as `novel` or every book from the nineteenth century:

```
{
 "query": {
  "filtered" : {
   "query": { "matchAll" : {} },
   "filter" : {
    "or" : [
     { "and" : [
      { "term": { "available" : true } },
      { "term": { "tags" : "novel" } }
      ]},
     { "range" : { "year" : { "from": 1800, "to" : 1899 } } }
    ]
   }
  }
 }
}
```

We are using the "filtered" version of the query because this is the only version where ElasticSearch can add information about filters that were used. Let's rewrite this query and name each filter:

```
{
 "query": {
  "filtered" : {
   "query": { "matchAll" : {} },
   "filter" : {
    "or" : {
     "filters" : [
     {
      "and" : {
       "filters" : [
       {
        "term": {
```

```
        "available" : true,
        "_name" : "avail"
        }
     },
     {
      "term": {
       "tags" : "novel",
       "_name" : "tag"
      }
     }
    ],
    "_name" : "and"
    }
   },
   {
     "range" : {
      "year" : {
       "from": 1800,
       "to" : 1899
      },
      "_name" : "year"
     }
    }
   ],
   "_name" : "or"
   }
  }
 }
}
}
```

It's much longer, isn't it? We've added the _name element to every filter. In the case of the and and or filters, we needed to change the syntax; we wrapped the enclosed filters by an additional object to make the JSON format correct. After sending a query to ElasticSearch, we should get a response similar to the following one:

```
{
  "took" : 2,
  "timed_out" : false,
  "_shards" : {
    "total" : 2,
    "successful" : 2,
    "failed" : 0
  },
```

```
  "hits" : {
    "total" : 2,
    "max_score" : 1.0,
    "hits" : [ {
      "_index" : "library",
      "_type" : "book",
      "_id" : "1",
      "_score" : 1.0, "_source" : { "title": "All Quiet on the
Western Front","otitle": "Im Westen nichts Neues","author": "Erich
Maria Remarque","year": 1929,"characters": ["Paul Bäumer", "Albert
Kropp", "Haie Westhus", "Fredrich Müller", "Stanislaus Katczinsky",
"Tjaden"],"tags": ["novel"],"copies": 1, "available": true},
      "matched_filters" : [ "or", "tag", "avail", "and" ]
    }, {
      "_index" : "library",
      "_type" : "book",
      "_id" : "4",
      "_score" : 1.0, "_source" : { "title": "Crime and
Punishment","otitle": "Преступле́ние и наказа́ние","author": "Fyodor
Dostoevsky","year": 1886,"characters": ["Raskolnikov", "Sofia
Semyonovna Marmeladova"],"tags": [],"copies": 0, "available" : true},
      "matched_filters" : [ "or", "year", "avail" ]
    } ]
  }
```

You can see that every document in addition to standard information also contains a an array with filter names that were matched for that document.

Caching filters

The last thing about filters that we want to mention in this chapter is caching. Caching increases speed for the queries that use filters, but at the cost of memory and query time during the first execution of such a filter. Because of this, the best candidates for caching are filters that can be reused, for example, the ones that we will use frequently (which also includes the parameter values).

Caching can be turned on for the and, bool, and or filters (but it is usually a better idea to cache the enclosed filters instead). In this case, the required syntax is the same as described for the named filters.

Some filters don't support the _cache parameter because their results are always cached. This is true for the exists, missing, range, term, and terms filters that are cached by default, but this behavior can be modified and caching can be turned off. Caching also doesn't make sense for the ids, matchAll, and limit filters.

Compound queries

As we have already discussed, in addition to simple queries, ElasticSearch exposes a few compound queries that can be used to connect multiple queries together or are used to control the behavior of another query. You may wonder whether you need such functionality. In fact, if you are interested in making your search better, you'll use the following queries somewhere in your journey with ElasticSearch. A simple example is combining a simple term query with a phrase query in order to get better search results. But for now, let's stick to the query description.

The bool query

A bool query allows us to wrap a virtually unbounded number of queries and connect them with a logical value by using one of the following sections:

- `should`: The query wrapped into this section may or may not have a match (the number of the queries in the `should` section that need to match is controlled by the `minimum_should_match` parameter).

- `must`: The query wrapped into this section must match in order for the document to be returned.

- `must_not`: The query wrapped into this section must not match in order for the document to be returned.

Each of these sections can be present multiple times. Also, please remember that the score of the resulting document will be calculated as a sum of all the wrapped queries that the document matched. In addition to the preceding sections, we can add the following parameters to the query body:

- `boost`: This specifies the boost used with the query; it defaults to `1.0`.

- `minimum_should_match`: This integer value describes the minimum number of should clauses that have to match in order for the checked document to be counted as a match.

- `disable_coord`: This parameter defaults to `false` and allows us to enable or disable the score factor computation that is based on the fraction of all query terms that a document contains.

Imagine that we would like to find all the documents that have the term crime in the title field. In addition, they may or may not have a range of 1900 to 2000 in the year field and must not have the term "nothing" in the otitle field. Such a query made with the bool query may look like the following code:

```
{
  "query" : {
   "bool" : {
    "must" : {
     "term" : {
      "title" : "crime"
     }
    },
    "should" : {
     "range" : {
      "year" : {
       "from" : 1900,
       "to" : 2000
      }
     }
    },
    "must_not" : {
     "term" : {
      "otitle" : "nothing"
     }
    }
   }
  }
}
```

The boosting query

The boosting query is designed to wrap around two queries and lower the score of the documents that were returned by one of the queries. There are three sections of the boosting query that need to be defined – the positive section, which should hold the query whose document score will be left unchanged, the negative section whose resulting documents will have their score lowered, and the negative_boost section, which holds the boost value that will be used to lower the second section's query score. The advantage of the boosting query is that the results of both queries will be present in the results although some of them will have their score lowered. For example, if we used the bool query with the must_not section, we wouldn't get the results for such a query.

Let's see some examples. Say that we would like to have the results of a simple term query for the term `crime` in the `title` field and that we would like the score of such documents to not be changed. But say also that we would like to have the documents that range from 1800 to 1900 in the `year` field and that we would like the scores of documents returned by such a query to have an additional boost of `0.5`. Combining these specifications, we arrive at a query that looks like this:

```
{
  "query" : {
    "boosting" : {
      "positive" : {
        "term" : {
          "title" : "crime"
        }
      },
      "negative" : {
        "range" : {
          "year" : {
            "from" : 1800,
            "to" : 1900
          }
        }
      },
      "negative_boost" : 0.5
    }
  }
}
```

The constant score query

A constant score query is used to wrap another query (or filter) and return a constant score for each document returned by the wrapped query (or filter). It allows us to strictly control the score value assigned for a document matched by a query or filter. For example, if we want to have a score of `2.0` for all the documents that have the term "crime" in the `title` field, we can send the following query:

```
{
  "query" : {
    "constant_score" : {
      "query" : {
        "term" : {
```

```
      "title" : "crime"
     }
    },
    "boost" : 2.0
   }
  }
 }
```

The indices query

This functionality is useful when executing a query against multiple indices. It allows us to provide an array of indices (the indices property) and two queries— one that will be executed if we query the index from the list (the query property) and one that will be executed on all the other indices (the no_match_query property). For example, let's assume that we have an alias name, books, holding two indices—library and a new one called users— and we want to use that alias but we want to run different queries to those indices. To do that, we will send the following query:

```
{
 "query" : {
  "indices" : {
   "indices" : [ "library" ],
   "query" : {
    "term" : {
     "title" : "crime"
    }
   },
   "no_match_query" : {
    "term" : {
     "user" : "crime"
    }
   }
  }
 }
}
```

In the preceding query, the query described in the query property would be run against the library index, and no_match_query would be run against all the other indices present in the cluster.

The custom filters score query

The custom filters score query allows us to wrap a query and filters. It works in such a way that if a document from the wrapped query matches a filter, we can influence the score of such a document with either a boost or a defined script. For example, if we run the match all query and want to use a boost value of 10 for the documents that have crime in the title field, and in addition to that, want to set the score of the documents that have values between 1900 and 1950 in the year field, we will send the following query:

```
{
 "query" : {
  "custom_filters_score" : {
   "query" : {
    "match_all" : {}
   },
   "filters" : [
    {
     "filter" : {
      "term" : {
       "title" : "crime"
      }
     },
     "boost" : 10.0
    },
    {
     "filter" : {
      "range" : {
       "year" : {
        "from" : 1900,
        "to" : 1950
       }
      }
     },
     "script" : "_source.year"
    }
   ],
   "score_mode" : "first"
  }
 }
}
```

Let's stop for a bit and discuss the query structure. At the main level of the `custom_filters_score` query, we have three sections, the `query` section, which holds the actual query we run, the `filters` section, which is an array of ordered filters that will be used to match the documents from the query and modify their score, and the `score_mode` section, which we will discuss. The `filters` array is built on one or more `filter` objects and the boost value or a script used to modify the score of the document that matches the filter. In our case, we used the script (the `script` parameter) to calculate the score for the range filter—the document will have a score equal to the value of its `year` field.

The `score_mode` section allows us to control how the defined filters affect the score of the matched documents. By default, it is set to `first`, which means that only the first matching filter will modify the score. The other values are aggregation-based and are as follows:

- `min`: The score of the document will be influenced by the minimum scoring filter
- `max`: The score of the document will be influenced by the maximum scoring filter
- `total`: The score of the document will be influenced by the sum of the scores of the matching filters
- `avg`: The score of the document will be influenced by the average of the score of the matching filters
- `multiply`: The score of the document will be influenced by the multiplication of the scores of the matching filters

There is also another parameter in addition to the one mentioned, that is, the `max_boost` parameter, which allows one to set the maximum boost value a document can have.

The custom boost factor query

The custom boost factor query allows us to wrap another query into it and multiply the score of the documents returned by that query by a provided factor. The difference between this and the boost given to queries is that the boost given to a custom boost factor query is not normalized, which can be desired sometimes. So, if we would like to multiply the boost of a simple term query by 10, we could run a query like this one:

```
{
  "query" : {
   "custom_boost_factor" : {
    "query" : {
     "term" : {
      "title" : "crime"
     }
    },
    "boost_factor" : 10.0
   }
  }
}
```

As you can see, in the query body, we have new sections—the custom_boost_ factor section (which has the query property nested and holds the actual query) and the boost_factor section, which holds the boost multiplier).

The custom score query

A custom score query can be used to customize scoring for another query with the use of script. For example, if we want to add the year field to the score calculated by our simple term query and multiply it by the value 2 (of course, it doesn't make much sense right?), we could send the following query:

```
{
  "query" : {
   "custom_score" : {
    "query" : {
     "term" : {
      "title" : "crime"
     }
    },
    "params" : {
     "multiply" : 2
    },
    "script" : "_score * _source.year * multiply"
   }
  }
}
```

We wrapped our term query with a `custom_score` query. In addition to that, we provided two additional sections—the `params` section, which holds additional parameters used in the score calculation script, and the `script` section, which holds the actual score calculation script. The value calculated by the script (as the result of multiplication of the score, the `year` field, and the `multiply` parameter) will be assigned as the score of all the documents that match the query. As you may have noticed, because we don't store the `year` field, we get it from `_source`.

Sorting data

Now we can build quite complex queries for the whole index, or to part of it, by using filters. We can send these queries to ElasticSearch and analyze the returned data. Until now, this data was organized in the order determined by scoring. This is exactly what we want in most cases. Search should give us the most appropriate documents first. But what can we do if we want to use our search more like a database or set a more sophisticated algorithm for data ordering? Let's check what ElasticSearch can do with sorting.

Default sorting

Let's look at the following query, which returns all the books with at least one of the specified words:

```
{
  "query" : {
    "terms" : {
      "title" : [ "crime", "front", "punishment" ],
      "minimum_match" : 1
    }
  }
}
```

Under the hood, ElasticSearch sees this as follows:

```
{
  "query" : {
    "terms" : {
      "title" : [ "crime", "front", "punishment" ],
      "minimum_match" : 1
    }
  },
  "sort" : [
    { "_score" : "desc" }
  ]
}
```

Note the highlighted section. This is the default sorting used by ElasticSearch. This means that the return matched documents will show the ones with the highest score first. The simplest modification is reversing the ordering using this:

```
"sort" : [
  { "_score" : "asc" }
]
```

Selecting fields used for sorting

Default sorting is boring, isn't it? Let's change this into something a bit more engaging:

```
"sort" : [
  { "title" : "asc" }
]
```

Unfortunately, this doesn't work. In the server response, you can find JSON with the reason key, where ElasticSearch says:

```
[Can't sort on string types with more than one value per doc, or more
than one token per field]
```

Of course, ElasticSearch allows adding documents with multiple values in one field, but such fields cannot be used for sorting because the search doesn't know which values should be used to determine the order. Another reason may be that the field is analyzed and divided into multiple tokens. This is what happened in the preceding case. To avoid this, we can add an additional, non-analyzed version of the title field. To do that, let's change our title field to multi_field, which we already discussed. For example, the title field definition could look like this:

```
"title" : {
  "type": "multi_field",
  "fields": {
    "title": { "type" : "string" },
    "sort": { "type" : "string", "index": "not_analyzed" }
  }
}
```

After changing the `title` field in the mappings that we've shown in the beginning of the chapter, we can try sorting on the `title.sort` field and see if it will work. To do that, we will need to send the following query:

```
{
  "query" : {
    "match_all" : { }
  },
  "sort" : [
    {"title.sort" : "asc" }
  ]
}
```

Now, it works properly. In the response from ElasticSearch, every document contains information about the value used for sorting, for example:

```
"_index" : "library",
"_type" : "book",
"_id" : "1",
"_score" : null, "_source" : { "title": "All Quiet on the
Western Front","otitle": "Im Westen nichts Neues","author": "Erich
Maria Remarque","year": 1929,"characters": ["Paul Bäumer", "Albert
Kropp", "Haie Westhus", "Fredrich Müller", "Stanislaus Katczinsky",
"Tjaden"],"tags": ["novel"],"copies": 1, "available": true, "section"
: 3},
"sort" : [ "All Quiet on the Western Front" ]
```

Note that `sort`, in request and response, is given as an array. This suggests that we can use several different orderings. It is true; ElasticSearch will use the next elements in the list to determine ordering between documents having the same previous field value.

Specifying behavior for missing fields

What about ordering? What about when some of the documents that match the query don't have defined the field we want to run the sort on? By default, documents without the given field are returned first in case of ascending order and last in case of descending order. But sometimes, this is not exactly what we want to achieve. when running sort on a numeric field, this can be changed easily. For example:

```
{
  "query" : {
    "match_all" : { }
  },
  "sort" : [
    { "section" : { "order" : "asc", "missing" : "_last" } }
  ]
}
```

Note the extended form of defining the field for sorting; it allows adding other parameters, such as `missing`. It is worth mentioning that, besides the `_last` and `_first` values, ElasticSearch allows us to use any number. In such a case, documents without a defined field will be treated as documents with this given value.

You are probably wondering what we can do in the case of fields that aren't numbers. Don't worry, we will try to avoid this problem, although in a less elegant way.

Dynamic criteria

We've promised an example of how to force ElasticSearch to put documents without the defined fields at the bottom of the result list. In order to achieve that, we will show you how ElasticSearch allows one to calculate the value that should be used for sorting. In our example, we are sorting a field that is an array (as we mentioned before, we can't run sort on multiple values), and we assume that we want to run sort by comparing the first element of that array. So let's look at the request:

```
{
"query" : {
   "match_all" : { }
},
"sort" : {
    "_script" : {
       "script" : "doc['tags'].values.length > 0 ? doc['tags'].
values[0] : '\u19999'",
       "type" : "string",
       "order" : "asc"
    }
 }
}
```

In the preceding example, we've replaced every nonexistent value by the Unicode code of a character that should be low enough in the list. The main idea of this code is that we check whether our array contains at least a single element. If it does, the first value from the array is returned. If the array is empty, we return the Unicode character that should be placed at the bottom of the results list. Besides the script, this option of sorting requires us to specify the ordering (ascending in our case) and type that will be used for comparison (we return `string` from our script).

Collation and national characters

If you want to use languages other than English, you can face the problem of incorrect order of characters. It happens because many languages have a different alphabetical order defined. ElasticSearch supports many languages, but proper collation requires an additional plugin. It's easy to install and configure, but we will discuss it in the *ElasticSearch plugins* section in *Chapter 7, Administrating Your Cluster*.

Using scripts

ElasticSearch has a few functionalities where scripts can be used. You've already seen examples such as updating documents, filtering, and searching. Regardless of the fact that this seems to be advanced, we will take a look at the possibilities given by ElasticSearch. Looking into any request that use scripts, we can spot several fields:

- `script`: This field contains the script code.
- `lang`: This field informs the engine which language is used. If it is omitted, ElasticSearch assumes `mvel`.
- `params`: This is an object containing parameters. Every defined parameter is available for script by its name. By using parameters, we can write cleaner code. Due to caching, code with parameters performs better than code with embedded constant values.

Available objects

During the execution of the script, ElasticSearch exposes several objects. The ones available for operations connected with searching are as follows:

- `doc` (also available as `_doc`): This is an instance of the `org.elasticsearch.search.lookup.DocLookup` object. It gives us access to the current document found with calculated score and field values.
- `_source`: This is an instance of `org.elasticsearch.search.lookup.SourceLookup`. This provides access to the source of the current document and values defined in this source.
- `_fields`: This is an instance of `org.elasticsearch.search.lookup.FieldsLookup`. Again, it is used for access to document values.

In an update operation, ElasticSearch exposes only the `ctx` object with the `_source` property, which provides access to the current document.

As we have previously seen, several methods are mentioned in the context of document fields and their values. Let's show several examples of ways of getting the value for the `title` field (in the brackets you can see what ElasticSearch would return for one of our sample documents from the library index):

- `_doc.title.value` (crime)
- `_source.title` (Crime and Punishment)
- `_fields.title.value` (null)

A bit confusing, isn't it? Let's stop for a moment and recall the previous information about fields. During indexing, a field value is sent to ElasticSearch as a part of the `_source` document. The search engine can store this information as a whole in the index (this is the default behavior but can be turned off). In addition, this source is parsed and every field may be stored in an index if it is marked as stored (meaning that the `store` property is set to `true`, that is, by default not marked). Finally, the field value may be configured as indexed. This means that the field value is analyzed, cut into tokens, and placed in the index again. To sum up, one field may be stored in an index as:

- A part of `_source`
- A stored, unparsed value
- An indexed value, parsed into tokens

In scripts, except the script for updating, we have access to all these representations. You may wonder which version we should use. Well, if we want access to the processed form, the answer would be as simple as `_doc`. What about `_source` and `_fields`? In most cases, `_source` is a good choice. It is usually fast and needs fewer disk operations than reading the original field values from the index.

MVEL

ElasticSearch can use several languages for scripting when declared; otherwise, it assumes that MVEL is used. MVEL is fast, easy to use and embed, and simple, but it is a powerful expression language used in open source projects. It allows us to use Java objects, automatically maps properties to a getter/setter call, converts simple types, and maps collections and maps to arrays and associative arrays. For more information, refer to the following link:

```
http://mvel.codehaus.org/Language+Guide+for+2.0
```

Other languages

Using MVEL for scripting is a simple and sufficient solution, but if you would like to use something different, you can choose between JavaScript, Python, and Groovy. Before using other languages, we must install an appropriate plugin. For now, we'll just run the following command from the ElasticSearch directory:

```
bin/plugin -install elasticsearch/elasticsearch-lang-javascript/1.1.0
```

The only change we should make in the request is to add the additional information about which language we are using for scripting, and of course, to modify the script itself to be correct in the new language. Look at the following example:

```
{
  "query" : {
    "match_all" : { }
  },
  "sort" : {
      "_script" : {
        "script" : "doc.tags.values.length > 0 ? doc.tags.values[0]
:'\u19999';",
        "lang" : "javascript",
        "type" : "string",
        "order" : "asc"
      }
  }
}
```

As you can see, we used JavaScript for scripting instead of the default MVEL.

Script library

Usually, scripts are small, and it is quite convenient to put them in the request. But sometimes applications grow, and you want to give the developers something that they can reuse in their modules. If the scripts are large and complicated, it is generally better to place them in files and only refer to them in API requests. The first thing to do is to place our script in the proper place with a proper name. Our tiny script should be placed in the ElasticSearch directory `config/scripts`. Let's name our example file `text_sort.js`, where the extension of the file should indicate the language used for scripting. The content of this example file is very simple:

```
doc.tags.values.length > 0 ? doc.tags.values[0] :'\u19999';
```

And the query using the preceding script can be a little easier:

```
{
  "query" : {
    "match_all" : { }
  },
  "sort" : {
      "_script" : {
        "script" : "text_sort",
        "type" : "string",
        "order" : "asc"
      }
  }
}
```

We can use `text_sort` as a method name. In addition, we can omit the script language; ElasticSearch will figure it out from the file extension.

Native code

For occasions when scripts are too slow or when you don't like scripting languages, ElasticSearch allows you to write Java classes and use them instead of scripts.

To create a new native script, we should implement at least two classes. The first one is a factory for our script. Let's focus on it for now and see some sample code:

```
package pl.solr.elasticsearch.examples.scripts;

import java.util.Map;

import org.elasticsearch.common.Nullable;
import org.elasticsearch.script.ExecutableScript;
import org.elasticsearch.script.NativeScriptFactory;

public class HashCodeSortNativeScriptFactory implements
NativeScriptFactory {

  @Override
  public ExecutableScript newScript(@Nullable Map<String, Object>
params) {
    return new HashCodeSortScript(params);
  }

}
```

The essential parts are highlighted. This class should implement `org.elasticsearch.script.NativeScriptFactory`. The interface forces us to implement the `newScript()` method. It takes parameters defined in the API call and returns an instance of our script.

Now, let's see the main class, our script. It will be used for sorting. Documents will be ordered by the `hashCode()` value of the chosen field. Documents without a field defined will be the first. We know the logic doesn't have too much sense, but it is good for presentation. The source code for our native script is like this:

```
package pl.solr.elasticsearch.examples.scripts;

import java.util.Map;

import org.elasticsearch.script.AbstractSearchScript;

public class HashCodeSortScript extends AbstractSearchScript {
  private String field = "name";

  public HashCodeSortScript(Map<String, Object> params) {
    if (params != null && params.containsKey("field")) {
      this.field = params.get("field").toString();
    }
  }

  @Override
  public Object run() {
    Object value = source().get(field);
    if (value != null) {
      return value.hashCode();
    }
    return 0;
  }

}
```

First of all the class inherits from `org.elasticsearch.script.AbstractSearchScript` and implements the `run()` method. This is the place where we get appropriate values from the current document, process them according to our strange logic, and return the result. You may notice the `source()` call. Yes, it is exactly the same _source parameter that we meet in the non-native scripts, and yes, there are also `doc()` and `fields()` available. Look at how we've used the parameters. We assume that a user can provide the `field` parameter, telling us which document field will be used for manipulation. We also provide a default value for this parameter.

Now it's time to install our native script. After packing the compiled classes as a JAR archive, we should put it in the ElasticSearch `lib` directory. This makes our code visible to the class loader. What we should do after that is to register our script. This can be done by using the settings API call or by adding a single line to the `elasticsearch.yml` configuration file, as shown in the following code:

```
script.native.native_sort.type: pl.solr.elasticsearch.examples.
scripts.HashCodeSortNativeScriptFactory
```

Note the `native_sort` fragment. This is our script name, which will be used during requests and will be passed to the `script` parameter. The value for this property is the full class name of the factory whose server should be used to create the script.

The last thing is the need to restart the ElasticSearch instance and send our queries. For the example that uses our previously indexed data, we can try running the following query:

```
{
  "query" : {
     "match_all" : { }
  },
  "sort" : {
      "_script" : {
         "script" : "native_sort",
         "params" : {
            "field" : "otitle"
         },
         "lang" : "native",
         "type" : "string",
         "order" : "asc"
      }
  }
}
```

Note the `params` part of the query. In this call, we want to sort on the `otitle` field. We provide the script name, `native_sort`, and the script language, `native`. This is required. If everything goes well, we should see our results sorted by our custom sort logic. If we look at the response from ElasticSearch, we will see that documents without the `otitle` field are in the first positions of the results list and their sort value is 0.

Summary

In this chapter we've looked at simple and compound query types that are available in ElasticSearch. In addition to that, we've learned how to filter query results and alter the way documents are sorted. We've also learned how to use scripts in ElasticSearch. In the next chapter, we will look at some of the ways to extend our index structure and search results, such as highlighting, using geographical queries or implementing autocomplete functionality with ElasticSearch.

3
Extending Your Structure and Search

Till now we've learned how to install, configure, and query our ElasticSearch cluster. We also prepared some more sophisticated mappings. We've also used aliasing to make querying easier and in addition to that we used routing to control where the data is placed. In this chapter, we will extend our knowledge of ElasticSearch by looking at how to index data that is not flat, how to handle geographical data, and how to deal with files. We will also learn how to distinguish the text fragment that was matched and how to implement commonly used autocomplete features. By the end of this chapter you will learn:

- How to index data that is not flat
- How to extend your index with additional data such as time-to-live and document identifier
- How to handle highlighting
- How to implement the autocomplete feature
- How to handle files
- How to handle geographical data

Indexing data that is not flat

Not all data is flat like that which we have been using since *Chapter 2, Searching Your Data*. Of course if we are building our system, which ElasticSearch will be a part of, we can create a structure that is convenient for ElasticSearch. However, it doesn't need to be flat, it can be more object-oriented. Let's see how to create mappings that use fully structured JSON objects.

Data

Let's assume we have the following data (we store it in the file called `structured_data.json`):

```json
{
  "book" : {
   "author" : {
    "name" : {
     "firstName" : "Fyodor",
     "lastName" : "Dostoevsky"
    }
   },
   "isbn" : "123456789",
   "englishTitle" : "Crime and Punishment",
   "originalTitle" : "Преступление и наказание",
   "year" : 1886,
   "characters" : [
    {
     "name" : "Raskolnikov"
    },
    {
     "name" : "Sofia"
    }
   ],
   "copies" : 0
  }
}
```

As you can see, the data is not flat. It contains arrays and nested objects, so we can't use our mappings that we used previously. But we can create mappings that will be able to handle such data.

Objects

The previous example data shows a structured JSON file. As you can see, the root object in our file is `book`. The root object is a special one, which allows us to define additional properties. The `book` root object has some simple properties such as `englishTitle`, `originalTitle`, and so on. Those will be indexed as normal fields in the index. In addition to that it has the `characters` array type, which we will discuss in the next paragraph. For now, let's focus on `author`. As you can see, `author` is an object that has another object nested in it, that is, the `name` object, which has two properties `firstName` and `lastName`.

Arrays

We have already used array type data, but we didn't talk about it. By default all fields in Lucene and thus in ElasticSearch are multivalued, which means that they can store multiple values. In order to send such fields for indexing to ElasticSearch we use the JSON array type, which is nested within the opening and closing square brackets []. As you can see in the previous example, we used the array type for `characters` property for our book.

Mappings

So, what can we do to index such data as that shown previously? To index arrays we don't need to do anything, we just specify the properties for such fields inside the array name. So in our case in order to index the `characters` data present in the data we would need to add such mappings as these:

```
"characters" : {
 "properties" : {
  "name" : {"type" : "string", "store" : "yes"}
 }
}
```

Nothing strange, we just nest the `properties` section inside the array's name (which is `characters` in our case) and we define fields there. As a result of this mapping, we would get the `characters.name` multivalued field in the index.

We perform similar steps for our `author` object. We call the section by the same name as is present in the data, but in addition to the `properties` section we also tell ElasticSearch that it should expect the object type by adding the `type` property with the value `object`. We have the `author` object, but it also has the `name` object nested in it, so we do the same; we just nest another object inside it. So, our mappings for that would look like the following code:

```
"author" : {
 "type" : "object",
 "properties" : {
  "name" : {
   "type" : "object",
   "properties" : {
    "firstName" : {"type" : "string", "store" : "yes"},
    "lastName" : {"type" : "string", "store" : "yes"}
   }
  }
 }
}
```

The firstName and lastName fields would appear in the index as author.name. firstName and author.name.lastName. We will check if that is true in just a second.

The rest of the fields are simple core types, so I'll skip discussing them as they were already discussed in the *Schema mapping* section of *Chapter 1, Getting Started with ElasticSearch Cluster.*

Final mappings

So our final mappings file that we've called structured_mapping.json looks like the following:

```
{
 "book" : {
  "properties" : {
   "author" : {
    "type" : "object",
    "properties" : {
     "name" : {
      "type" : "object",
      "properties" : {
       "firstName" : {"type" : "string", "store" : "yes"},
       "lastName" : {"type" : "string", "store" : "yes"}
      }
     }
    }
   },
   "isbn" : {"type" : "string", "store" : "yes"},
   "englishTitle" : {"type" : "string", "store" : "yes"},
   "originalTitle" : {"type" : "string", "store" : "yes"},
   "year" : {"type" : "integer", "store" : "yes"},
   "characters" : {
    "properties" : {
     "name" : {"type" : "string", "store" : "yes"}
    }
   },
   "copies" : {"type" : "integer", "store" : "yes"}
  }
 }
}
```

To be or not to be dynamic

As we already know, ElasticSearch is schemaless, which means that it can index data without the need of first creating the mappings (although we should do so if we want to control the index structure). The dynamic behavior of ElasticSearch is turned on by default, but there may be situations where you may want to turn it off for some parts of your index. In order to do that, one should add the `dynamic` property set to `false` on the same level of nesting as the `type` property for the object that shouldn't be dynamic. For example, if we would like our `author` and `name` objects not to be dynamic, we should modify the relevant parts of the mappings file so that it looks like the following code:

```
"author" : {
 "type" : "object",
 "dynamic" : false,
 "properties" : {
  "name" : {
   "type" : "object",
   "dynamic" : false,
   "properties" : {
    "firstName" : {"type" : "string", "store" : "yes"},
    "lastName" : {"type" : "string", "store" : "yes"}
   }
  }
 }
}
```

However, please remember that in order to add new fields for such objects, we would have to update the mappings.

 You can also turn off the dynamic mapping functionality by adding the `index.mapper.dynamic : false` property to your `elasticsearch.yml` configuration file.

Sending the mappings to ElasticSearch

The last thing I would like to do is test if all the work we did actually works. This time we will use a slightly different technique of creating an index and adding the mappings. First, let's create the `library` index with the following command:

```
curl -XPUT 'localhost:9200/library'
```

Now, let's send our mappings for the book type:

```
curl -XPUT 'localhost:9200/library/book/_mapping' -d @structured_mapping.
json
```

Now we can index our example data:

```
curl -XPOST 'localhost:9200/library/book/1' -d @structured_data.json
```

If we would like to see how our data was indexed, we can run a query like the following:

```
curl -XGET 'localhost:9200/library/book/_search?q=*:*&fields=*&pretty=tr
ue'
```

It will return the following data:

```
{
    "took" : 1,
    "timed_out" : false,
    "_shards" : {
        "total" : 5,
        "successful" : 5,
        "failed" : 0
    },
    "hits" : {
        "total" : 1,
        "max_score" : 1.0,
        "hits" : [ {
            "_index" : "library",
            "_type" : "book",
            "_id" : "1",
            "_score" : 1.0,
            "fields" : {
                "copies" : 0,
                "characters.name" : [ "Raskolnikov", "Sofia" ],
                "englishTitle" : "Crime and Punishment",
                "author.name.lastName" : "Dostoevsky",
                "isbn" : "123456789",
                "originalTitle" : "Преступле́ние и наказа́ние",
                "year" : 1886,
                "author.name.firstName" : "Fyodor"
            }
        } ]
    }
}
```

As you can see, all the fields from arrays and object types are indexed properly. Please notice that there is, for example, the `author.name.firstName` field present, because ElasticSearch did flatten the data.

Extending your index structure with additional internal information

All the information provided in the previous chapters gave us a good look at what ElasticSearch is capable of, both in terms of indexing and querying. But their coverage was not nearly complete. One thing we would like to discuss in more detail is the functionalities of ElasticSearch that are not used every day, but can make our life easier when it comes to data handling.

 Each of the following field types should be defined on an appropriate type level. So if you recall our sample mappings for our small library from *Chapter 2, Searching Your Data*, we would add any of the following types under the `book` type mappings.

The identifier field

As you recall, each document indexed in ElasticSearch has its own identifier and type. In ElasticSearch there are two types of internal identifiers for the documents.

The first one is the `_uid` field, which is the unique identifier of the document in the index and is composed of the document's identifier and the document type. This basically means that documents of different types that are indexed into the same index can have the same document identifier yet ElasticSearch will be able to distinguish them. This field doesn't require any additional settings; it is always indexed, but it's good to know that it exists.

The second field holding an identifier is the `_id` field. This field stores the actual identifier set during index time. In order to enable the indexing of the `_id` field (and storing it if possible), we need to add the `_id` field definition just like any other property in our mappings (although as said before, please add it in the body of the type definition).

So, our sample book type definition will look like the following:

```
{
  "book" : {
   "_id" : {
    "index": "not_analyzed",
    "store" : "no"
   },
   "properties" : {
    .
    .
    .
   }
  }
}
```

As you can see, in the previous example, we said that we want our _id field to be indexed, but not analyzed and we don't want to store it.

In addition to specifying an ID during indexing time, we can specify that we want it to be fetched from one of the fields of the indexed documents (although this will be slightly slower because of the additional parsing needed). In order to do that we need to specify the path property with the name of the field we want to use as the identifier value provider. For example, if we have the book_id field in our index and we would like to use it as the value for the _id field, we could change the previous mappings to something like the following:

```
{
  "book" : {
   "_id" : {
    "path": "book_id"
   },
   "properties" : {
    .
    .
    .
   }
  }
}
```

One last point to remember is that even when disabling the _id field, all the functionalities requiring the document's unique identifier will still work because they will be using the _uid field instead.

The _type field

Let's say it one more time, each document in ElasticSearch is at least described by an identifier and type and if we want, we may include the type name as the internal _type field of our indices. By default the _type field is indexed, but not stored. If we would like to store that field we will have to change our mappings file to one like the following:

```
{
  "book" : {
   "_type" : {
    "store" : "yes"
   },
   "properties" : {
    .
    .
    .
   }
  }
}
```

We can also change the _type field in such a way that it will not be indexed, but then some queries like term queries and filters will not work.

The _all field

The _all field allows us to create a field where the contents of other fields will be copied as well. This kind of field may be useful when we want to implement a simple search feature and search all the data (or only the fields we copy to the _all field), but we don't want to think about field names and things like that. By default the _all field is enabled and it contains all the data from all the fields from the index. In order to exclude a certain field from the _all field, one should use the include_ in_all property, which was discussed in *Chapter 2, Searching Your Data*.

In order to completely turn off the _all field functionality (our index will be smaller without the _all field) we will modify our mappings file to one looking like the following:

```
{
  "book" : {
   "_all" : {
    "enabled" : false
   },
   "properties" : {
     .

     .

     .
   }
  }
}
```

In addition to the enabled property, the _all field supports the following ones:

- store
- term_vector
- analyzer
- index_analyzer
- search_analyzer

For information about these properties please refer to *Chapter 2, Searching Your Data.*

The _source field

The _source field allows us to store the original JSON document that was sent to ElasticSearch during indexing. By default the _source field is turned on because some of the ElasticSearch functionalities depend on it, for example, the partial update feature that was already described in *Chapter 1, Getting Started with ElasticSearch Cluster*. In addition to that, the _source field can be used as the source of data for the highlighting functionality if a field is not stored. But if we don't need such functionality, we can disable those fields because it causes some storage overhead. In order to do that, we will need to set the enabled property of the _source object to false, for example, as shown in the following code:

```
{
  "book" : {
    "_source" : {
      "enabled" : false
    },
    "properties" : {
      .
      .
      .
    }
  }
}
```

Because the _source field causes some storage overhead we may choose to compress information stored in that field. In order to do that, we would have to set the compress parameter to true. Although this will shrink the index, it will make the operations made on the _source field a bit more CPU-intensive. However, ElasticSearch allows us to decide when to compress the _source field. Using the compress_threshold property, we can control how big the _source field's content needs to be in order for ElasticSearch to compress it. This property accepts a size value in bytes (for example, 100b, 10kb).

The _boost field

As you may suspect, the _boost field allows us to set a default boost value for all the documents of a certain type. Imagine that we would like our book's documents to have a higher value than all the other types of documents in the index. You may wonder, why increase the boost value of the document? If some of your documents are more important than others, you can increase their boost value in order for ElasticSearch to know that they are more valuable. To achieve that for every single document we can use the _boost field. So if we would like all our book documents to have the value 10.0, we can modify our mappings to something like the following:

```
{
  "book" : {
    "_boost" : {
      "name" : "_boost",
      "null_value" : 10.0
    },
    "properties" : {
      .
      .
      .
    }
  }
}
```

This mapping change says that if we don't add an additional field named `_boost` to our documents sent for indexing the `null_value` value will be used as boost. If we do add such a field, its value will be used instead of the default one.

The _index field

ElasticSearch allows us to store information about the index that the document is indexed in. We can do that by using the internal `_index` field. Imagine that we create daily indices, use aliasing, and are interested to know in which daily index the returned document is stored. In such a case the `_index` field can be useful.

By default, the indexing of the `_index` field is disabled. In order to enable it, we need to set the `enabled` property of the `_index` object to `true`, for example:

```
{
  "book" : {
   "_index" : {
    "enabled" : true
   },
   "properties" : {
    .

    .

    .
   }
  }
}
```

The _size field

The `_size` field, which is disabled by default, allows you to automatically index the original, uncompressed size of the `_source` field and store it along with the documents. If we would like to enable the `_size` field, we need to add the `_size` property and wrap the `enabled` property with the value of `true`. In addition to that, we can also set the `_size` field to be stored by using the usual `store` property. So, if we would like our mapping to include the `_size` field and also want to store it, we have to change our mappings to something like the following:

```
{
  "book" : {
   "_size" : {
    "enabled": true,
    "store" : "yes"
   },
```

```
    "properties" : {
        .
        .
        .
    }
  }
}
```

The _timestamp field

The `_timestamp` field, which is disabled by default, allows us to store information about when the document was indexed. Enabling that functionality is as simple as adding the `_timestamp` section to our mappings and setting the `enabled` property to `true`, for example:

```
{
  "book" : {
  "_timestamp" : {

  "enabled" : true

  },
  "properties" : {
      .
      .
      .
  }
 }
}
```

The `_timestamp` field is not stored, indexed, and also not analyzed by default, but you can change those two parameters to match your needs. In addition to that, the `_timestamp` field is just like the normal date field so we can change its format just like we do with the usual date-based fields. In order to change the format, we need to specify the `format` property with the desired format.

One more thing, instead of automatically creating the `_timestamp` field during document indexation, we can add the `path` property and set it to the name of the field from which the date should be taken. So if we would like our `_timestamp` field to be based on the `year` field, we need to modify our mappings to something like the following:

```
{
  "book" : {
   "_timestamp" : {
    "enabled" : true,
    "path" : "year",
    "format" : "YYYY"
   },
   "properties" : {
    .
    .
    .
   }
  }
}
```

As you may notice, we also modify the format of the `_timestamp` field in order to match the values stored in the `year` field.

> If you use the `_timestamp` field and you let ElasticSearch create it automatically, the value of that field will be set to the time of indexation of that document. Please note that when using the partial document update functionality the `_timestamp` field will also be updated.

The _ttl field

The `_ttl` field stands for time to live, that is, a functionality that allows us to define a life period of a document after which it will be automatically deleted. As you may expect, by default the `_ttl` field is disabled and to enable it we need to add the `_ttl` JSON object with its `enabled` property set to `true`, just like in the following example:

```
{
  "book" : {
   "_ttl" : {
    "enabled" : true
   },
   "properties" : {
    .
    .
    .
   }
  }
}
```

If you need to provide the default expiration time for documents, just add the default property to the _ttl field definition with the desired expiration time. For example, to have our documents deleted after 30 days, we would set the following parameters:

```
{
  "book" : {
   "_ttl" : {
    "enabled" : true,
    "default" : "30d"
   },
   "properties" : {
    .
    .
    .
   }
  }
}
```

By default, the _ttl field is stored and indexed, but not analyzed and you can change those two parameters, but remember that this field needs to be not analyzed in order to work.

Highlighting

You have probably heard of highlighting or even if you are not familiar with the name you've probably seen highlighting results on the usual web pages that you visit. **Highlighting** is the process of showing which word or words for the query were matched in the resulting documents. For example, if we search Google for the word `lucene` you will see it in bold in the results list, for example:

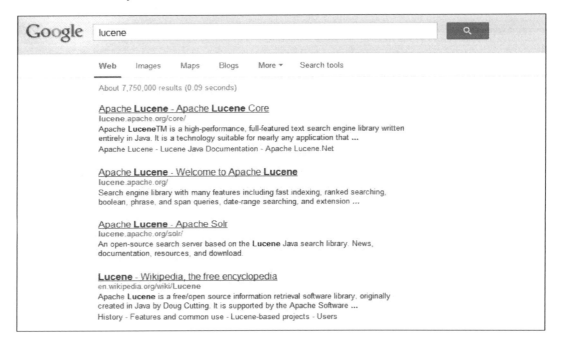

In this chapter, we will see how to use the ElasticSearch highlighting capabilities to enhance our application with highlighted results.

Getting started with highlighting

There is no better way of showing how highlighting works than making a query and looking at the results returned by ElasticSearch. So let's do that. Let's assume that we would like to highlight the words that were matched in the `title` field of our documents to increase the search experience of our users. We are again looking for the word `crime` and we would like to get highlighted results, so the following query would have to be sent:

```
{
 "query" : {
  "term" : {
   "title" : "crime"
  }
 },
 "highlight" : {
  "fields" : {
   "title" : {}
  }
 }
}
```

The response for such a query would be as follows:

```
{
  "took" : 2,
  "timed_out" : false,
  "_shards" : {
    "total" : 5,
    "successful" : 5,
    "failed" : 0
  },
  "hits" : {
    "total" : 1,
    "max_score" : 0.19178301,
    "hits" : [ {
      "_index" : "library",
      "_type" : "book",
      "_id" : "4",
      "_score" : 0.19178301, "_source" : { "title": "Crime and
Punishment","otitle": "Преступление и наказáние","author": "Fyodor
Dostoevsky","year": 1886,"characters": ["Raskolnikov", "Sofia
Semyonovna Marmeladova"],"tags": [],"copies": 0, "available" : true},
      "highlight" : {
        "title" : [ "<em>Crime</em> and Punishment" ]
      }
    } ]
  }
}
```

As you can see, apart from the standard information we got from ElasticSearch, there is a new section called highlight. Here, ElasticSearch used the <em> HTML tag as the beginning of the highlight section and its closing counterpart to close the section. This is the default behavior of ElasticSearch, but we will learn how to change that.

Field configuration

In order to perform highlighting, the original content of the field needs to be present — we have to set to store the fields that we will use for highlighting. However, it is possible to use the `_source` field if fields are not stored and ElasticSearch will use one or the other automatically.

Under the hood

ElasticSearch uses Apache Lucene under the hood and highlighting is one of the features of that library. Lucene provides two types of highlighting implementation — the standard one, which we just used and the second one called `FastVectorHighlighter`, which needs term vectors and positions to be able to work. ElasticSearch chooses the right highlighter implementation automatically. If the field is configured with the `term_vector` property set to `with_positions_offsets`, `FastVectorHighlighter` will be used; otherwise the default Lucene highlighter will be used.

However, you have to remember that having term vectors will cause your index to be larger, but the highlighting will take less time to be executed. Also, `FastVectorHighlighter` is recommended for fields that store a lot of data in them.

Configuring HTML tags

As we already mentioned, it is possible to change the default HTML tags to the ones we would like to use. For example, let's assume that we would like to use the standard HTML `<b>` tag for highlighting. In order to do that, we should set the `pre_tags` and `post_tags` properties (those are arrays) to `<b>` and `</b>`. Because both of these properties are arrays, we can include more than one tag and ElasticSearch will use each of the defined tags to highlight different words. So our example query would be like the following:

```
{
  "query" : {
   "term" : {
    "title" : "crime"
   }
  },
  "highlight" : {
   "pre_tags" : [ "<b>" ],
   "post_tags" : [ "</b>" ],
   "fields" : {
    "title" : {}
   }
  }
}
```

The result returned by ElasticSearch to the previous query would be the following:

```
{
  "took" : 2,
  "timed_out" : false,
  "_shards" : {
    "total" : 5,
    "successful" : 5,
    "failed" : 0
  },
  "hits" : {
    "total" : 1,
    "max_score" : 0.19178301,
    "hits" : [ {
      "_index" : "library",
      "_type" : "book",
      "_id" : "4",
      "_score" : 0.19178301, "_source" : { "title": "Crime and
Punishment","otitle": "Преступление и наказа́ние","author": "Fyodor
Dostoevsky","year": 1886,"characters": ["Raskolnikov", "Sofia
Semyonovna Marmeladova"],"tags": [],"copies": 0, "available" : true},
      "highlight" : {
        "title" : [ "<b>Crime</b> and Punishment" ]
      }
    } ]
  }
}
```

As you can see, the word `Crime` in `title` was surrounded by the tags of our choice.

Controlling highlighted fragments

ElasticSearch allows us to control the number of highlighted fragments returned, their sizes, and also exposes two of the properties we are allowed to use. The first one, `number_of_fragments`, defines the number of fragments returned by ElasticSearch (it defaults to 5). Setting this property to 0 causes the whole field to be returned, which can be handy for short fields; however, it can be expensive for longer fields.

The second property, `fragment_size`, lets us specify the maximum length of the highlighted fragments in characters and defaults to 100.

Global and local settings

The highlighting properties we discussed previously can be set both on a global basis and on a per field basis. The global ones will be used for all the fields that don't overwrite them and should be placed on the same level as the `fields` section of your highlighting, for example:

```
{
 "query" : {
  "term" : {
   "title" : "crime"
  }
 },
 "highlight" : {
  "pre_tags" : [ "<b>" ],
  "post_tags" : [ "</b>" ],
  "fields" : {
   "title" : {}
  }
 }
}
```

You can also set the properties for each field. For example, if we would like to keep the default behavior for all the fields except our `title` field, we would do the following:

```
{
 "query" : {
  "term" : {
   "title" : "crime"
  }
 },
 "highlight" : {
  "fields" : {
   "title" : { "pre_tags" : [ "<b>" ], "post_tags" : [ "</b>" ] }
  }
 }
}
```

As you can see, instead of placing the properties on the same level as the `fields` section we placed them inside the empty JSON object that specifies the `field` title's behavior. Of course, each field can be configured to use different properties.

Require matching

One last thing about highlighting, sometimes there may be a need (especially when using multiple highlighted fields) to show only the fields that matched our query. In order to have such behavior, we need to set the `require_field_match` property to `true`. Setting this property to `false` will cause all the terms to get highlighted even if a field didn't match the query.

To see how that works, let's create a new index called `users` and let's index a single document there. We will do that by sending the following command:

```
curl -XPUT 'http://localhost:9200/users/user/1' -d '{
 "name" : "Test user",
 "description" : "Test document"
}'
```

So, let's assume we want to highlight the hits in both of the previous fields, so our query will look like the following:

```
{
  "query" : {
   "term" : {
    "name" : "test"
   }
  },
  "highlight" : {
   "fields" : {
    "name" : { "pre_tags" : [ "<b>" ], "post_tags" : [ "</b>" ] },
    "description" : { "pre_tags" : [ "<b>" ], "post_tags" : [ "</b>" ]
  }
   }
  }
}
```

The result of the query would be as follows:

```
{
   "took" : 3,
   "timed_out" : false,
   "_shards" : {
     "total" : 5,
     "successful" : 5,
     "failed" : 0
   },
```

```
    "hits" : {
      "total" : 1,
      "max_score" : 0.19178301,
      "hits" : [ {
        "_index" : "users",
        "_type" : "user",
        "_id" : "1",
        "_score" : 0.19178301, "_source" : {"name" : "Test
user","description" : "Test document"},
        "highlight" : {
          "description" : [ "<b>Test</b> document" ],
          "name" : [ "<b>Test</b> user" ]
        }
      } ]
    }
  }
```

Notice, that even though we only matched the name field, we got highlighting results in both fields. In most cases we want to avoid that. So now let's modify our query to use the require_field_match property:

```
{
  "query" : {
   "term" : {
    "name" : "test"
   }
  },
  "highlight" : {
   "require_field_match" : true,
   "fields" : {
    "name" : { "pre_tags" : [ "<b>" ], "post_tags" : [ "</b>" ] },
    "description" : { "pre_tags" : [ "<b>" ], "post_tags" : [ "</b>" ]
}
   }
  }
}
```

And now let's look at the modified query results:

```
{
  "took" : 2,
  "timed_out" : false,
  "_shards" : {
    "total" : 5,
    "successful" : 5,
    "failed" : 0
  },
  "hits" : {
    "total" : 1,
    "max_score" : 0.19178301,
    "hits" : [ {
      "_index" : "users",
      "_type" : "user",
      "_id" : "1",
      "_score" : 0.19178301, "_source" : {"name" : "Test
user","description" : "Test document"},
      "highlight" : {
        "name" : [ "<b>Test</b> user" ]
      }
    } ]
  }
}
```

As you can see, ElasticSearch returned only the field that was matched, in our case the name field.

Autocomplete

Modern searching doesn't go without the autocomplete functionality. Thanks to it, users are provided with a convenient way to find items whose spelling isn't known. Autocomplete can also be a good marketing tool. For these reasons, sooner or later, you'll want to know how to implement this feature.

Before we configure autocomplete, we should ask ourselves a few questions: what data do we want to use for suggestions? Do we have a set of suggestions already prepared (such as country names) or do we want to generate them dynamically, based on indexed documents? Do we want to suggest words or whole documents? Do we need information about the number of suggested items? And finally, do we want to display only one field from the document or a few (for example, product name and price)? Each possible solution has its pros and cons and supports one requirement at the cost of another. Now, let's go through three common ways to implement the autocomplete functionality in ElasticSearch.

The prefix query

The simplest way of building an autocomplete solution is using a prefix query, which we have already discussed. For example, if we want to suggest country names, we just index them (for example, into the country_code field) and search like the following:

```
curl -XGET 'localhost:9200/countries/_search' -d '
{
  "query" : {
   "prefix" : {
    "country": "r"
   }
  }
}'
```

This returns every country that starts with the letter r. This is very simple, but not ideal. If you have more data, you will notice that the prefix query is expensive. It is not suitable for open datasets where individual values can be repeated. Fortunately, if we run into performance problems, we can modify this method to the one using edge ngrams.

Edge ngrams

The prefix query works well; but in order for it to work, ElasticSearch must iterate through the list of terms to find the ones that match the given prefix. The idea for optimizing this is quite simple. Since finding particular terms is less costly, we can split terms into smaller parts. For example, the word Britain can be stored as a series of terms such as Bri, Brit, Brita, Britai, and Britain. Thanks to this, we can find documents containing the whole word only by supplying a part of that word. You may wonder why we start with three-letter tokens. In real-case scenarios, suggestions for shorter user input is not very useful due to too many suggestions being returned.

Let's see a full-index configuration for a simple address book application:

```
{
  "settings" : {
    "index" : {
      "analysis" : {
        "analyzer" : {
          "autocomplete" : {
            "tokenizer" : "engram",
            "filter" : ["lowercase"]
          }
        },
        "tokenizer" : {
          "engram" : {
            "type" : "edgeNGram",
            "min_gram" : 3,
            "max_gram" : 10
          }
        }
      }
    }
  },
  "mappings" : {
    "contact" : {
      "properties" : {
        "name" : {
          "type" : "string",
          "index_analyzer" : "autocomplete",
          "index" : "analyzed", "search_analyzer" : "standard"
        },
        "country" : { "type" : "string" }
      }
    }
  }
}
```

The mapping for this index contains the name field. This is the field that we'll use to generate suggestions. As you can see, this field has a different analyzer defined for indexing and searching. During indexing, ElasticSearch cuts input words into edge ngrams but while searching this is not necessary (and not desired) as the user already provides a part of the field. Note the engram tokenizer configuration.

There are two options we are currently interested in. They are:

- `min_gram`: Tokens that are shorter than the value of this parameter won't be built. This value directly influences the minimum number of characters that will have to be provided in order to get suggestions. In our case it's 3.

- `max_gram`: The tokenizer will ignore tokens for longer than the value given by this parameter. This is the maximum number of characters for which suggestions will be available. You can use any reasonable limit. In this example, we assume that no one will need suggestions for longer queries because the user probably knows what he or she wants to find.

Now, let's look at how it works. For this example, we can use the simplest form of query, as follows:

```
curl -XGET 'localhost:9200/addressbook/_search?q=name:joh&pretty'
```

For names shorter than three characters, the search returns no results. For more than three, the number of results will be equal to the available suggestions.

If you look again at the specified analyzer, you'll notice that the analyzer used for the `name` field doesn't split the text into words before changing it to ngrams. Because of that, this version of autocomplete suits well for situations where we assume that our users will write the exact content of the field. This is usually the case when our users use the autocomplete functionality as a tool for faster choice of a particular value. This is useful for countries, but for an address book and people's names we need to suggest something regardless of whether the user starts to type the first name or the last name. After small changes done to our mapping, it will look like the following:

```
{
  "settings" : {
    "index" : {
      "analysis" : {
        "analyzer" : {
          "autocomplete" : {
            "tokenizer" : "whitespace",
            "filter" : ["lowercase", "engram"]
          }
        },
```

```
        "filter" : {
          "engram" : {
            "type" : "edgeNGram",
            "min_gram" : 3,
            "max_gram" : 10
          }
        }
      }
    }
  },
  "mappings" : {
    "contact" : {
      "properties" : {
        "name" : { "type" : "string", "index_analyzer" :
"autocomplete", "index" : "analyzed", "search_analyzer" : "standard"
},
        "country" : { "type" : "string" }
      }
    }
  }
}
```

Note the highlighted fragments. First, we see that the tokenizer was changed to
whitespace. This provides the functionality of dividing our document field's data
into words on the basis of whitespace characters. Because there can be only one
tokenizer, we moved the engram definition to a filter. Remember that the tokenizer
and the filters are different objects with different usage (the tokenizer takes input
and divides it into tokens and the filters operate on the token stream provided by the
tokenizer and can change tokens), but fortunately ElasticSearch provides edgeNGram
both as a tokenizer and as a filter so the changes are simple. The rest is the same as
in the previous example. But now we can fetch suggestions for part of every word
in the name field. For example, the following query will find the record with Joseph
Heller unlike the previous example query:

```
curl -XGET 'localhost:9200/addressbook/_search?q=name:jos&pretty'
```

The following query finds the record with Joseph Heller as well:

```
curl -XGET 'localhost:9200/addressbook/_search?q=name:hell&pretty'
```

Faceting

The third possible way of implementing the autocomplete functionality is based on faceting. We haven't written about faceting yet, so don't worry if you have no idea of how it works. Everything will be explained in the chapter dedicated to faceting (*Chapter 6, Beyond Searching*). For now, let's assume that faceting is a functionality that allows us to get information about the distribution of a particular document value in the result set. In fact, this solution is an extension of the previous idea. It introduces the possibility of working with repeatable tokens and it is suitable for suggestions based on non-dictionary data. First let's look at the rewritten index configuration:

```
{
  "settings" : {
   "index" : {
    "analysis" : {
     "analyzer" : {
      "autocomplete" : {
       "tokenizer" : "whitespace",
       "filter" : ["lowercase", "engram"]
      }
     },
     "filter" : {
      "engram" : {
       "type" : "edgeNGram",
       "min_gram" : 3,
       "max_gram" : 10
      }
     }
    }
   }
  },
  "mappings" : {
   "contact" : {
    "properties" : {
     "name" : {
      "type" : "multi_field",
      "fields" : {
       "name" : { "type" : "string", "index" : "not_analyzed" },
       "autocomplete" : { "type" : "string", "index_analyzer" :
"autocomplete", "index" : "analyzed", "search_analyzer" : "standard" }
      }
     },
     "country" : { "type" : "string" }
    }
   }
  }
}
```

The only difference from the previous example is the additional `not_analyzed` field, which we will use as a facet label. This is a common technique for functionalities such as autocomplete. We prepare several forms of one field where each form has its own use. For example, if we want to search on this field as well, we can add another `analyzed` copy.

Since this time the query will be more complicated, we put it in the `facet_query.json` file. Its contents are:

```
{
  "size" : 0,
  "query" : {
   "term" : { "name.autocomplete" : "jos" }
  },
  "facets" : {
   "name" : {
    "terms" : {
     "field" : "name"
    }
   }
  }
}
```

We are searching for every name starting with `jos`. This is exactly the same as in the previous example. But look at the `size` parameter. We don't want any document to be returned. Why? Because all the information is in facets and document data is only an additional ballast. Now, let's execute our search by sending the following command:

```
curl -XGET 'localhost:9200/addressbook/_search?pretty' -d @facet_query.json
```

You know a little about faceting, so this time we'll show the returned data:

```
{
  "took" : 1,
  "timed_out" : false,
  "_shards" : {
    "total" : 5,
    "successful" : 5,
    "failed" : 0
  },
  "hits" : {
    "total" : 1,
    "max_score" : 0.095891505,
    "hits" : [ ]
  },
```

```
    "facets" : {
      "name" : {
        "_type" : "terms",
        "missing" : 0,
        "total" : 1,
        "other" : 0,
        "terms" : [ {
          "term" : "Joseph Heller",
          "count" : 1
        } ]
      }
    }
  }
```

As you can see in the highlighted part we have a single suggestion returned. And in addition to the suggestion, you can also see the count parameter, which holds the information about how many times it appeared in the matched documents. If we had more suggestions, the first 10 of them would show as the values in the terms array. Why 10? How to change this? This is something you can learn in *Chapter 6, Beyond Searching*, in the section dedicated to faceting.

Handling files

The next use case we will discuss is searching in the contents of files. The most obvious method is adding logic to an application that will be responsible for fetching files, extracting valuable information from them, building JSON objects, and indexing them to ElasticSearch.

Of course the previously mentioned method is valid and you can go this way, but there is another way we would like to show you. We can send documents to ElasticSearch for content extraction and indexing. This requires us to install an additional plugin. Note that we will describe plugins in *Chapter 7, Administrating Your Cluster*, so we'll skip the detailed description here. For now, just run the following command to install the attachments plugin:

```
bin/plugin -install elasticsearch/elasticsearch-mapper-attachments/1.6.0
```

After restarting ElasticSearch, it miraculously gains new skills!

Let's begin with preparing a new index with the following mappings:

```
{
  "mappings" : {
    "file" : {
      "properties" : {
        "note" : { "type" : "string", "store" : "yes" },
        "book" : {
          "type" : "attachment",
          "fields" : {
            "file" : { "store" : "yes", "index" : "analyzed" },
            "date" : { "store" : "yes" },
            "author" : { "store" : "yes" },
            "keywords" : { "store" : "yes" },
            "content_type" : { "store" : "yes" },
            "title" : { "store" : "yes" }
          }
        }
      }
    }
  }
}
```

As we can see, we have the book type, which we will use to store the contents of our file. In addition to that we've defined some nested fields as follows:

- file: The file content itself
- date: The file creation date
- author: The author of the file
- keywords: The additional keywords connected with the document
- content_type: The MIME type of the document
- title: The title of the document

These fields will be extracted from files, if available. In our example, we marked all fields as stored; this allows us to see their values in the search results. In addition, we defined the note field. This is an ordinary field, which will be used not only by the plugin but by us as well.

Now we should prepare our document. Look at the example placed in the index. json file:

```
{
  "book" : "UEsDBBQABgAIAAAAIQDpURCwjQEAAMIFAAATAAgCW0NvbnRlbnRfVHlw
ZXNdLnhtbCCiBAIooAA...",
  "note" : "just a note"
}
```

As you can see, we have some strange content in the book field. This is the content of the file encoded with the base64 algorithm (please note that this is only a small part of it; for clarity we omitted the rest of this field). Because the file contents can be binary and thus cannot be easily included in the JSON structure, the authors of ElasticSearch require us to encode the file contents with the mentioned algorithm. On the Linux operating system there is a simple command that we use to encode document contents into base64, for example, with a command like the following:

```
base64 -i example.docx -o example.docx.base64
```

We will assume that you successfully created a proper base64 version of our document. Now we can index this document by running the following command:

```
curl -XPUT 'localhost:9200/media/file/1?pretty' -d @index.json
```

It was simple. In the background, ElasticSearch decoded the file, extracted its contents and created proper entries in the index. Now, let's create the query (we've placed it in the query.json file):

```
{
  "fields" : ["title", "author", "date", "keywords", "content_type",
"note"],
  "query" : {
    "term" : { "book" : "example" }
  }
}
```

If you have read the previous chapters carefully, the previous query should be simple to understand. We searched for the word example in the book field. Our example document contains the text This is an example document for "ElasticSearch Server" book; we need to find this document. In addition, we requested all the stored fields to be returned in the results. Let's execute our query:

```
curl -XGET 'localhost:9200/media/_search?pretty' -d @query.json
```

If everything goes well, we should see something like the following:

```
{
    "took" : 2,
    "timed_out" : false,
    "_shards" : {
      "total" : 5,
      "successful" : 5,
      "failed" : 0
    },
    "hits" : {
      "total" : 1,
      "max_score" : 0.13424811,
      "hits" : [ {
        "_index" : "media",
        "_type" : "file",
        "_id" : "1",
        "_score" : 0.13424811,
        "fields" : {
          "book.content_type" : "application/vnd.openxmlformats-
officedocument.wordprocessingml.document",
          "book.title" : "ElasticSearch Server",
          "book.author" : " Rafał Kuć, Marek Rogoziński",
          "book.keywords" : "ElasticSearch, search, book",
          "book.date" : "2012-10-08T17:54:00.000Z",
          "note" : "just a note"
        }
      } ]
    }
}
```

Looking at the result, you see content type `application/vnd.openxmlformats-officedocument.wordprocessingml.document`. You can guess that our document was created in Microsoft Office and probably had the `.docx` extension. We also see additional fields such as authors or modification date extracted from the document. And again everything works!

Additional information about a file

When we are indexing files, the obvious requirement is the possibility of returning the filename in the result list. Of course we can add the filename as another field in the document, but ElasticSearch allows us to store this information within the file object. We can just add the `_name` field to the document in the following manner:

```
{
```

```
   "book" : "UEsDBBQABgAIAAAAIQDpURCwjQEAAMIFAAATAAgCW0NvbnRlbnRfVHlw
ZXNdLnhtbCCiBAIooAA...",
 "_name" : "example.docx",
 "note" : "just a note"
}
```

Thanks to it being available in the result list, the filename will be available as a part of the _source field. But if you use the fields option in the query, don't forget to add _source to this array.

And finally, you can use the content_type field for information about MIME type, just as the _name field.

Geo

Search servers such as ElasticSearch are usually looked at from the perspective of full text search. This is only partially true. Sometimes the text search is not enough. Imagine searching for local services. For the end user the most important thing is the accuracy of results, but by accuracy we not only mean the proper results of full text search, but also the results being as near as they can in terms of location. In some cases this is the same as text search on geographical names such as cities or streets, but in other cases we can find it very useful to be able to search on the basis of geographical coordinates of our indexed documents. As you can guess, this is of course also something that is supported by ElasticSearch.

Mapping preparation for spatial search

In order to discuss the spatial search functionality, let's prepare an index with a list of cities. This will be a very simple index with one type named poi (which stands for point of interest) with name of the city and its coordinates. The mappings are as follows:

```
{
 "mappings" : {
  "poi" : {
   "properties" : {
    "name" : { "type" : "string" },
    "location" : { "type" : "geo_point" }
   }
  }
 }
}
```

Assuming that we put this definition into the `mapping.json` file, we can create an index by running the following command:

```
curl -XPUT localhost:9200/map -d @mapping.json
```

The only new thing is the `geo_point` type, which is used for the `location` field. By using it we can store the geographical position of our city.

Example data

Our example file with documents looks like the following:

```
{ "index" : { "_index" : "map", "_type" : "poi", "_id" : 1 }}
{ "name" : "New York", "location" : "40.664167, -73.938611" }
{ "index" : { "_index" : "map", "_type" : "poi", "_id" : 2 }}
{ "name" : "London", "location" : [-0.1275, 51.507222] }
{ "index" : { "_index" : "map", "_type" : "poi", "_id" : 3 }}
{ "name" : "Moscow", "location" : { "lat" : 55.75, "lon" : 37.616667
}}
{ "index" : { "_index" : "map", "_type" : "poi", "_id" : 4 }}
{ "name" : "Sydney", "location" : "-33.859972, 151.211111" }
{ "index" : { "_index" : "map", "_type" : "poi", "_id" : 5 }}
{ "name" : "Lisbon", "location" : "eycs0p8ukc7v" }
```

In order to perform a bulk request, we've added information about index name, type, and the unique identifier of our documents. So we can now easily import this data using the following command:

```
curl -XPOST http://localhost:9200/_bulk --data-binary @documents.json
```

Look at this data and the `location` field. We use various notations for coordinates. We can provide the latitude and longitude as a string, as a pair of numbers, or as an object. Note that the string and array method have a different order for the latitude and longitude parameters. The last record shows that there is also a possibility to give coordinates as a geohash value.

Sample queries

Now let's look at several examples of how to use coordinates and solve common requirement problems in modern applications that require searching geographical data along with full text searching.

Let's start from a very common requirement of sorting results by distance from the given point. In our example, we want to get all the cities and sort them by the distance from the capital of France, that is, Paris. In order to do that, we send the following query to ElasticSearch:

```
{
  "query" : {
   "matchAll" : {}
  },
  "sort" : [{
   "_geo_distance" : {
    "location" : "48.8567, 2.3508",
    "unit" : "km"
   }
  }]
}
```

If you remember the *Sorting data* section from *Chapter 2, Searching Your Data*, you'll notice that the format is slightly different. We are using the _geo_distance key to indicate sorting by distance. We must give the base location (the location attribute, which holds the information of the Paris location in our case) and we specify units that could be used in results. The available values are km and mi, which stand for kilometers and miles. The result of such a query will be as follows:

```
{
  "took" : 102,
  "timed_out" : false,
  "_shards" : {
    "total" : 5,
    "successful" : 5,
    "failed" : 0
  },
  "hits" : {
    "total" : 5,
    "max_score" : null,
    "hits" : [ {
      "_index" : "map",
      "_type" : "poi",
      "_id" : "2",
      "_score" : null, "_source" : { "name" : "London", "location" :
[-0.1275, 51.507222] },
      "sort" : [ 343.46748684411773 ]
    }, {
```

```
        "_index" : "map",
        "_type" : "poi",
        "_id" : "5",
        "_score" : null, "_source" : { "name" : "Lisbon", "location" :
"eycs0p8ukc7v" },
        "sort" : [ 1453.6450747751787 ]
    }, {
        "_index" : "map",
        "_type" : "poi",
        "_id" : "3",
        "_score" : null, "_source" : { "name" : "Moscow", "location" : {
"lat" : 55.75, "lon" : 37.616667 }},
        "sort" : [ 2486.2560754763977 ]
    }, {
        "_index" : "map",
        "_type" : "poi",
        "_id" : "1",
        "_score" : null, "_source" : { "name" : "New York", "location" :
"40.664167, -73.938611" },
        "sort" : [ 5835.763890418129 ]
    }, {
        "_index" : "map",
        "_type" : "poi",
        "_id" : "4",
        "_score" : null, "_source" : { "name" : "Sydney", "location" :
"-33.859972, 151.211111" },
        "sort" : [ 16960.04911335322 ]
    } ]
}
```

As for the other examples with sorting, ElasticSearch shows information about the values used for sorting. Let's look at the highlighted record. As we can see, the distance between Paris and London is about 343 km; you can check that the map agrees with ElasticSearch in this case.

Bounding box filtering

The next example that we want to show is narrowing the results to a selected area that is bounded by a given rectangle. This is very handy if we want to show results on the map or when we allow the user to mark a map area for searching. You have already read about filters in the *Filtering your results* section in *Chapter 2, Searching Your Data*, so you can probably guess that we need to use this functionality. This is how we can do it:

```
{
  "filter" : {
    "geo_bounding_box" : {
      "location" : {
        "top_left" : "52.4796, -1.903",
        "bottom_right" : "48.8567, 2.3508"
      }
    }
  }
}
```

In this example, we selected the map fragment between Birmingham and Paris by providing the top-left and bottom-right corners' coordinates. Those two corners are enough to specify any rectangle we want and ElasticSearch will do the rest of the calculation for us. The following screenshot shows the specified rectangle on the map:

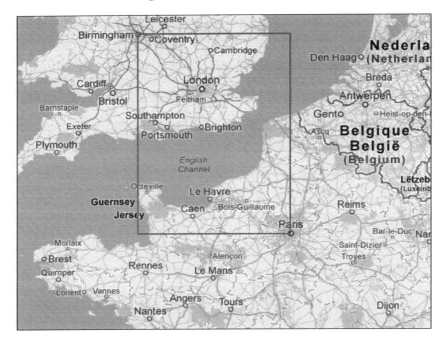

As we can see, the only city from our data that meets the criteria is **London**. So let's check if ElasticSearch knows about that by running the previous query and checking the results:

```
{
  "took" : 9,
  "timed_out" : false,
  "_shards" : {
    "total" : 5,
    "successful" : 5,
    "failed" : 0
  },
  "hits" : {
    "total" : 1,
    "max_score" : 1.0,
    "hits" : [ {
      "_index" : "map",
      "_type" : "poi",
      "_id" : "2",
      "_score" : 1.0, "_source" : { "name" : "London", "location" :
[-0.1275, 51.507222] }
    } ]
  }
}
```

As you can see, once again ElasticSearch agrees with the map.

Limiting the distance

The previous example shows the next common requirement, that is, how to limit the result to places that are located within the selected distance from the base point. Let's see all the cities closer than 500km from Paris:

```
{
  "filter" : {
  "geo_distance" : {
   "location" : "48.8567, 2.3508",
   "distance" : "500km"
  }
  }
}
```

If everything goes well, ElasticSearch should return only a single record for this query and that record should be that for London; however, we will leave it for you as a reader to check that.

Summary

In this chapter, we've looked at how to extend your indices with additional data such as timestamp, index name, or time-to-live information. We've also learned how to index data that is not flat and how to deal with geographical data and files. In addition to that, we've implemented the autocomplete functionality for our application. In the next chapter, we will learn how to use information provided by ElasticSearch and how to use query and index-time boosting. We'll learn about the possibility of using synonyms and span queries. And finally, we'll discuss multilingual data handling.

4

Make Your Search Better

In the previous chapter, we learned how to extend our index with additional information and how to handle highlighting and indexing data that is not flat. We also implemented an autocomplete mechanism using ElasticSearch, indexed files, and geographical information. However, by the end of this chapter, you will have learned the following:

- Why your document was matched
- How to influence document score
- How to use synonyms
- How to handle multilingual data
- How to use term position aware queries (span queries)

Why this document was found

Compared to databases, using systems capable of performing full-text search can often be anything other than obvious. We can search in many fields simultaneously and the data in the index can vary from those provided for indexing because of the analysis process, synonyms, language analysis, abbreviations, and others. It's even worse; by default, search engines sort data by scoring—a number that indicates how many current documents fit into the current searching criteria. For this, "how much" is the key; search takes into consideration many factors such as how many searched words were found in the document, how frequent is this word in the whole index, and how long is the field. This seems complicated and finding out why a document was found and why another document is "better" is not easy. Fortunately, ElasticSearch has some tools that can answer these questions. Let's take a look at them!

Understanding how a field is analyzed

One of the common questions asked is why a given document was not found. In many cases, the problem lies in the definition of the mappings and the configuration of the analysis process. For debugging an analysis, ElasticSearch provides a dedicated REST API endpoint. Let's see a few examples on how to use this API.

The first query asks ElasticSearch for information about the analysis process, using the default analyzer:

```
curl -XGET 'localhost:9200/_analyze?pretty' -d 'Crime and Punishment'
```

In response, we get the following data:

```
{
  "tokens" : [ {
    "token" : "crime",
    "start_offset" : 0,
    "end_offset" : 5,
    "type" : "<ALPHANUM>",
    "position" : 1
  }, {
    "token" : "punishment",
    "start_offset" : 10,
    "end_offset" : 20,
    "type" : "<ALPHANUM>",
    "position" : 3
  } ]
}
```

As we can see, ElasticSearch divided the input phrase into two tokens. During processing, the and common word was omitted (because it belongs to the stop words list) and the other words were changed to lowercase versions. Now let's take a look at something more complicated. In *Chapter 3, Extending Your Structure and Search*, when we talked about the autocomplete feature, we used the edge engram filter. Let's recall this index and see how our analyzer works in that case:

```
curl -XGET 'localhost:9200/addressbook/_analyze?analyzer=autocomplete&pre
tty' -d 'John Smith'
```

In the preceding call, we used an additional parameter named `analyzer`, which you should already be familiar with—it tells ElasticSearch which analyzer should be used instead of the default one. Look at the returned result:

```
{
  "tokens" : [ {
    "token" : "joh",
```

```
    "start_offset" : 0,
    "end_offset" : 3,
    "type" : "word",
    "position" : 1
}, {
    "token" : "john",
    "start_offset" : 0,
    "end_offset" : 4,
    "type" : "word",
    "position" : 2
}, {
    "token" : "smi",
    "start_offset" : 5,
    "end_offset" : 8,
    "type" : "word",
    "position" : 3
}, {
    "token" : "smit",
    "start_offset" : 5,
    "end_offset" : 9,
    "type" : "word",
    "position" : 4
}, {
    "token" : "smith",
    "start_offset" : 5,
    "end_offset" : 10,
    "type" : "word",
    "position" : 5
} ]
}
```

This time, in addition to lowercasing and splitting words, we used the edge engram filter. Our phrase was divided into tokens and lowercased. Please note that the minimum length of the generated prefixes was three letters.

It is worth noting that there is another form of analysis API available—one that allows us to provide tokenizers and filters. It is very handy when we want to experiment with a configuration before creating the target mappings. An example of such a call is as follows:

```
curl -XGET 'localhost:9200/addressbook/_analyze?tokenizer=whitespace&filt
ers=lowercase,engram&pretty' -d 'John Smith'
```

In the preceding example, we used an analyzer that was built from the `whitespace` tokenizer and the two filters `lowercase` and `engram`.

As we can see, an analysis API can be very useful for tracking down bugs in the mapping configuration, but when we want to solve problems with queries and search relevance, explanation from the API is invaluable. It can show us how our analyzers work, what terms they produce, and what are the attributes of those terms. With such information, analyzing query problems will be easier to track down.

Explaining the query

Let's look at the following example:

```
curl -XGET 'localhost:9200/library/book/1/_explain?pretty&q=quiet'
```

In the preceding call, we provided a specific document and a query to run. Using the _explain endpoint, we ask ElasticSearch for an explanation about how the document was matched (or not matched) by ElasticSearch. For example, should the preceding document be found by the provided query? If it is found, ElasticSearch will provide the information why the document was matched with the details about how its score was calculated:

```
{
  "ok" : true,
  "matches" : true,
  "explanation" : {
    "value" : 0.057534903,
    "description" : "fieldWeight(_all:quiet in 0), product of:",
    "details" : [ {
      "value" : 1.0,
      "description" : "tf(termFreq(_all:quiet)=1)"
    }, {
      "value" : 0.30685282,
      "description" : "idf(docFreq=1, maxDocs=1)"
    }, {
      "value" : 0.1875,
      "description" : "fieldNorm(field=_all, doc=0)"
    } ]
  }
}
```

Looks complicated, doesn't it? Well, it is complicated and is even worse if we realize that this is only a simple query! ElasticSearch, and more specifically the Lucene library, shows the internal information of the scoring process. We will only scratch the surface and will explain the most important things.

The most important part is the total score calculated for a document. If it is equal to 0, the document won't match the given query. Another important element is the description that tells us about different scoring components. Depending on the query type, components may affect the final score in a different way. In our case, the total score is a product of the scores calculated by all the components.

The detailed information about components and knowing where we should seek for an explanation and why our document matches the query is also important. In this example, we were looking for the `quiet` word. It was found in the `_all` field. It is obvious because we searched in the default field, which is `_all` (you should remember from *Chapter 3, Extending Your Structure and Search*, that this is the field where all indexed data is copied by default to make a default search field available). In the preceding response, you can also read information about the term frequency in the given field (which was 1 in our case). This means that the field contained only a single occurrence of the searched term. And finally, the last piece of information; `maxDocs` equals to 1, which means that only one document was found with the specified term. This usually means that we are dealing with a small index or we've searched with the use of very rare word.

Influencing scores with query boosts

In the previous chapter, we learned how to check why the search returns a given document and what factors had influence on its position in the result list. When an application grows, the need for improving the quality of search also increases—so-called search experience. We need to gain knowledge about what is more important to the user and to see how users use the search functionality. This leads to various conclusions; for example, we see that some parts of the documents are more important than the others or that particular queries emphasize one field at the cost of others. This is where boosting can be used. In the previous chapters, we've seen some information about boosting. In this chapter, we'll summarize this knowledge and we will show how to use it in practice.

What is boost?

Boost is an additional value used in the process of scoring. We can apply this value to the following:

- **Query**: This is a way to inform the search engine that the given query that is a part of a complex query is more significant than the others.
- **Field**: Several document fields are important for the user. For example, searching e-mails by Bill should probably list those from Bill first, next those with Bill in subject, and then e-mails mentioning Bill in contents.

- **Document**: Sometimes some documents are more important. In our example, with e-mail searching, e-mails from our friend are usually more important than e-mails from an unknown man.

Values assigned by us to a query, field, or document are only one factor used when we calculate the resulting score. We will now look at a few examples of query boosting.

Adding boost to queries

Let's imagine that our index has two documents:

```
{
  "id" : 1,
  "to" : "John Smith",
  "from" : "David Jones",
  "subject" : "Top secret!"
}
```

And:

```
{
  "id" : 2,
  "to" : "David Jones",
  "from" : "John Smith",
  "subject" : "John, read this document"
}
```

This data is trivial, but it should describe our problem very well. Now let's assume we have the following query:

```
{
  "query" : {
    "query_string" : {
      "query" : "john",
      "use_dis_max" : false
    }
  }
}
```

In this case, ElasticSearch will create a query to the `_all` field and will find
documents that contain desired words. We also said that we don't want a disjunction
query to be used by specifying the `use_dis_max` parameter to `false` (if you don't
remember what a disjunction query is, please refer to the *Explaining the query string*
section dedicated to querying a string query in *Chapter 2, Searching Your Data*). As we
can easily guess, both our records will be returned and the record with ID equals to 2
will be first because of two occurrences of `John` in the `from` and `subject` fields. Let's
check this out in the following result:

```
"hits" : {
  "total" : 2,
  "max_score" : 0.16273327,
  "hits" : [ {
    "_index" : "messages",
    "_type" : "email",
    "_id" : "2",
    "_score" : 0.16273327, "_source" :
    { "to" : "David Jones", "from" :
    "John Smith", "subject" : "John, read this document"}
  }, {
    "_index" : "messages",
    "_type" : "email",
    "_id" : "1",
    "_score" : 0.11506981, "_source" :
    { "to" : "John Smith", "from" :
    "David Jones", "subject" : "Top secret!" }
  } ]
}
```

Is everything all right? Technically, yes. But I think that the second document should
be positioned as the first one in the result list, because when searching for something,
the most important factor (in many cases) is matching people, rather than the
subject of the message. You can disagree, but this is exactly why full-text searching
relevance is a difficult topic—sometimes it is hard to tell which ordering is better for
a particular case. What can we do? First, let's rewrite our query to implicitly inform
ElasticSearch what fields should be used for searching:

```
{
  "query" : {
    "query_string" : {
      "fields" : ["from", "to", "subject"],
      "query" : "john",
      "use_dis_max" : false
    }
  }
}
```

This is not exactly the same query as the previous one. If we run it, we will get the same results (in our case), but if you look carefully, you will notice differences in scoring. In the previous example, ElasticSearch only used one field, _all. Now we are searching in three fields. This means that several factors, such as field lengths, are changed. Anyway, this is not so important in our case. ElasticSearch, under the hood, generates a complex query made of three queries—one to each field so that fields are treated equally. Of course, the score contributed by each query depends on the number of terms found in this field and the length of this field. Let's introduce some differences between fields. Compare the following query to the previous one:

```
{
  "query" : {
    "query_string" : {
      "fields" : ["from^5", "to^10", "subject"],
      "query" : "john",
      "use_dis_max" : false
    }
  }
}
```

Look at the highlighted parts (^5 and ^10). In this way, we can tell ElasticSearch how important a given field is. We see that the most important field is to and the from field is less important. The subject field has the default value for boost, which is 1.0. Always remember that this value is only one of various factors. You may be wondering why we choose 5, not 1000 or 1.23. Well, this value depends on the effect we want to achieve, what query we have, and most importantly, what data we have in our index. This is the important part because this means that when data changes in the meaningful parts, we should probably check and tune our relevance once again.

Finally, let's look at a similar example, but using the bool query:

```
{
  "query" : {
    "bool" : {
      "should" : [
        { "term" : { "from": { "value" : "john", "boost" : 5 }}},
        { "term" : { "to": { "value" : "john", "boost" : 10  }}},
        { "term" : { "subject": { "value" : "john" }}}
      ]
    }
  }
}
```

Modifying the score

The preceding example shows how to affect the result list by boosting particular query components. Another technique is to run a query and affect the score of the documents returned by this query. In the following sections, we will summarize the possibilities offered by ElasticSearch. In the examples, we will use our library data from the second chapter.

Constant score query

A constant score query allows us to take any filter or query and explicitly set the value that should be used as the score that will be given for each matching document.

At first, this query doesn't seem to be practical. But when we think about building complex queries, this query allows us to set how many documents matching this query can affect the total score. Look at the following example:

```
{
  "query" : {
    "constant_score" : {
      "query": {
        "query_string" : {
          "query" : "available:false author:heller"
        }
      },
      "boost": 5.0
    }
  }
}
```

In our library data that we have used, we have two documents with the `available` field set to `false`. One of these documents has an additional value in the `author` field. But thanks to the constant score query, ElasticSearch will ignore that information. Both documents will be given a score equal to... `1.0`. Strange? Not if we think about normalization that happens during indexing. In this stage, ElasticSearch saved additional information and changed the resulting score in order for this score to be comparable with the other parts of this query. It doesn't matter if our query contains only a single part. Note that in our example, we've used a query, but we can also use a filter. This is also better for performance reasons. For clarity, let's look at the following example with a filter:

```
{
  "query" : {
    "constant_score" : {
      "filter": {
```

```
        "term" : {
          "available" : false
        }
      },
      "boost": 5.0
    }
  }
}
```

Custom boost factor query

This query is similar to the previous one. Let's start with an example:

```
{
  "query" : {
    "custom_boost_factor" : {
      "query": {
        "query_string" : {
          "query" : "available:false author:heller"
        }
      },
      "boost_factor": 5.0
    }
  }
}
```

In this case, the resulting score is multiplied by boost_factor. Unlike the previous query, this version doesn't support filters instead of queries.

Boosting query

The next type of query connected with boosting is the boosting query. The idea is to allow us to define an additional part of a query, where the score of every matched document decreases. The following example lists all the available books, but books written by E. M. Remarque will have a score of 10 times lower:

```
{
  "query" : {
    "boosting" : {
      "positive" : {
        "term" : {
          "available" : true
        }
      },
      "negative" : {
```

```
        "term" : {
          "author" : "remarque"
        }
      },
      "negative_boost" : 0.1
    }
  }
}
```

Custom score query

The custom score query gives us the simple possibility to set a score for all matched documents. It allows us to attach additional logic defined by a script to every matching document. Of course, this way of influencing a score is much slower, but sometimes it is the most convenient and the simplest way, so we should be aware of its existence and its possible usage. For example:

```
{
  "query" : {
    "custom_score" : {
      "query" : {
        "matchAll" : {}
      },
      "script" : "doc['copies'].value * 0.5"
    }
  },
  "fields" : ["title", "copies"]
}
```

This query matches all documents in the index. We've wrapped this query with the custom_score element and thanks to it, we can use an additional script for score calculation. In our example, we've used a very simple script. We just return the score as a half of the copies field value. For clarity, we use the fields element to get only the values for the title and copies fields. And now, what we obtain in return is as follows:

```
"hits" : [ {
    "_index" : "library",
    "_type" : "book",
    "_id" : "2",
    "_score" : 3.0,
    "fields" : {
      "title" : "Catch-22",
      "copies" : 6
    }
```

```
    }, {
      "_index" : "library",
      "_type" : "book",
      "_id" : "1",
      "_score" : 0.5,
      "fields" : {
        "title" : "All Quiet on the Western Front",
        "copies" : 1
      }
    }, {
      "_index" : "library",
      "_type" : "book",
      "_id" : "4",
      "_score" : 0.0,
      "fields" : {
        "title" : "Crime and Punishment",
        "copies" : 0
      }
    }, {
      "_index" : "library",
      "_type" : "book",
      "_id" : "3",
      "_score" : 0.0,
      "fields" : {
        "title" : "The Complete Sherlock Holmes",
        "copies" : 0
      }
    } ]
```

ElasticSearch did what we wanted, but look what happens when the copies field is set to 0. The score is also 0! Normally this means that document doesn't match the query. We should remember that score manipulation doesn't allow us to reject any documents from the result.

Custom filters score query

The last query that we will discuss in this chapter is the custom filters score query. This query contains the base query and an array of filters. Each of these filters has a boost value defined. For example:

```
{
  "query" : {
    "custom_filters_score" : {
      "query" : {
        "matchAll" : {}
```

```
      },
      "filters" : [
        {
          "filter" : { "term" : { "available" : true }},
          "boost" : 10
        },
        {
          "filter" : { "term" : { "copies" : 0 }},
          "boost" : 100
        }

      ]
    }
  },
  "fields" : ["title", "copies", "available"]
}
```

We have a base query that simply selects all documents. In addition to that, we've
defined two filters. The first filter selects all available books and the second one
selects all the books without copies. Let's look at the result:

```
"hits" : {
  "total" : 4,
  "max_score" : 100.0,
  "hits" : [ {
    "_index" : "library",
    "_type" : "book",
    "_id" : "3",
    "_score" : 100.0,
    "fields" : {
      "title" : "The Complete Sherlock Holmes",
      "copies" : 0,
      "available" : false
    }
  }, {
    "_index" : "library",
    "_type" : "book",
    "_id" : "4",
    "_score" : 10.0,
    "fields" : {
      "title" : "Crime and Punishment",
      "copies" : 0,
      "available" : true
    }
  }, {
```

```
      "_index" : "library",
      "_type" : "book",
      "_id" : "1",
      "_score" : 10.0,
      "fields" : {
        "title" : "All Quiet on the Western Front",
        "copies" : 1,
        "available" : true
      }
    }, {
      "_index" : "library",
      "_type" : "book",
      "_id" : "2",
      "_score" : 1.0,
      "fields" : {
        "title" : "Catch-22",
        "copies" : 6,
        "available" : false
      }
    } ]
  }
```

As you can see, ElasticSearch checks each document against the defined filters. When
the filter matches, ElasticSearch takes the defined boost value and applies it to the
resulting score. When a filter doesn't match, it takes the next filter. If none of them
match, ElasticSearch returns the score from the base query. The more filters matched,
the better the document is for a given query. Let's look at another example:

```
{
 "query" : {
  "custom_filters_score" : {
   "query" : {
    "matchAll" : {}
   },
   "filters" : [
    {
     "filter" : { "term" : { "available" : true }},
     "boost" : 10
    },
    {
     "filter" : { "term" : { "copies" : 0 }},
     "boost" : 100
    }

   ],
```

```
      "score_mode" : "total"
  }
},
  "fields" : ["title", "copies", "available"]
}
```

There is only a single change, namely, the `score_mode` attribute. In the previous example, we used the default value, `first`. Now, the `score_mode` value of `total` tells ElasticSearch that all matching filters should be used for the boosting query. We've discussed different score modes in the *Compound queries* section in *Chapter 2, Searching Your Data*. However, let's check the results to illustrate this example:

```
"hits" : {
  "total" : 4,
  "max_score" : 110.0,
  "hits" : [ {
    "_index" : "library",
    "_type" : "book",
    "_id" : "4",
    "_score" : 110.0,
    "fields" : {
      "title" : "Crime and Punishment",
      "copies" : 0,
      "available" : true
    }
  }, {
    "_index" : "library",
    "_type" : "book",
    "_id" : "3",
    "_score" : 100.0,
    "fields" : {
      "title" : "The Complete Sherlock Holmes",
      "copies" : 0,
      "available" : false
    }
  }, {
    "_index" : "library",
    "_type" : "book",
    "_id" : "1",
    "_score" : 10.0,
    "fields" : {
      "title" : "All Quiet on the Western Front",
      "copies" : 1,
      "available" : true
    }
```

```
    }, {
      "_index" : "library",
      "_type" : "book",
      "_id" : "2",
      "_score" : 1.0,
      "fields" : {
        "title" : "Catch-22",
        "copies" : 6,
        "available" : false
      }
    } ]
}
```

The `Crime and Punishment` book is available and has no copies. The resulting score reflects this fact.

The `score_mode` parameter gives us even more possibilities. In addition to the mentioned values, it can also take the value `min`, `max`, `avg`, or `multiply`.

When does index-time boosting make sense

In the previous section, we talked about boosting queries. This type of boosting is very handy and powerful and fulfills its role in most situations. However, there is one case where the more convenient way is to use the index-time boosting. This situation is where important documents are a part of input data. We gain a boost independent from a query at the cost of re-indexing, when the boost value is changed. In addition to that, the performance is slightly better because some parts needed in the boosting process are already calculated at index time. ElasticSearch stores information about the boost as a part of normalization information. This is important because if we set `omit_norms` to `true`, we can't use index-time boosting.

Defining field boosting in input data

Let's look at the typical document definition:

```
{
  "title" : "The Complete Sherlock Holmes",
  "author" : "Arthur Conan Doyle",
  "year" : 1936
}
```

If we want to boost the `author` field for this particular document, the structure should be slightly changed and should look like the following:

```
{
   "title" : "The Complete Sherlock Holmes",
   "author" : {
     "_value" : "Arthur Conan Doyle",
     "_boost" : 10.0
   },
   "year": 1936
}
```

Defining document boosting in input data

As you've seen, field boosting during indexing is simple. In my opinion, the more useful way is to boost a whole document. For example, we want to promote some items in our shop application. Another example is when we desire to improve search relevance. Sometimes, we note that statistically people are more likely to seek popular products, so there is a lot of sense to boost popular products a bit by placing them at a higher level in the result list. How to do it? Let's look at following example:

```
{
   "title" : "The Complete Sherlock Holmes",
   "author" : "Arthur Conan Doyle",
   "year" : 1936,
   "_boost" : 10.0
}
```

As you can see, this is as simple as it can be. We've just added a new field named `_boost`. ElasticSearch will automatically apply its value as a document boost.

Defining boosting in mapping

It is worth mentioning that it is possible to directly define a field's boost in our mappings. The following example shows that:

```
{
   "mappings" : {
     "book" : {
       "properties" : {
         "title" : { "type" : "string" },
         "author" : { "type" : "string", "boost" : 10.0 }
       }
     }
   }
}
```

Thanks to the preceding boost, all queries will favor values found in the field named `author`. This also applies to queries using the `_all` field.

The words having the same meaning

You may have heard about synonyms—words that have the same or similar meaning. Sometimes you would want to have some words to be matched when one of those words is entered into the search box. Let's recall our sample data from *Chapter 2, Searching Your Data*; there was a book called "Crime and Punishment". What if we want that book to be matched not only when the words `crime` or `punishment` are used, but also when using words like `criminality` and `abuse`. However silly it may sound, let's use that example to see how synonyms can be used in ElasticSearch.

Synonym filter

In order to use the synonym filter, we need to define our own analyzer (please refer to *Chapter 1, Getting Started with ElasticSearch Cluster*, in order to see how to do that). Our analyzer will be called `synonym` and will use the `whitespace` tokenizer and a single filter called synonym. Our filter's `type` property needs to be set to `synonym`, which tells ElasticSearch that this filter is a synonym filter. In addition to that, we want to ignore the case so that upper- and lowercased synonyms will be treated equally (set the `ignore_case` property to `true`). So, in order to define our custom synonym analyzer that uses a synonym filter, we need to have the following mappings done:

```
{
  "index" : {
    "analysis" : {
      "analyzer" : {
        "synonym" : {
          "tokenizer" : "whitespace",
          "filter" : [
            "synonym"
          ]
        }
      },
      "filter" : {
        "synonym" : {
          "type" : "synonym",
```

```
        "ignore_case" : true,
        "synonyms" : [
          "crime => criminality"
        ]
      }
    }
  }
 }
}
```

Synonyms in mappings

In the preceding definition, we've specified the synonym rule in the mappings we send to ElasticSearch. In order to do that, we need to add the synonyms property, which is an array of synonym rules, for example, the following:

```
"synonyms" : [
  "crime => criminality"
]
```

We will discuss defining the synonym rules in just a second.

Synonyms in files

ElasticSearch allows us to use file-based synonyms. In order to use a file, we need to specify the synonyms_path property instead of the synonyms one. The synonyms_path property should be set to the name of the file that holds the synonym's definition and the specified file path is relative to the ElasticSearch config directory. So, if we store our synonyms in the synonyms.txt file and we save that file in the config directory, in order to use it, we should set synonyms_path to the value of synonyms.txt.

For example, this is how the synonym filter (the one from the preceding mappings) will be, if we want to use the synonyms stored in a file:

```
"filter" : {
  "synonym" : {
    "type" : "synonym",
    "synonyms_path" : "synonyms.txt"
  }
}
```

Defining synonym rules

Till now, we have discussed what we have to do in order to use synonym expansions in ElasticSearch. Now, let's see what formats of synonyms can be used.

Using Apache Solr synonyms

The most common synonym structure in the Apache Lucene world is probably the one used by Apache Solr—the search engine build on top of Lucene, just like ElasticSearch. This is the default way of handling synonyms in ElasticSearch and the possible ways of defining a new synonym are discussed in the following sections.

Explicit synonyms

A simple mapping allows us to map a list of words into other words. So, in our case, if we want the `criminality` word to be mapped to `crime` and the `abuse` word to be mapped to `punishment`, we need to define the following entries:

```
criminality => crime
abuse => punishment
```

Of course, a single word can be mapped into multiple ones and multiple ones can be mapped into a single one, for example:

```
star wars, wars => starwars
```

The preceding example means that `star wars` and `wars` will be changed to `starwars` by the synonym filter.

Equivalent synonyms

In addition to the explicit mapping, ElasticSearch allows us to use equivalent synonyms. For example, the following definition will make all the words exchangeable so that you can use any of them to match a document that has one of them in its contents:

```
star, wars, star wars, starwars
```

Expanding synonyms

A synonym filter allows us to use one additional property when it comes to Apache Solr format synonyms—the expand property. When this is set to `true` (by default, it is set to `false`), all synonyms will be expanded by ElasticSearch to all equivalent forms. For example, let's say we have the following filter configuration:

```
"filter" : {
  "synonym" : {
    "type" : "synonym",
```

```
    "expand": false,
    "synonyms" : [
      "one, two, three"
    ]
  }
}
```

ElasticSearch will map the preceding synonym definition to the following:

```
one, two, thee => one
```

This means that the words one, two, and three will be changed to one. However, if we set the expand property to true, the same synonym definition will be interpreted in the following way:

```
one, two, three => one, two, three
```

Which means that each of the words from the left side of the definition will be expanded to all the words.

Using WordNet synonyms

If we want to use WordNet-structured synonyms (to learn more about WordNet, please visit http://wordnet.princeton.edu/), we need to provide an additional property for our synonym filter. The property name is format, and we should set its value to wordnet in order for ElasticSearch to understand that format.

Query- or index-time synonym expansion

As with all the analyzers, one can wonder when we should use our synonym filter—during indexing, during querying, or maybe during both indexing and querying. Of course, it depends on your needs. However, please remember that using index-time synonyms requires data re-indexing after each synonym change, because they need to be reapplied to all the documents. If we use only query-time synonyms, we can update the lists of synonyms and have them applied (for example, after updating the mappings, which we will talk about later in this book).

Searching content in different languages

Till now, we've talked mostly in theory about language analysis, for example, handling multiple languages our data can consist, and things like that. This will now change as we will now discuss how we can handle multiple languages in our data.

Why we need to handle languages differently

As you already know that ElasticSearch allows us to choose different analyzers for our data, we can have our data divided into words on the basis of whitespaces, have them lowercased, and so on. This can usually be done with the data regardless of the language—you should have the same tokenization on the basis of whitespaces for English, German, and Polish (that doesn't apply to Chinese though). However, what if you want to find documents that contain words like cat and cats by only sending the cat word to ElasticSearch? This is where language analysis comes into play with stemming algorithms for different languages, which allow reducing the analyzed words into their root forms.

And now the worst part—we can't use one general stemming algorithm for all the languages in the world; we have to choose the one appropriate for each language. The following chapter will help you with some parts of the language analysis process.

How to handle multiple languages

There are a few ways of handling multiple languages in ElasticSearch and all of them have some pros and cons. We won't be discussing everything, but just for the purpose of giving you an idea, some of those ways are as follows:

- Storing documents in different languages as different types
- Storing documents in different languages in separate indices
- Storing different versions of fields in a single document so that they contain different languages

However, we will focus on a single method that allows us to store documents in different languages in a single index (with some slight modifications). We will focus on a problem where we have a single type of documents, but they may come from all over the world and thus be written in multiple languages. Also we would like to enable our users to use all the analysis capabilities, like stemming and stop words for different languages, not only for English.

Detecting a document's language

If you don't know the language of your documents and queries (and this is mostly the case), you can use software for language detection that can detect (with some probability) the language of your documents and queries.

If you use Java, you can use one of the few available language detection libraries. Some of them are as follows:

- Apache Tika (`http://tika.apache.org/`)
- Language Detection (`http://code.google.com/p/language-detection/`)

Language Detection claims to have over 99 percent precision for 53 languages, so that's a lot if you ask me.

You should remember, though, that for longer text, data language detection will be more precise. Because of that, you'll probably have your document's language identified correctly. However, because the text of queries is usually short, you'll probably have some degree of errors during query language identification.

Sample document

Let's start with introducing a sample document, which would be as follows:

```
{
    "title" : "First test document",
    "content" : "This is a test document",
    "lang" : "english"
}
```

As you can see, the document is pretty simple; it contains three fields:

- `title`: Holds the title of the document
- `content`: Holds the actual content of the document
- `lang`: The language identified

The first two fields are created from our user's documents and the third one is the language our hypothetical user has chosen when he/she uploaded the document.

In order to inform ElasticSearch which analyzer is to be used, we map the `lang` field to one of the analyzers that exist in ElasticSearch (full list of these analyzers can be found at `http://www.elasticsearch.org/guide/reference/index-modules/analysis/lang-analyzer.html`) and if the user enters a language that is not supported, we don't specify the `lang` field at all, so that ElasticSearch uses the default analyzer.

Mappings

So now, let's look at the mappings created for holding the preceding documents (we stored them in mappings.json):

```json
{
  "mappings" : {
    "doc" : {
      "_analyzer" : {
        "path" : "lang"
      },
      "properties" : {
        "title" : {
          "type" : "multi_field",
          "fields" : {
            "title" : {
              "type" : "string",
              "index" : "analyzed",
              "store" : "no"
            },
            "default" : {
              "type" : "string",
              "index" : "analyzed",
              "store" : "no",
              "analyzer" : "simple"
            }
          }
        },
        "content" : {
          "type" : "multi_field",
          "fields" : {
            "content" : {
              "type" : "string",
              "index" : "analyzed",
              "store" : "no"
            },
            "default" : {
              "type" : "string",
              "index" : "analyzed",
              "store" : "no",
              "analyzer" : "simple"
            }
          }
        },
        "lang" : {
```

```
                    "type" : "string",
                    "index" : "not_analyzed",
                    "store" : "yes"
                }
            }
        }
    }
}
```

In the preceding mappings, the things we are most interested in are the analyzer definition and the `title` and `description` fields (if you are not familiar with any parts of mappings, please refer to *Chapter 1, Getting Started with ElasticSearch* and *Chapter 3, Extending Your Structure and Search*). We want the analyzer to be based on the `lang` field. Because of that, we need to add a value in the `lang` field that is equal to one of the names of the analyzers known to ElasticSearch (the default one or another one defined by us).

Now come the definitions of two fields that hold the actual data. As you can see, we've used the multi field definition in order to index the `title` and `description` fields. The first one of the multi fields is indexed with the analyzer specified by the `lang` field (because we didn't specify the exact analyzer name, so the one defined globally will be used). We will use that field when we know in which language the query is specified. The second of the multi-fields uses a simple analyzer and will be used for searching when a query language is unknown. However, the simple analyzer is only an example and you can also use a standard analyzer or any other of your choice.

In order to create the `docs` index with the preceding mappings, we used the following command:

```
curl -XPUT 'localhost:9200/docs' -d @mappings.json
```

Querying

Now let's see how we can query our data. We can divide the querying situation into two different cases.

Queries with a known language

Let's assume we identified that our user has sent a query written in English and we know that English matches the `english` analyzer. In such a case, our query could be as follows:

```
curl -XGET 'localhost:9200/docs/_search?pretty=true ' -d '{
  "query" : {
```

```
      "match" : {
        "content" : {
          "query" : "documents",
          "analyzer" : "english"
        }
      }
    }
  }
}'
```

Notice the `analyzer` parameter, which indicates which analyzer we need to use. We set that parameter to the name of the analyzer corresponding with the identified language. Notice that the term we are searching for is `documents`, while the term in the document is `document`, but the `english` analyzer should take care of it and find that document:

```
{
  "took" : 2,
  "timed_out" : false,
  "_shards" : {
    "total" : 5,
    "successful" : 5,
    "failed" : 0
  },
  "hits" : {
    "total" : 1,
    "max_score" : 0.19178301,
    "hits" : [ {
      "_index" : "docs",
      "_type" : "doc",
      "_id" : "1",
      "_score" : 0.19178301
    } ]
  }
}
```

As you can see, that document was found.

Queries with an unknown language

Now let's assume that we don't know the language with which the user is sending the query. In this case, we can't use the field analyzed with the analyzer specified by our `lang` field, because we don't want to analyze the query with an analyzer that is language-specific. In that case, we will use our standard simple analyzer and we will send the query to the `contents.default` field instead of `content`. The query could be as follows:

```
curl -XGET 'localhost:9200/docs/_search?pretty=true ' -d '{
  "query" : {
    "match" : {
      "content.default" : {
        "query" : "documents",
        "analyzer" : "simple"
      }
    }
  }
}'
```

However, we didn't get any results this time, because the simple analyzer can't deal in searching with a singular form of a word when we are searching with a plural form.

Combining queries

To additionally boost the documents that perfectly match our default analyzer, we can combine the two preceding queries with the `bool` query, so that they look like the following:

```
curl -XGET 'localhost:9200/docs/_search?pretty=true ' -d '{
  "query" : {
    "bool" : {
      "minimum_number_should_match" : 1,
      "should" : [
        {
          "match" : {
            "content" : {
              "query" : "documents",
              "analyzer" : "english"
```

```
            }
          }
        },   .
        {
          "match" : {
            "content.default" : {
              "query" : "documents",
              "analyzer" : "simple"
            }
          }
        }
      ]
    }
  }
}'
```

At least one of those queries must match, and if both match, the document will have a higher value for the results.

There is one additional advantage to the preceding combined query—if our language analyzer won't find a document (for example, when the analysis is different from the one used during indexing), the second query has a chance to find the terms that are tokenized only by whitespace characters and lowercased.

Using span queries

ElasticSearch leverages the Lucene span queries, which basically allow us to create queries that match when some tokens or phrases are placed near other tokens or phrases. When using the standard non-span queries, we are not able to make queries that are position aware—to some extent phrase queries allow that, but only to some extent.

There are five span queries exposed in ElasticSearch:

- Span term query
- Span first query
- Span near query
- Span or query
- Span not query

Before we continue with the description, let us index a new document that we will be using in order to show how span queries work. To do that, we send the following command to ElasticSearch:

```
curl -XPOST 'localhost:9200/library/book/5' -d '{
  "title" : "Test book",
  "author" : "Test author",
  "description" : "The world breaks everyone, and afterward,
  some are strong at the broken places"
}'
```

As you can see, we used ElasticSearch's ability to update our index structure automatically and we've added the description field. We did that to have a field that has more content than a book's title usually has.

What is a span?

A **span**, in our context, is a starting and ending token position in a field. For example, in our case, world breaks everyone can be a single span, world can be a single span too. As you may know, during analysis, Lucene, in addition to token, includes some additional parameters—such as distance from the previous token. Position information combined with terms allows us to construct spans, using the ElasticSearch span queries (which are mapped to Lucene span queries). In the next few sections, we will learn how to construct spans by using different span queries and how to control which documents are matched.

Span term query

A span term query is a query similar to the already-discussed term query. On its own, it works just like the mentioned term query—it matches a term. Its definition is simple and looks as follows (I omitted some parts of the query on purpose, because we will discuss it in a few lines of text):

```
{
  "query" : {
    ...
    {
      "span_term" : {
        "description" : {
          "value" : "world",
          "boost" : 5.0
        }
      }
    }
  }
}
```

As you can see, this query is very similar to a term query. The preceding query is run against the `description` field and we want to have the documents that have the `world` term returned. We also specified a boost, which is also allowed. Of course, similar to a term query, we can use a simplified version if we don't want to use boosts:

```
{
  "query" : {
    ...
    {
      "span_term" : {
        "description" : "world"
      }
    }
  }
}
```

Span first query

The span first query allows matching only documents that have matched in the first positions of the field. In order to define a span first query, we need to nest any other span queries inside it, for example, a span term query that we already know. So, let's find documents that have the term `world` in the first two positions in the `description` field. We do that by sending the following query:

```
{
  "query" : {
    "span_first" : {
      "match" : {
        "span_term" : { "description" : "world" }
      },
      "end" : 2
    }
  }
}
```

In the results, we will get our document that we indexed at the beginning of this chapter. In the `match` section of the span first query, we should include at least a single span query that should be matched at the maximum position specified by the `end` parameter.

So, if we understand everything well and if we set the end parameter to 1, we will not get our document with the preceding query. So let's check it by sending the following query:

```
{
  "query" : {
    "span_first" : {
      "match" : {
        "span_term" : { "description" : "world" }
      },
      "end" : 1
    }
  }
}
```

The response to the preceding query will be as follows:

```
{
  "took" : 1,
  "timed_out" : false,
  "_shards" : {
    "total" : 5,
    "successful" : 5,
    "failed" : 0
  },
  "hits" : {
    "total" : 0,
    "max_score" : null,
    "hits" : [ ]
  }
}
```

So it's working as expected, hurrah!

Span near query

The span near query allows us to match documents that have other spans near each other and this is also a compound query that wraps other span queries. For example, if we want to find documents that have the term `world` near the term `everyone`, we can run the following query:

```
{
  "query" : {
    "span_near" : {
      "clauses" : [
        { "span_term" : { "description" : "world" } },
        { "span_term" : { "description" : "everyone" } }
      ],
      "slop" : 0,
      "in_order" : true
    }
  }
}
```

As you can see, we specified our queries in the `clauses` section of the span near query. It is an array of other span queries. The `slop` parameter specified in the preceding query is similar to the one used in the phrase queries—it allows us to control the number of allowed terms between spans. The `in_order` parameter can be used to limit the matches only to those documents that match our queries in the same order they were defined, so in our case, we will get documents that have `world everyone`, but not `everyone world` in the `description` field.

So let's get back to our query—that will return 0 results. If you look at our example document, you will notice that between the terms `world` and `everyone`, an additional term is present. We have set the `slop` parameter to 0 (slop was discussed during description of the phrase query in *Chapter 2, Searching Your Data*). If we increase it to 1, we will get our result. To test it, let's send the following query:

```
{
  "query" : {
    "span_near" : {
      "clauses" : [
        { "span_term" : { "description" : "world" } },
        { "span_term" : { "description" : "everyone" } }
      ],
      "slop" : 1,
      "in_order" : true
    }
  }
}
```

And the results returned by ElasticSearch are as follows:

```
{
    "took" : 4,
    "timed_out" : false,
    "_shards" : {
        "total" : 5,
        "successful" : 5,
        "failed" : 0
    },
    "hits" : {
        "total" : 1,
        "max_score" : 0.095891505,
        "hits" : [ {
            "_index" : "library",
            "_type" : "book",
            "_id" : "5",
            "_score" : 0.095891505, "_source" : {"title" : "Test book",
            "author" : "Test author","description" :
            "The world breaks everyone, and afterward,
            some are strong at the broken places" }
        } ]
    }
}
```

As you can see, it works!

Span or query

The span or query allows us to wrap other span queries and aggregate matches of all those that we've wrapped — it makes a union of span queries. This also uses the clauses array to specify other span queries for which matches should be aggregated. For example, if we want to get the documents that have the world term in the first two positions of the description field or the ones that have the term world not further than a single position from the term everyone, we will send the following query:

```
{
    "query" : {
        "span_or" : {
            "clauses" : [
                {
                    "span_first" : {
                        "match" : {
                            "span_term" : { "description" : "world" }
                        },
```

```
            "end" : 2
          }
        },
        {
          "span_near" : {
            "clauses" : [
                { "span_term" : { "description" : "world" } },
                { "span_term" : { "description" : "everyone" } }
            ],
            "slop" : 1,
            "in_order" : true
          }
        }
      ]
    }
  }
}
```

The result of the preceding query should be our example document that we indexed at the beginning:

```
{
  "took" : 3,
  "timed_out" : false,
  "_shards" : {
    "total" : 5,
    "successful" : 5,
    "failed" : 0
  },
  "hits" : {
    "total" : 1,
    "max_score" : 0.16608895,
    "hits" : [ {
      "_index" : "library",
      "_type" : "book",
      "_id" : "5",
      "_score" : 0.16608895, "_source" : {"title" : "Test book",
      "author" : "Test author","description" :
      "The world breaks everyone, and afterward,
      some are strong at the broken places" }
    } ]
  }
}
```

Span not query

The last type of span queries, the span not query, allows us to specify two sections of queries. The first is the `include` section, which specifies which span queries should be matched and the second section, `exclude`, specifies span queries that shouldn't overlap with the first ones. To keep it simple, if a query from the `exclude` section matches the same span (or a part of it) as a query from the `include` section, such a document won't be returned as a match for that span not query. Each of those sections can contain multiple span queries.

So to illustrate that query, let's create a query that will return all the documents that have the span constructed from a single term `breaks` in the `description` field. And let's exclude the documents that have a span that matches the `world` and `everyone` terms that are at a maximum of a single position from each other, when such a span overlaps the one defined in the first span query.

```
{
   "query" : {
     "span_not" : {
       "include" : {
         "span_term" : { "description" : "breaks" }
       },
       "exclude" : {
         "span_near" : {
            "clauses" : [
               { "span_term" : { "description" : "world" } },
               { "span_term" : { "description" : "everyone" } }
            ],
            "slop" : 1
         }
       }
     }
   }
}
```

And the result is as follows:

```
{
   "took" : 1,
   "timed_out" : false,
   "_shards" : {
     "total" : 5,
     "successful" : 5,
     "failed" : 0
   },
```

```
    "hits" : {
      "total" : 0,
      "max_score" : null,
      "hits" : [ ]
    }
  }
}
```

As you may have noticed, the result of the query is as we had expected—our document wasn't found because the span query from the exclude section was overlapping the span from the include section.

Performance considerations

A few words at the end of the discussion about span queries—remember that they are more costly when it comes to processing power, because not only do terms have to be matched, but also positions have to be calculated and checked.

Summary

In this chapter, we looked at how to use boosting to improve the relevance and importance of queries, documents, and individual fields. We also learned how to check why our document was found or not found, which can come in handy when dealing with relevance problems. We took a look at how synonyms can be used, how we can handle content in different languages, and finally how to use span queries to make queries where positions matter.

In the next chapter, we will take a look at nested objects and parent-child relationships and how to handle them. We will also discuss how to use batch indexing and modify our existing index structure.

5
Combining Indexing, Analysis, and Search

In the previous chapter, we learned how to improve our user's search experience by influencing a document's score, how to use synonyms, and how to handle multilingual data. We also saw what span queries are and why your document was returned. In this chapter, we will look at the possibility of indexing data that is not flat or that is related to other data. We will also use the index update API to modify already created indices, and we will finally learn how to index data in the most efficient way. By the end of this chapter, you will have learned:

- How to index tree-like structures
- How to modify indices with the update API
- How to use nested objects
- How to use the parent-child relationship
- How to fetch data from external systems
- How to use batch processing to speed up indexing

Indexing tree-like structures

Trees! Trees are everywhere. If you develop a shop application, you probably have categories. If you look at the filesystem, the files and directories are arranged in tree-like structures. This book may also be represented as a tree; chapters contain topics and subtopics. ElasticSearch has functionalities that help us handle tree-like structures. Let's check how we can navigate such data using `path_analyzer`.

First we'll create a simple mapping:

```
{
  "settings" : {
   "index" : {
    "analysis" : {
     "analyzer" : {
      "path_analyzer" : {"tokenizer" : "path_hierarchy"}
     }
    }
   }
  },
  "mappings" : {
   "category" : {
    "properties" : {
     "category" : {
      "type" : "multi_field",
      "fields" : {
       "name" : { "type" : "string", "index" : "not_analyzed" },
       "path" : { "type" : "string", "analyzer" : "path_analyzer",
"store" : true }
      }
     }
    }
   }
  }
}
```

In order to put those mappings during index creation use the following command:

```
curl -XPOST 'localhost:9200/path/' --data-binary '...'
```

The above mappings should be put as the request body.

As you can see, we have configured only one field, that is, `category`, which represents where in the tree structure our document is placed. The idea is simple; we can show the position in a tree as a path, exactly the same as how files and directories are presented on your hard disk drive. For example, in an automotive shop, we can have `/cars/passenger/sport`, `/cars/passenger/camper`, or `/cars/delivery_truck/`. We will index this value in two ways, namely, as a name without additional processing and as a path using `path_analyzer`.

Now we will see what ElasticSearch will do with a category path during the analysis process. To see this, we will use the analysis API described in the *Why this document was found* topic in *Chapter 3, Extending Your Structure and Search*:

```
curl -XGET 'localhost:9200/path/_analyze?field=category.path&pretty' -d
'/cars/passenger/sport'
```

And the following results were returned by ElasticSearch:

```
{
  "tokens" : [ {
    "token" : "/cars",
    "start_offset" : 0,
    "end_offset" : 5,
    "type" : "word",
    "position" : 1
  }, {
    "token" : "/cars/passenger",
    "start_offset" : 0,
    "end_offset" : 15,
    "type" : "word",
    "position" : 1
  }, {
    "token" : "/cars/passenger/sport",
    "start_offset" : 0,
    "end_offset" : 21,
    "type" : "word",
    "position" : 1
  } ]
}
```

As we can see, our category path, /cars/passenger/sport, was processed by ElasticSearch and it was divided into three tokens. Thanks to that, we can simply find every document that belongs to a given category or its subcategories using the term filter, such as:

```
{
  "filter" : {
    "term" : { "category.path" : "/cars" }
  }
}
```

Note that we also have the original value indexed in the category.name field. This is handy when we want to find documents from a particular path, ignoring documents that are deeper in the hierarchy.

As we've seen how tree-like structures can be handled in ElasticSearch, we would like to move on to the next section, that is, index modification with the update API.

Modifying your index structure with the update API

In the previous chapters, we discussed how to create index mappings and index the data. But what if you already have the mappings created, data indexed, but you want to modify the structure of the index? This is possible to some extent and soon we will learn how to do it.

The mapping

Let's assume that we have the following mappings for our `users` index stored in the `user.json` file:

```
{
  "user" : {
   "properties" : {
    "name" : {"type" : "string", "store" : "yes", "index" : "analyzed"}
    }
   }
}
```

This is nothing unusual, just a simple type that stores the username. Let's create our index and let's create the type with the preceding mappings:

```
curl -XPOST 'localhost:9200/users'
curl -XPUT 'localhost:9200/users/user/_mapping' -d @user.json
```

If everything went well, we will have our index and type created. So now let's try adding a new field to the mappings.

Adding a new field

Let's assume that we want to add a new field that will store our user's phone number so we can show it in our application. In order to do that, we need to send an HTTP PUT command to the `/index_name/type_name/_mapping` REST endpoint with the proper body that will include our new field. For example, to add the `phone` field, we would run the following command:

```
curl -XPUT 'http://localhost:9200/users/user/_mapping' -d '
{
  "user" : {
   "properties" : {
    "phone" : {"type" : "string", "store" : "yes", "index" : "not_
analyzed"}
   }
  }
}'
```

Once again, everything went well and we have a new field added to our index structure.

 After adding a new field to the existing type, we need to index all the documents again, because ElasticSearch didn't update them automatically. This is crucial to remember. You can use your primary source of data to do that or use the _source field to get the original data from it and index it once again.

Modifying fields

So now our index structure contains two fields, namely, the name and phone fields. We have indexed some data, but after a while, we decide that we want to search the phone field, and we would like to change its index property from not_analyzed to analyzed. So we run the following command:

```
curl -XPUT 'http://localhost:9200/users/user/_mapping' -d '
{
  "user" : {
   "properties" : {
    "phone" : {"type" : "string", "store" : "yes", "index" : "analyzed"}
   }
  }
}'
```

And ElasticSearch returns the following:

```
{"error":"MergeMappingException[Merge failed with failures {[mapper
[phone] has different index values, mapper [phone] has different index_
analyzer, mapper [phone] has different search_analyzer]}]","status":400}
```

This is because we can't change the `not_analyzed` field to `analyzed`. And not just that, in most cases, you won't be able to update the field's mapping.

For example, the following modification can be safely made:

- Updating a field to the `multi_field` type
- Adding a new type definition
- Adding a new field
- Adding a new analyzer

The following modifications are prohibited or will not work:

- Changing the type of the field (for example, from text to numeric)
- Changing "stored to field" to "not stored" and vice versa
- Changing the value of the indexed property
- Changing the analyzer of an already indexed document

 Please remember that the aforementioned examples of allowed and not allowed modifications do not mention all the possibilities of update API usage, and you have to try it for yourself to see if the update you are trying to carry out will work.

If you want to ignore conflicts and just make the new mappings, you can set the `ignore_conflicts` parameter to `true`. This will cause ElasticSearch to overwrite your mappings with the one you send. So our previous command with the additional parameter would look like this:

```
curl -XPUT 'http://localhost:9200/users/user/_mapping?ignore_
conflicts=true' -d '...'
```

Using nested objects

Nested objects can come in handy in certain situations. Basically, with nested objects, ElasticSearch allows us to connect multiple documents together—one main document and multiple dependent ones. Now, imagine that we have a shop with clothes and we store the size and color of each T-shirt. Our standard, non-nested mappings could look like the following code (stored in `cloth.json`):

```
{
 "cloth" : {
  "properties" : {
    "name" : {"type" : "string", "store" : "yes", "index" :
"analyzed"},
    "size" : {"type" : "string", "store" : "yes", "index" : "not_
analyzed"},
    "color" : {"type" : "string", "store" : "yes", "index" : "not_
analyzed"}
  }
 }
}
```

Now imagine that we have a T-shirt in our shop that we only have in the XXL size in "red" and XL size in "black". So our example document could look like the following code:

```
{
 "name" : "Test shirt",
 "size" : [ "XXL", "XL" ],
 "color" : [ "red", "black" ]
}
```

But if one of our clients were to search our shop in order to find the XXL T-shirt in black, a query similar to the following one could be run:

```
curl -XGET 'localhost:9200/shop/cloth/_search?pretty=true' -d '{
 "query" : {
  "bool" : {
   "must" : [
    {
     "term" : { "size" : "XXL" }
    },
    {
     "term" : { "color" : "black" }
    }
   ]
  }
 }
}'
```

We should get no results right? But in fact ElasticSearch returned the following document:

```
{
  (...)
  "hits" : {
    "total" : 1,
    "max_score" : 0.2712221,
    "hits" : [ {
      "_index" : "shop",
      "_type" : "cloth",
      "_id" : "1",
      "_score" : 0.2712221, "_source" : { "name" : "Test shirt", "size" :
[ "XXL", "XL" ], "color" : [ "red", "black" ]}
    } ]
  }
}
```

So, let's modify our mappings to use nested objects to separate color and size to different, nested documents (we store these mappings in the cloth_nested.json file):

```
{
  "cloth" : {
   "properties" : {
    "name" : {"type" : "string", "store" : "yes", "index" :
"analyzed"},
    "variation" : {
     "type" : "nested",
     "properties" : {
      "size" : {"type" : "string", "store" : "yes", "index" : "not_
analyzed"},
      "color" : {"type" : "string", "store" : "yes", "index" : "not_
analyzed"}
     }
    }
   }
  }
}
```

As you can see, we've introduced a new object inside our `cloth` type, `variation`. This is a nested object (type `property` set to `nested`). It basically says that we will want to index nested documents. Now, let's modify our document to something like the following code:

```
{
  "name" : "Test shirt",
  "variation" : [
    { "size" : "XXL", "color" : "red" },
    { "size" : "XL", "color" : "black" }
  ]
}
```

We've structured the document so that each size and its matching color is a separate document. However, if you were to run our previous query, it wouldn't return any documents. This is because in order to query for nested documents, we need to use a specialized query. So now our query looks like this:

```
curl -XGET 'localhost:9200/shop/cloth/_search?pretty=true' -d '{
  "query" : {
    "nested" : {
      "path" : "variation",
      "query" : {
        "bool" : {
          "must" : [
            { "term" : { "variation.size" : "XXL" } },
            { "term" : { "variation.color" : "black" } }
          ]
        }
      }
    }
  }
}'
```

And now, the preceding query wouldn't return the indexed document, because we don't have a nested document that has a size equal to XXL and color black.

Lastly, let's look at the query. As you can see, we've used the `nested` query in order to search in the nested documents. The `path` property specifies the name of the nested object (yes, we can have multiple objects). As you can see, we just included a standard query section under the `nested` type. Please also note that we specified the full path for the field names in the nested objects, which is handy when you have multi-level nesting, which is also possible.

> If you would like to use the nested type functionality as a filter, you can use it as there is a `nested` filter that has the same functionality as the `nested` query. Please refer to the *Filtering your results* section in *Chapter 3, Extending Your Structure and Search*, for information about filtering.

Using parent-child relationships

In the previous section, we discussed the ability to index nested documents along with a parent one. However, even though the nested documents are indexed as separate documents in the index, we can't change a single nested document (unless we use the update API). However, ElasticSearch allows us to have a real parent-child relationship and we will look at it in the following sections.

Mappings and indexing

Let's use our previous example with the clothing store. However, what we would like to have is the ability to update sizes and colors without the need of indexing the whole document after each change. In order to do that, we will use the parent-child functionality of ElasticSearch.

Creating parent mappings

So now, the only field we need to have in our parent document is the name. We don't need anything more than that. So in order to create our mapping in the `shop` index, we would run the following command:

```
curl -XPUT 'localhost:9200/shop/cloth/_mapping' -d '{
  "cloth" : {
   "properties" : {
    "name" : {"type" : "string", "store" : "yes", "index" : "analyzed"}
   }
  }
}'
```

Creating child mappings

Now let's create the child mappings. In order to do that, we will need to add the _parent property with the name of the parent type, which is cloth in our case. So, the command that creates the variation type would look like the following:

```
curl -XPUT 'localhost:9200/shop/variation/_mapping' -d '{
 "variation" : {
  "_parent" : { "type" : "cloth" },
  "properties" : {
    "size" : {"type" : "string", "index" : "not_analyzed"},
    "color" : {"type" : "string", "index" : "not_analyzed"}
  }
 }
}'
```

And that's all. You don't need to specify which field will be used to connect a child document to the parent because, by default, ElasticSearch will use the unique identifier for that, and if you remember from the previous chapters, that information is present in the index by default.

Parent document

Now let's index our parent document. It's very simple; in order to do that, we just run the usual indexing command, for example, one like the following command:

```
curl -XPOST 'localhost:9200/shop/cloth/1' -d '{
 "name" : "Test document"
}'
```

If you look at the above command, you'll notice that our document will be given the identifier of 1.

Child documents

In order to index child documents, we need to provide information about the parent document with the use of the parent request parameter and set that parameter value to the identifier of the parent document. So in order to index two child documents to our parent document, we would need to run the following commands:

```
curl -XPOST 'localhost:9200/shop/variation/1000?parent=1' -d '{
 "color" : "red",
 "size" : "XXL"
}'
```

And:

```
curl -XPOST 'localhost:9200/shop/variation/1001?parent=1' -d '{
 "color" : "black",
 "size" : "XL"
}'
```

And that's all. We've indexed two additional documents, which are of a new type, but we've specified that our documents have a parent.

Querying

We've indexed our data and now we need to use appropriate queries in order to match documents with the data stored in their children. However, please note that when running queries against parents, child documents won't be returned and vice versa.

Querying for data in the child documents

So if we would like to get clothes that are of XXL size and in red, we would run the following query:

```
{
  "query" : {
   "has_child" : {
    "type" : "variation",
    "query" : {
     "bool" : {
      "must" : [
       { "term" : { "size" : "XXL" } },
       { "term" : { "color" : "red" } }
      ]
     }
    }
   }
  }
}
```

The query is quite simple—it is of a `has_child` type, which tells ElasticSearch that we want to search in the child documents. In order to specify which type of child documents we are interested in, we specify the `type` property with the name of the child type. Then we have a standard `bool` query, which we've already discussed.

The top children query

There is one additional query that returns parent documents, but is run against child documents—the `top_children` query. That query can be used to run against a specified number of child documents. Let's look at the following query:

```
{
  "query" : {
   "top_children" : {
    "type" : "variation",
    "query" : {
     "term" : { "size" : "XXL" }
    },
    "score" : "max",
    "factor" : 10,
    "incremental_factor" : 2
   }
  }
}
```

The preceding query will be run first against a total of 100 child documents (`factor` multiplied by the default `size` of `10`). If there are 10 parent documents found (because of the default `size` parameter being equal to `10`), then those will be returned and the query execution will end. However, if there are less parents returned and there are still child documents that were not queried, then another 20 documents will be queried (the `incremental_factor` parameter multiplied by the result's size). And so on until the requested number of parent documents is found or there are no child documents left to query.

The `top_children` query offers the ability to specify how the score should be calculated with the use of the `score` parameter, with the following value of `max`, `sum`, or `avg` possible. Because ElasticSearch wraps the `top_children` query in the custom filter's score query, please refer to that query in order to see what the values mean (this query has been discussed in the *Custom score query* and *Custom filters score query* sections in *Chapter 2, Searching Your Data*).

Querying for data in the parent documents

If we would like to return child documents that match the given data in the parent document, we should use the `has_parent` query. It is similar to the `has_child` query, however, instead of the type property, we specify the `parent_type` parameter with the value of the parent document type. For example, the following query will return both the child documents we've indexed:

```
{
  "query" : {
   "has_parent" : {
    "parent_type" : "cloth",
    "query" : {
     "term" : { "name" : "test" }
    }
   }
  }
}
```

Parent-child relationship and filtering

If you would like to use parent- child queries as filters, you can use them. There are `has_child` and `has_parent` filters that have the same functionality as the queries with corresponding names. Actually ElasticSearch wraps those filters in the constant score query to allow them to be used as queries.

Performance considerations

When using the ElasticSearch parent-child functionality, one has to be aware of the performance impact that it has. The first thing you need to remember is that the parent and the child documents need to be stored in the same shard in order for the queries to work. If you happen to have a high number of child documents for a single parent, you may end up with shards not having a similar number of documents. Because of that, your query performance can be lower on one of the nodes resulting in entire queries being slower. Also please remember that the parent-child queries will be slower than those run against documents that don't have a relationship between them.

The second very important thing is that when running queries, such as the `has_child` one, ElasticSearch needs to preload and cache document identifiers. Those identifiers will be stored in memory and you have to be sure that you have given ElasticSearch enough memory to store those identifiers. Otherwise, you can expect `OutOfMemory` exceptions being thrown and your nodes or the whole cluster not being operational.

Finally, as we mentioned, the first query will preload the cache document identifiers, and it takes time. In order to improve performance of the first queries that use the parent-child relationship, the Warmer API can be used. You can find more information about how to add warming queries to ElasticSearch in the *Warming up* section of *Chapter 8, Dealing with Problems*.

Fetching data from other systems: river

In the first chapter, we've seen how to create and update indices using the REST API. Loading the data to ElasticSearch is the main task (except, of course, searching), which should be solved when building a search application. It would be good to have some infrastructure or plugins that can handle integration of the search engine with various sources of data. ElasticSearch is a relatively new project, but already addresses this goal with a functionality called **river**.

What we need and what a river is

You can guess that there are two approaches for putting the data into your search system. We can pop the data from the source system, or the source system could push the data into our system. In the first case, we need some kind of service in our ElasticSearch cluster that could monitor the changes of an external data source or check these sources periodically. River is such a service. ElasticSearch takes care of this service and makes sure that only a single instance is running across the whole cluster. If any node dies, all rivers running on this node are moved to another node. A particular river instance is described by its name and type. There are several types available but except for dummy river, which is a simple example river, every one of them should be installed as an additional plugin.

 Please consider that when using a river, you are bound to the performance of a single node. So for heavy processing of documents, a standalone indexing application is preferred.

Installing and configuring a river

As we said, there are several rivers already available. Some of them are created by the ElasticSearch team and some of them are available as external projects. You can check the official list at http://www.elasticsearch.org/guide/reference/modules/plugins.html.

In this chapter, we will use the MongoDB river as an example. Let's start by installing this river using the ElasticSearch plugins system. In order to do that, we first run the following command:

```
bin/plugin -install richardwilly98/elasticsearch-river-mongodb/1.6.1
```

Please note that this command doesn't work with ElasticSearch newer than 0.20.1 because of the binary plugin location changes. Until this is resolved, you can use the following command:

```
bin/plugin -url https://github.com/downloads/
richardwilly98/elasticsearch-river-mongodb/
elasticsearch-river-mongodb-1.6.1.zip -install river-
mongodb
```

After restarting our ElasticSearch instance, we are ready to configure our new river.

All the rivers' configuration is stored in the _river index. By default, this index doesn't exist, but we may easily create it just like any other index. In this index every instance of the river can store its data. ElasticSearch assumes that every instance of river has its own configuration data stored under the type in the index equal to the name of the river. Another assumption is that the document indexed in the mentioned index has the _meta identifier. The third assumption is that ElasticSearch handles an additional document with the _status identifier for every configured river. Let's configure our river and see what this index looks like after this operation.

We've prepared the config.json file, which will be loaded into ElasticSearch. Its contents are as follows:

```
{
  "type" : "mongodb",
  "mongodb" : {
    "servers" : [
      { "host" : "localhost", "port" : 27017 }
    ],
    "db" : "esbook",
    "collection" : "products"
  },
  "index" : {
    "name" : "esbook"
  }
}
```

As we can see, there are three keys in this JSON object: type – which tells ElasticSearch which river plugin should be used, mongodb – with the river configuration (available MongoDB servers, database, and collection names), and index – with information about the index where fetched data should be indexed. There are some more options described in the river documentation, but these are sufficient for our example.

If you would like to test this example on your computer, make sure that your MongoDB instance is available and it is configured as a replica set (for more information, go to `http://docs.mongodb.org/manual/tutorial/deploy-replica-set/`). This is necessary because this river uses a special system collection, `oplog`, for tracking changes in the database.

Now let's run our river. As we said before, this means creation of a document with an identifier named `_meta` in the `_river` index, for example, with this command:

```
curl -XPUT 'localhost:9200/_river/mongolink/_meta' -d @config.json
```

If everything went well, you should see information in the ElasticSearch log about the river creation. There should also be an empty `esbook` index. Let's see the status information about our river:

```
curl -XGET 'localhost:9200/_river/mongolink/_status?pretty'
```

We should see something like the following result:

```
{
  "_index" : "_river",
  "_type" : "mongolink",
  "_id" : "_status",
  "_version" : 1,
  "exists" : true, "_source" : {"ok":true,"node":{"id":"VhN9duujSdOkQdAEC
lNgpg","name":"Lancer","transport_address":"inet[/192.168.1.101:9300]"}}
}
```

As you can see, ElasticSearch automatically created the `_status` document that tells us where our river is running (which instance) and what its status is. Now going to the most important part of our test, let's run the Mongo console and create an example document:

```
PRIMARY> use esbook
switched to db esbook
PRIMARY> db.products.insert({ "name" : "book", "value" : 200 })
PRIMARY>
```

And now let's query ElasticSearch:

```
curl 'localhost:9200/esbook/_search?pretty'
```

And again, if everything was done correctly, we should see something like the following result:

```
{
  "took" : 1,
  "timed_out" : false,
  "_shards" : {
    "total" : 5,
    "successful" : 5,
    "failed" : 0
  },
  "hits" : {
    "total" : 1,
    "max_score" : 1.0,
    "hits" : [ {
      "_index" : "esbook",
      "_type" : "esbook",
      "_id" : "5092cc65e629448dce7212d5",
      "_score" : 1.0, "_source" : {"_id":"5092cc65e629448dce7212d5","name":"book","value":200.0}
    } ]
  }
}
```

As we can see, there is one document in our index and this has exactly the same data as we created in Mongo. You can check it for yourself to see that the update and delete operations also work as expected.

One last thing—we can of course perform some housekeeping and stop and remove our configured river with the use of the following command:

```
curl -XDELETE localhost:9200/_river/mongolink/
```

Batch indexing to speed up your indexing process

In the first chapter, we've seen how to index a particular document into ElasticSearch. Now it's time to tell how to index many documents in a more convenient and efficient way than doing it one by one.

Some of the information in this chapter should not be new to us. We've already used it when preparing test data in the previous parts of this book, but now we'll summarize this knowledge.

How to prepare data

ElasticSearch allows us to merge many requests into one packet and send this in one request. In this way, we can mix three operations: adding or replacing existing documents in the index (index), removing documents from the index (delete), or adding new documents to the index when there is not another definition of the document in the index (create). The format of the request was chosen for processing efficiency and assumes that every line of the request contains a JSON object with the operation description followed by the second line with a JSON object, which contains document data for this operation. The exception to this rule is the delete operation, which, for obvious reasons, doesn't have the second line. Let's look at the example data:

```
{ "index": { "_index": "addr", "_type": "contact", "_id": 1 }}
{ "name": "Fyodor Dostoevsky", "country": "RU" }
{ "create": { "_index": "addr", "_type": "contact", "_id": 2 }}
{ "name": "Erich Maria Remarque", "country": "DE" }
{ "create": { "_index": "addr", "_type": "contact", "_id": 2 }}
{ "name": "Joseph Heller", country: "US" }
{ "delete": { "_index": "addr", "_type": "contact", "_id": 4 }}
{ "delete": { "_index": "addr", "_type": "contact", "_id": 1 }}
```

It is very important that every document or action description is placed in one line. This means that the document cannot be pretty-printed. There is a default limitation on the size of the bulk indexing file, which is set to 100 megabytes and can be changed by specifying the `http.max_content_length` property in the ElasticSearch configuration file. This lets us avoid issues with possible request timeouts and memory problems when dealing with over-large requests.

Please note that with a single batch indexing file, we can load the data into many indices and that documents can have different types.

Indexing the data

In order to execute the bulk request, ElasticSearch provides the `_bulk` endpoint. This can be used as `/_bulk` or with an index as `/index_name/_bulk` or even with a type as `/index_name/type_name/_bulk`. The second and third forms define the default values for the index name and type name, and if we would like, we can omit those in data in the operation description line.

If we have our example data in the `documents.json` file, execution would look as follows:

```
curl -XPOST 'localhost:9200/_bulk?pretty' --data-binary @documents.json
```

The `?pretty` parameter is of course not necessary. We've used this parameter only for the ease of analyzing the result of this command. What is important, in this case, is using `curl` with the `--data-binary` parameter instead of using `-d`. This is because the standard `-d` parameter ignores new line characters, which, as we said earlier, are important for parsing commands by ElasticSearch. Now let's look at the result returned by ElasticSearch:

```
{
  "took" : 113,
  "items" : [ {
    "index" : {
      "_index" : "addr",
      "_type" : "contact",
      "_id" : "1",
      "_version" : 1,
      "ok" : true
    }
  }, {
```

```
      "create" : {
        "_index" : "addr",
        "_type" : "contact",
        "_id" : "2",
        "_version" : 1,
        "ok" : true
      }
   }, {
      "create" : {
        "_index" : "addr",
        "_type" : "contact",
        "_id" : "2",
        "error" : "DocumentAlreadyExistsException[[addr][3] [contact][2]:
document already exists]"
      }
   }, {
      "delete" : {
        "_index" : "addr",
        "_type" : "contact",
        "_id" : "4",
        "_version" : 1,
        "ok" : true
      }
   }, {
      "delete" : {
        "_index" : "addr",
        "_type" : "contact",
        "_id" : "1",
        "_version" : 2,
        "ok" : true
      }
   } ]
}
```

As we can see, every result is a part of the `items` array. Let's briefly compare these results with our input data. The first two commands, namely, `index` and `create`, were executed without any problems. The third operation failed because we wanted to create a record with an identifier that already existed in the index. The next two operations were deletions. Both succeeded. Note that the first of them tried to delete a nonexistent document; as you can see, this wasn't a problem.

Is it possible to do it quicker?

Bulk operations are fast, but if you are wondering if there is a more efficient and quicker way of indexing, you can take a look at the **User Datagram Protocol (UDP)** bulk operations. Note that using UDP doesn't guarantee that no data was lost during communication with the ElasticSearch server. So this is useful only in some cases where performance is critical and more important than accuracy.

Summary

In this chapter, we've looked at how to index tree-like structures and how to modify existing index mappings. In addition to that, we've used nested documents and parent-child relationships to index data that can have relationship and structure. Finally, we've looked at the river functionality, which gives us the possibility of fetching data from other systems. We've also learned how to speed up our indexing process by using the batch indexing API. In the next chapter, we will take a look at faceting—a mechanism that allows us to calculate the aggregated data for our query results – and we will see the possibilities that give us the `_mlt` endpoint. Finally, we will look at the percolator functionality that allows us to use prospective search.

6
Beyond Searching

In the previous chapter we've looked at how to index tree-like structures, how to use nested objects, and the parent-child relationship. We've also discussed fetching data from external systems using the river plugins and batch processing to speed up indexing. We've seen how to use the index update API. In this chapter, we will learn how to use faceting, which will allow us to get aggregated data about our search results. We will also see how to get similar documents with the "more like this" functionality and how to use prospective search to store queries, not documents. By the end of this chapter you will have learned:

- How to use faceting
- How to use the "more like this" REST endpoint
- What a percolator is and how to use it

Faceting

ElasticSearch is a full text search engine that aims to provide search results on the basis of our queries. However, sometimes we would like to get more. For example, we would like to get aggregated data that is calculated on the result set we get, such as the number of documents priced between 100 and 200 dollars or the most common tags in the results documents. In order to do that, ElasticSearch provides a faceting module that is responsible for providing such data. In this chapter we will discuss different faceting methods provided by ElasticSearch.

Document structure

For the purpose of discussing faceting, we'll use a very simple index structure for our documents. It will contain the identifier of the document, document date, a multivalued field that can hold words describing our document (the `tags` field), and a field holding numeric information (the `total` field). Our mappings could look like this:

```
{
  "mappings" : {
   "doc" : {
    "properties" : {
     "id" : { "type" : "long", "store" : "yes" },
     "date" : { "type" : "date", "store" : "no" },
     "tags" : { "type" : "string", "store" : "no", "index" : "not_
analyzed" },
     "total" : { "type" : "long", "store" : "no" }
    }
   }
  }
}
```

 Keep in mind that when dealing with string fields you should avoid doing faceting on analyzed fields. Such results may not be human readable, especially when using stemming or any other heavy processing analyzers or filters.

Returned results

Before we get into how to run faceting, let's take a look on what to expect from ElasticSearch as a result of faceting requests. In most cases you'll only be interested in the data specific to the faceting type. However in most faceting types, in addition to information specific to a given faceting type, you'll get the following as well:

- `_type`: This specifies the faceting type used and will be provided for each faceting type
- `missing`: This specifies the number of documents that didn't have enough data (for example, a missing field) to calculate faceting

- total: This specifies the number of tokens in the facet calculation
- other: This specifies the number of facet values (for example, terms in terms faceting) not included in the returned counts

In addition to these types, you'll get an array of calculated facets such as count for your terms, queries, or spatial distance. For example, this is what the usual faceting results look like:

```
{
    .
    .
    .
    "facets" : {
      "tags" : {
        "_type" : "terms",
        "missing" : 54715,
        "total" : 151266,
        "other" : 143140,
        "terms" : [ {
          "term" : "test",
          "count" : 1119
        }, {
          "term" : "personal",
          "count" : 1063
        },
        (...)
        ]
      }
    }
}
```

As you can see in the results, our faceting was run against the tags field. We've got a total number of 151,266 tokens processed by the faceting module, and 143,140 that were not included in the results. We also have 54,715 documents that didn't have the value in the tags field. The term "test" appeared in 1,119 documents and the term "personal" appeared in 1,063 documents. This is what you can expect from a faceting response.

Query

Query is one of the simplest faceting types that allows us to get the number of documents that match the query in the faceting results. The query itself can be expressed using the ElasticSearch query language, which we discussed in *Chapter 2, Searching Your Data*. For example, faceting that would return the number of documents for a simple term query could look like this:

```
{
 "query" : { "match_all" : {} },
 "facets" : {
  "my_query_facet" : {
   "query" : {
    "term" : { "tags" : "personal" }
   }
  }
 }
}
```

As you can see, we've included the query type faceting with a simple term query.

A sample response for the preceding query could look like this:

```
{
  .
  .
  .
  "facets" : {
    "my_query_facet" : {
      "_type" : "query",
      "count" : 1081
    }
  }
}
```

As you can see, in the response, we've got the faceting type and the count of the documents that matched the facet query, and of course, the main query.

Filter

A **filter** is a simple faceting type that allows us to get the number of documents that match the filter. The filter itself can be expressed using the ElasticSearch query language. For example, faceting that would return the number of documents for a simple term filter could look like this:

```
{
  "query" : { "match_all" : {} },
  "facets" : {
   "my_filter_facet" : {
    "filter" : {
     "term" : { "tags" : "personal" }
    }
   }
  }
}
```

As you can see, we've included the `filter` type faceting with a simple term filter. When talking about performance, filter facets are faster than query facets or filter facets that wrap queries.

An example response for the preceding query could look like this:

```
{
  .
  .
  .
  "facets" : {
    "my_filter_facet" : {
      "_type" : "filter",
      "count" : 1081
    }
  }
}
```

As you can see in the response, we've got the faceting type and the count of the documents that matched the facet filter, and of course, the main query.

Terms

Terms faceting allows specifying a field, and ElasticSearch will return the most frequent terms for that field. For example, if we want to calculate terms faceting for the `tags` field, we could run the following query:

```
{
  "query" : { "match_all" : {} },
  "facets" : {
   "tags_facet_result" : {
    "terms" : {
     "field" : "tags"
    }
   }
  }
}
```

The following faceting response will be returned by ElasticSearch for the preceding query:

```
{
    .
    .
    .
  "facets" : {
    "tags_facet_result" : {
      "_type" : "terms",
      "missing" : 54716,
      "total" : 151266,
      "other" : 143140,
      "terms" : [ {
        "term" : "test",
        "count" : 1119
      }, {
        "term" : "personal",
        "count" : 1063
      }, {
        "term" : "feel",
        "count" : 982
```

```
    }, {
      "term" : "hot",
      "count" : 923
    },
    (...)
    ]
  }
 }
}
```

As you can see, our terms faceting results were returned in the `tags_facet_result` section and we've got the information that was already described.

There are a few additional parameters we can use for `terms` faceting:

- `size`: This specifies how many most frequent terms should be returned at most. The documents with subsequent terms will be included in the count of the `other` field in the result.
- `order`: This specifies the faceting ordering. The possible values are:
    - ◦ `count` (the default order by frequency, starting from the most frequent)
    - ◦ `term` (alphabetical order, ascending)
    - ◦ `reverse_count` (order by frequency, starting from the less frequent)
    - ◦ `reverse_term` (alphabetical order, descending)
- `all_terms`: This parameter, when set to `true`, will return all the terms in the result.
- `exclude`: This is an array of terms that should be excluded from facet calculation.
- `regex`: This is a regular expression that will control the terms to be included in the calculation.
- `script`: This specifies the script that will be used to process the term used in facet calculation.
- `fields`: This is an array that allows specifying multiple fields for faceting calculation (which should be used instead of the `field` property). ElasticSearch will return aggregation across multiple fields.
- `_script_field`: This specifies the script that will provide the actual term for calculation. For example, any term based from the `_source` field may be used.

Range

Range faceting allows us to get the number of documents for a defined set of ranges, and in addition to that, get data aggregated for the specified field. For example, if we wanted to get the number of documents that have the value in the `total` field falling into the ranges (lower bound inclusive, upper exclusive) up to 90, 90 to 180, and above 180, we would send the following query:

```
{
  "query" : { "match_all" : {} },
  "facets" : {
   "ranges_facet_result" : {
    "range" : {
     "field" : "total",
     "ranges" : [
      { "to" : 90 },
      { "from" : 90, "to" : 180 },
      { "from" : 180 }
     ]
    }
   }
  }
}
```

As you can see in the preceding query, we've defined the name of the field by using the `field` property and the array of ranges using the `ranges` property. Each range can be defined using the `to` or `from` properties or both at the same time.

The response for the preceding query could look like this:

```
{

  .
  .
  .

  "facets" : {
    "ranges_facet_result" : {
      "_type" : "range",
      "ranges" : [ {
        "to" : 90.0,
        "count" : 18210,
        "min" : 0.0,
        "max" : 89.0,
        "total_count" : 18210,
```

```
      "total" : 39848.0,
      "mean" : 2.1882482152663374
  }, {
      "from" : 90.0,
      "to" : 180.0,
      "count" : 159,
      "min" : 90.0,
      "max" : 178.0,
      "total_count" : 159,
      "total" : 19897.0,
      "mean" : 125.13836477987421
  }, {
      "from" : 180.0,
      "count" : 274,
      "min" : 182.0,
      "max" : 57676.0,
      "total_count" : 274,
      "total" : 585961.0,
      "mean" : 2138.543795620438
  } ]
 }
 }
}
```

As you can see, because we've defined three ranges in our query for the range faceting, we've got those in response. For each range the following statistics were returned:

- from: The left boundary of the range
- to: The right boundary of the range
- min: The minimum field value of the field used for faceting in the given range
- max: The maximum field value of the field used for faceting in the given range
- count: The number of documents with a value of the defined field that falls into the specified range
- total_count: The total number of values in the defined field that fall into the specified range (should be the same as count for single-valued fields and can be different for fields with multiple values)

- `total`: The sum of all the values in the defined field that fall into the specified range
- `mean`: The mean value calculated for the values in the given field used for range faceting calculation that falls into the specified range

Choosing different fields for aggregated data calculation

If we want to calculate the aggregated data statistics for a different field than we calculate the ranges for, we can use two properties—`key_field` and `key_value` (or `key_script` and `value_script`, which allow for script usage). The `key_field` property specifies which field value should be used to check whether the value falls into a given range and the `value_field` property specifies which field value should be used for aggregation calculation.

Numerical and date histogram

A histogram faceting allows us to build a histogram of values across intervals of the field value (for numerical and date-based fields). For example, if we wanted to see how many documents fall into intervals of 1000 in our `total` field, we would run the following query:

```
{
 "query" : { "match_all" : {} },
 "facets" : {
  "total_histogram" : {
   "histogram" : {
    "field" : "total",
    "interval" : 1000
   }
  }
 }
}
```

As you can see, we've used the `histogram` facet type, and in addition to the `field` property, we've included the `interval` property, which defines the interval we want to use.

A sample response for the preceding query could look like this:

```
{
 .
 .
 .
 "facets" : {
```

```
"total_histogram" : {
  "_type" : "histogram",
  "entries" : [ {
    "key" : 0,
    "count" : 18565
  }, {
    "key" : 1000,
    "count" : 33
  }, {
    "key" : 2000,
    "count" : 14
  }, {
    "key" : 3000,
    "count" : 5
  },
  (...)
  ]
    }
  }
}
```

As you can see in these results for the first bracket of 0 to 1000, we have 18,565 documents; for the second bracket of 1000 to 2000 we have 33 documents, and so on.

Date histogram

In addition to the histogram facets type, which can be used on numerical fields, ElasticSearch allows us to use the date_histogram faceting type, which can be used on date-based fields. The date_histogram type allows us to use constants such as year, month, week, day, hour, or minute as the value of the interval property. For example, one could send the following query:

```
{
  "query" : { "match_all" : {} },
  "facets" : {
   "date_histogram_test" : {
    "date_histogram" : {
     "field" : "date",
     "interval" : "day"
    }
   }
  }
}
```

In both numerical and date histogram faceting, we can use the key_field, key_value, key_script, and value_script properties, which we've discussed when talking about terms faceting earlier in this chapter.

Statistical

The statistical faceting allows us to compute statistical data for a numeric field type. In return, we get the count, total, sum of squares, average, minimum, maximum, variance, and standard deviation. For example, if we wanted to compute statistics for our total field, we would run the following query:

```
{
  "query" : { "match_all" : {} },
  "facets" : {
    "statistical_test" : {
      "statistical" : {
        "field" : "total"
      }
    }
  }
}
```

As a result we would get the following response:

```
{
  .
  .
  .
  "facets" : {
    "statistical_test" : {
      "_type" : "statistical",
      "count" : 18643,
      "total" : 645706.0,
      "min" : 0.0,
      "max" : 57676.0,
      "mean" : 34.63530547658639,
      "sum_of_squares" : 1.2490405256E10,
      "variance" : 668778.6853747752,
      "std_deviation" : 817.7889002516329
    }
  }
}
```

These are the statistics that were returned:

- `_type`: The faceting type
- `count`: The number of documents with the specified value in the defined field
- `total`: The sum of all the values in the defined field
- `min`: The minimum field value
- `max` The maximum field value
- `mean`: The mean value calculated for the values in the specified field
- `sum_of_squares`: The sum of squares calculated for the values in the specified field
- `variance`: The variance value calculated for the values in the specified field
- `std_deviation`: The standard deviation value calculated for the values in the specified field

 Please note that we are also allowed to use the `script` and `fields` properties in statistical faceting just like in terms faceting.

Terms statistics

The `terms_stats` faceting combines both `statistical` and `terms` faceting types as it provides the ability to compute statistics on a field for values got from another field. For example, if we wanted the faceting for the `total` field but to divide the value on the basis of the `tags` field, we would run the following query:

```
{
  "query" : { "match_all" : {} },
  "facets" : {
   "total_tags_terms_stats" : {
    "terms_stats" : {
     "key_field" : "tags",
     "value_field" : "total"
    }
   }
  }
}
```

We've specified the `key_field` property, which holds the name of the field that provides the terms, and the `value_field` property, which holds the name of the field with numerical data values. Here is a portion of the results we got from ElasticSearch:

```
{
  .
  .
  .
  "facets" : {
    "total_tags_terms_stats" : {
      "_type" : "terms_stats",
      "missing" : 54715,
      "terms" : [ {
        "term" : "personal",
        "count" : 1063,
        "total_count" : 254,
        "min" : 0.0,
        "max" : 322.0,
        "total" : 707.0,
        "mean" : 2.783464566929134
      }, {
        "term" : "me",
        "count" : 715,
        "total_count" : 218,
        "min" : 0.0,
        "max" : 138.0,
        "total" : 710.0,
        "mean" : 3.256880733944954
      }
      (...)
      ]
    }
  }
}
```

As you can see, the faceting results were divided on a per-term basis. Please note that the same set of statistics was returned for each term as the ones that are returned for the ranges faceting (please refer to the *Range* subsection in the *Faceting* section in this chapter for an explanation of what those values mean). This is because we've used a numerical field (`total`) to calculate the facet values for each field.

Spatial

The last faceting calculation type we would like to discuss is the `geo_distance` type. It allows us to get the information about the number of documents that fall into distance ranges from a given location. For example, let's assume that we have a `location` field in our documents in the index that stores the geographical point. And now imagine that we would like to get information about how many documents fall into the bracket of 10 kilometers from the 10.0,10.0 spatial point, how many fall into the bracket of 10 to 100 kilometers, and how many into that of more than 100 kilometers. In order to do that we will run the following query:

```
{
  "query" : { "match_all" : {} },
  "facets" : {
   "spatial_test" : {
    "geo_distance" : {
     "location" : {
      "lat" : 10.0,
      "lon" : 10.0
     },
     "ranges" : [
      { "to" : 10 },
      { "from" : 10, "to" : 100 },
      { "from" : 100 }
     ]
    }
   }
  }
}
```

In the preceding query we've defined the latitude (the `lat` property) and the longitude (the `lon` property) of the point from which we want to calculate the distance. We choose, as the name of the field that holds the location, the name of the object to which we pass the `lat` and `lon` properties. The second thing is the `ranges` array, which specifies the brackets; each range can be defined using the `to` or `from` properties or both at the same time.

In addition to the previously mentioned properties, we are also allowed to set the `unit` property (default: `km` for distance in kilometers and `mi` for distance in miles) and the `distance_type` property (default: `arc` for better precision and `plane` for faster execution).

Filtering faceting results

As we mentioned before, the filters you include in your queries don't narrow the faceting results, so you'll just get the documents matching your query. However, you may include the filters you want in your faceting definition. Basically, any filter we've discussed in *Chapter 2, Searching Your Data*, can be used with faceting. What you just need to do is include an additional section under the facet name.

For example, if we want our query to match all documents but have facets calculated for the multivalued `tags` field—only for those documents that have the term `fashion` in the `tags` field—we could run the following query:

```
{
  "query" : { "match_all" : {} },
  "facets" : {
   "tags" : {
    "terms" : { "field" : "tags" },
    "facet_filter" : {
     "term" : { "tags" : "fashion" }
    }
   }
  }
}
```

As you can see, there is an additional `facet_filter` section on the same level as the type of facet calculation (which is `terms` in the preceding query). You just need to remember that the `facet_filter` section is constructed with the same logic as any filter described in *Chapter 2*.

Scope of your faceting calculation

Imagine a situation where you would like to calculate facets, not on the information from the parent documents but instead using the information present in nested documents. In order to do that, ElasticSearch provides the `scope` and `nested` properties, allowing us to define what documents are seen by our facets.

In order to illustrate how to use those properties, let's recall our clothing store mappings, which we used in *Chapter 5, Combining Indexing, Analysis, and Search*, when we talked about nested objects (in the *Using nested objects* section). So let's recall it:

```
{
  "cloth" : {
    "properties" : {
      "name" : {"type" : "string", "store" : "yes", "index" :
"analyzed"},
      "variation" : {
```

```
      "type" : "nested",
      "properties" : {
        "size" : {"type" : "string", "store" : "yes", "index" : "not_
analyzed"},
        "color" : {"type" : "string", "store" : "yes", "index" : "not_
analyzed"}
      }
    }
   }
  }
 }
}
```

Facet calculation on all nested documents

The simplest way to calculate faceting on all the nested documents matching the parent documents that were returned by the query is to define the nested property and set its value to the name of the nested documents we are interested in. For example, let's look at the following query:

```
{
  "query": { "match_all": {} },
  "facets": {
   "size": {
    "terms" : { "field" : "size" },
    "nested": "variation"
   }
  }
}
```

As you can see, we want to calculate the terms facets on the size field. However, because this is a nested object, we've specified the nested property and have set its value to the name of the nested document we are interested in, which in our case was variation. The shortened response to the previous query (which shows the facets calculation) is as follows:

```
{
  .
  .
  .
  "facets" : {
    "size" : {
      "_type" : "terms",
      "missing" : 0,
```

```
        "total" : 2,
        "other" : 0,
        "terms" : [ {
          "term" : "XXL",
          "count" : 1
        }, {
          "term" : "XL",
          "count" : 1
        } ]
      }
    }
}
```

Facet calculation on nested documents that match a query

The method we've just used is good when we are interested in calculating facets for all the nested documents of a certain parent type that matched the query. However, sometimes we may be only interested in documents that match a certain part of the query. This is where the scope property comes into play. Let's look at the following query:

```
{
  "query" : {
   "nested" : {
    "path" : "variation",
    "query" : {
     "term" : { "variation.size" : "XL" }
    }
   }
  }
}
```

And now, let's introduce the scope. There are two places where we need to add it—first, in the query itself (where we need to introduce the _scope property with the name of our choice) and then in the facet calculation part (where we need to specify the scope we are interested in with the use of the scope property). Yes, you're right! We can have multiple _scope properties in different parts of the query and calculate different facets for different scopes. But let's get back to our modified query, which would look something like this:

```
{
  "query" : {
    "nested" : {
      "_scope": "es_book_scope",
      "path" : "variation",
      "query" : { "term" : { "variation.size" : "XL" } }
    }
  },
  "facets": {
    "size": {
      "terms" : {
        "field" : "size"
      },
      "scope": "es_book_scope"
    }
  }
}
```

The facets results for the preceding query should only be calculated on the nested documents that match the XL value in the size field; in fact, ElasticSearch returned what we expected:

```
{

  .

  .

  .

  "facets" : {
    "size" : {
      "_type" : "terms",
      "missing" : 0,
      "total" : 1,
      "other" : 0,
      "terms" : [ {
        "term" : "XL",
        "count" : 1
      } ]
    }
  }
}
```

Faceting memory considerations

Faceting can be memory-intensive, especially with large amounts of data in the indices and many distinct values. This is because ElasticSearch needs to load the data into the so-called **field data cache** in order to calculate faceting values. In the case of large amounts of data, you may be forced to change your index structure, for example, by lowering the cardinality of your fields by using less precise dates (not analyzed string fields or types such as `short`, `integer`, or `float` instead of `long` and `double`) when possible. If that doesn't help, you may need to give ElasticSearch more heap memory or even add more servers and divide your index to more shards.

More like this

The ElasticSearch functionality is not only about searching documents based on selected criteria. For example, we can use it in our application to find similar products to the ones that were returned by a user query.

In fact, we already know something about this functionality from *Chapter 2, Searching Your Data*, where we saw the "more like this" query. But, in the mentioned query, we have to construct the `like_text` field. ElasticSearch can generate this data based on the example document and provides a special endpoint for this.

Example data

For our example, let's imagine we have a travel agency where every available location is assigned a set of tags describing it. The simplified version of the data can look like this:

```
{ "index": { "_index" : "travel", "_type" : "loc", "_id" : 1}}
{ "name" : "beautiful hotel by the sea", "tags" : ["sea", "greece",
"beach"] }
{ "index": { "_index" : "travel", "_type" : "loc", "_id" : 2}}
{ "name" : "a small cottage in the mountains", "tags" : ["mountains",
"switzerland", "hiking"] }
{ "index": { "_index" : "travel", "_type" : "loc", "_id" : 3}}
{ "name" : "a small cottage in the mountains", "tags" : ["mountains",
"italy", "hiking"] }
{ "index": { "_index" : "travel", "_type" : "loc", "_id" : 4}}
{ "name" : "at the seaside", "tags" : ["sea", "italy"] }
```

As in previous examples, we've written this data to the `documents.json` file and loaded it into ElasticSearch using the following command:

```
curl -XPOST 'localhost:9200/_bulk' --data-binary @documents.json
```

Finding similar documents

Now we can use the `_mlt` endpoint and provide an identifier for a document for which we would like to find similar documents for. Look at the following command:

```
curl 'localhost:9200/travel/loc/3/_mlt?pretty&mlt_fields=tags&min_term_
freq=1&min_doc_freq=0'
```

We've tried to find documents similar to the one with ID equal to 3. The `mlt_fields` parameter tells ElasticSearch which fields (separated by a comma character) from this document should be used for searching. In our example we want to find the documents that have similar tags (the `tags` field). Let's look at the results returned by ElasticSearch:

```
{
  "took" : 2,
  "timed_out" : false,
  "_shards" : {
    "total" : 5,
    "successful" : 5,
    "failed" : 0
  },
  "hits" : {
    "total" : 2,
    "max_score" : 0.2169777,
    "hits" : [ {
      "_index" : "travel",
      "_type" : "loc",
      "_id" : "2",
      "_score" : 0.2169777,
      "_source" : { "name" : "a small cottage in the mountains", "tags" :
["mountains", "switzerland", "hiking"] }
    }, {
      "_index" : "travel",
      "_type" : "loc",
      "_id" : "4",
      "_score" : 0.19178301,
      "_source" : { "name" : "at he seaside", "tags" : ["sea", "italy"] }
    } ]
  }
}
```

As we can see, ElasticSearch thinks that if you are interested in hiking somewhere in the mountains in Italy, you can also consider a journey to Switzerland. Or maybe you should see more in Italy? You may wonder why we used additional parameters such as `min_term_freq` and `min_doc_freq`. This is because these parameters control which terms (words) should be ignored in comparison. ElasticSearch assumes that the given word should not be used too rarely in the index or too frequently (like common words such as and). Our index is very small, so we need it to slightly tune these parameters. In real cases, default values should work better (2 for the `min_term_freq` parameter and 5 for the `min_doc_freq` parameter), but you can also experiment for best results with other parameters described in the *The more like this query* section in *Chapter 2, Searching Your Data*.

Percolator

Did you ever wonder what would happen if we reversed the traditional model of using queries to find documents? Does it make sense to find documents that match the queries? It's no surprise that there is an entire range of solutions where this model is very useful. Wherever you operate on unbounded streams of input data, where you search for occurrences of particular events, you can use this approach. This can be the detection of failures in a monitoring system or a "tell me when this product with defined criteria will be available in this shop" functionality. Let's see how the ElasticSearch percolator works and how it can handle this last example.

Preparing the percolator

The percolator looks like an additional index in ElasticSearch. This means that we can store any documents in it and obtain its mappings. We can also search it like an ordinary index. However, we spoke about the reversal of the standard behavior and treating queries as documents. Let's get the library example from *Chapter 2, Searching Your Data*, and try to index this query in the percolator. We assume that our users need to be informed when any book matching a defined criterion is available. Of course, the challenge is to develop the user interface for defining such complicated queries, but happily, we are only search specialists, and this is not our problem.

Look at the `query1.json` file that contains the example query generated by the user:

```
{
  "query" : {
   "bool" : {
    "must" : {
     "term" : {
      "title" : "crime"
     }
    }
```

```
        },
        "should" : {
          "range" : {
           "year" : {
            "from" : 1900,
            "to" : 2000
           }
          }
        },
        "must_not" : {
          "term" : {
           "otitle" : "nothing"
          }
         }
        }
       }
      }
     }
```

The user interface can also use filters. This is not a problem. The second query should find all the books written before the year 2010 and that are currently available in our library. This is what the query2.json content looks like:

```
{
 "query" : {
  "filtered": {
   "query" : {
    "range" : {
     "from" : 0,
     "year" : {
      "to" : 2010
     }
    }
   },
   "filter" : {
    "term" : {
     "available" : true
    }
   }
  }
 }
}
```

Now let's register both the queries in the percolator. In order to do that we run the following commands:

```
curl -XPUT 'localhost:9200/_percolator/notifier/1' -d @query1.json
curl -XPUT 'localhost:9200/_percolator/notifier/old_books' -d @query2.json
```

ElasticSearch assumes that the target index (in our case, this index is named `notifier`) must be available, so let's create it now by running the following command:

```
curl -XPUT 'localhost:9200/notifier'
```

We are now ready to use our percolator. Our application will provide documents to the percolator and check whether ElasticSearch finds the corresponding queries. Let's use an example document that will match both the stored queries. It'll have the required title, the release date, and is currently available. It can look like the following code:

```
curl -XGET 'localhost:9200/notifier/x/_percolate?pretty' -d '{
  "doc" : {
    "title": "Crime and Punishment",
    "otitle": "Преступлéние и наказáние",
    "author": "Fyodor Dostoevsky",
    "year": 1886,
    "characters": ["Raskolnikov", "Sofia Semyonovna Marmeladova"],
    "tags": [],
    "copies": 0,
    "available" : true
  }
}'
```

As we expected, ElasticSearch responds with the result that lists the identifiers of the matching queries:

```
{
  "ok" : true,
  "matches" : [ "1", "old_books" ]
}
```

It works like a charm! Note the endpoint used in this query. The index name corresponds to the type name in the `_percolator` index. Type is irrelevant. We can use any name just to satisfy the index/type syntax in ElasticSearch.

Getting deeper

Because queries registered in the percolator are in fact documents, we can use a normal query sent to ElasticSearch to choose which queries stored in the _percolator index should be used in the percolate process! It may sound weird, but it really gives us a lot of possibilities. In our library we can have several groups of users. Let's assume some of them have permissions to borrow very rare books. Or we have several branches in the city, and the user can declare where he/she would like to go and get the book from. Look at the following query registration command:

```
curl -XPUT 'localhost:9200/_percolator/notifier/3' -d '{
  "query" : {
   "term" : {
    "title" : "crime"
   }
  },
  "branches" : ["bra", "brb", "brd"]
}'
```

In this example, the user is interested in any books with "crime" in the title. He/ she wants to borrow this book in one of the three listed branches. We will search in the branches field as we've already done with ordinary fields. In this particular case we have an array, so we must prepare mapping for that field. If you've already read *Chapter 1, Getting Started with ElasticSearch Cluster*, there shouldn't be a problem creating such a mapping. For example, we can do it like this:

```
    {
     "notifier" : {
      "properties" : {
       "branches" : {
        "type" : "string",
        "index" : "not_analyzed"
       }
      }
     }
    }
```

After updating the mappings and indexing our query, we can now test matching with our example document. We assume that the book was returned in the branch brB; now, let's check whether someone is interested in this book:

```
curl -XGET 'localhost:9200/notifier/x/_percolate?pretty' -d '{
  "doc" : {
   "title": "Crime and Punishment",
   "otitle": "Преступление и наказание",
```

```
    "author": "Fyodor Dostoevsky",
    "year": 1886,
    "characters": ["Raskolnikov", "Sofia Semyonovna Marmeladova"],
    "tags": [],
    "copies": 0,
    "available" : true
  },
  "query" : {
    "term" : {
      "branches" : "brb"
    }
  }
}'
```

If everything is right, the answer should be similar to this (we index our query with 3 as the identifier):

```
{
    "ok" : true,
    "matches" : [ "3" ]
}
```

 Please note that there are some limitations when it comes to the query types supported by the percolator functionality. In the current implementation, parent-child and nested queries are not available, so you can't use queries such as `has_child`, `top_children`, `has_parent`, and `nested`.

Summary

In this chapter we've looked at faceting—a mechanism that allows us to calculate aggregated data for our query results—and we saw the possibilities that give us the "more like this" functionality. Finally, we've discussed the percolator functionality, which allows us to use prospective search. In the next chapter, we'll learn how to control shards and replicas, how to use ElasticSearch gateway module, and what discovery is and how to configure it. In addition to that, we'll look at cluster monitoring possibilities and tools available, and finally, we'll learn how to install plugins.

7
Administrating Your Cluster

In the previous chapter, we've mainly looked at how to use the faceting functionality in ElasticSearch, which allowed us to get aggregated statistics about our search results. In addition to that, we've learned how to use the "more like this" REST endpoint to get a similar document to the ones we've found, and in addition to that we've also used the prospective search functionality called the **percolator** to store queries and check which queries matched the document sent to ElasticSearch. In this chapter, we will take a look at cluster health and cluster state monitoring. We will learn how to use tools to diagnose the state of our cluster. We will also use the shard and replica allocation mechanism to control the nodes on which they are placed by ElasticSearch. Finally we will learn what the **gateway** and **discovery** modules are and how to configure them. By the end of this chapter you will have learned:

- How to monitor your cluster state and health
- How to use tools for cluster state diagnosis
- How to control shard and replica allocation
- How to use the gateway module
- How to use the discovery module
- How to install plugins

Monitoring your cluster state and health

During the normal life of an application, a very important concern is monitoring. This allows the administrators of the system to detect possible problems and prevent them before they occur or at least know what happens during a failure.

ElasticSearch provides very detailed information that allows us to check and monitor the node or cluster as a whole. This includes statistics, information about the server, and node parameters, but first of all it includes complete information about the current cluster state. Let's look at this in more detail. But before that let's take a look at one piece of information: these APIs are very complex and in this book we've only described the basics. Please note that the amount of information regarding the cluster state and health monitoring is enormous; because of this we keep the information and details about ElasticSearch internal to the minimum that is needed to understand the described topic.

The cluster health API

ElasticSearch exposes information about the current node or cluster in the cluster health API. Let's see the reply for the following command:

```
curl localhost:9200/_cluster/health?pretty
```

In my notebook the answer is as follows:

```
{
    "cluster_name" : "elasticsearch",
    "status" : "yellow",
    "timed_out" : false,
    "number_of_nodes" : 1,
    "number_of_data_nodes" : 1,
    "active_primary_shards" : 103,
    "active_shards" : 103,
    "relocating_shards" : 0,
    "initializing_shards" : 0,
    "unassigned_shards" : 101
}
```

The most important piece of information is the one about the status of the cluster. In our example we see that the cluster is in the yellow state. What does that mean? Let's stop here and talk about a cluster and when a cluster, as a whole, is fully operational. As you already know, ElasticSearch always assumes that the current node is a part of a cluster. This means that the index is divided into separate parts called **shards** and can be allocated on a few nodes. In addition to that, ElasticSearch can create copies of these shards (replicas) to handle more requests and for data consistency.

A cluster is fully operational when ElasticSearch is able to allocate all shards and replicas on machines according to its configuration. This is the green state. The yellow state means that we are ready for handling requests because the primary shards are allocated, but some (or all) replicas aren't. The last state, red, means that the ElasticSearch cluster is not ready yet and at least one of the primary shards is not ready. When we have only one node and you have replicas, the yellow state is obvious. There are no other nodes to place replicas on. Let's start another node and check again:

```
{
   "cluster_name" : "elasticsearch",
   "status" : "green",
   "timed_out" : false,
   "number_of_nodes" : 2,
   "number_of_data_nodes" : 2,
   "active_primary_shards" : 103,
   "active_shards" : 205,
   "relocating_shards" : 0,
   "initializing_shards" : 0,
   "unassigned_shards" : 0
}
```

Now the cluster's state is green and our cluster is fully operational. This query can also be executed on a specific index or indices, for example:

```
curl 'localhost:9200/_cluster/health/library,map?pretty'
```

The state can be determined on several levels: shards, index (determined by the worst shard status), and cluster (determined by the worst index status). These levels can be used as the parameter in this API, affecting the level of detail of the information returned. Compare the results of the following commands:

```
curl 'localhost:9200/_cluster/health?pretty'
curl 'localhost:9200/_cluster/health?pretty&level=indices'
curl 'localhost:9200/_cluster/health?pretty&level=shards'
```

As we said, the "color of the cluster" has vital meaning for an application and direct connection with the availability of this application. As a result of this, during the bootstrap of the system, as a part of starting scripts, it is convenient to use this API to check whether the system is ready. ElasticSearch introduces additional parameters for that; one fo them is `wait_for_status` with a value corresponding to the color. The other interesting parameter is `wait_for_nodes` with a required number of nodes available. Both of these parameters cause that request not to end until the cluster attains the desired state/number of nodes, or the timeout exception is thrown. This timeout value can be changed using the `timeout` parameter (the default value is 30 seconds). For example:

```
curl 'localhost:9200/_cluster/health?wait_for_status=green&wait_for_
nodes=>=3&timeout=100s'
```

The previous command result will be returned only when the cluster has a green status and when there are at least three nodes available. The command will be canceled after 100 seconds if the mentioned conditions are not met. In this case, information about the timeout will be available in the returned JSON response.

The indices stats API

ElasticSearch can show various statistics concerning indices. All this information is available using the `/_stats` API endpoint. Queries sent to this endpoint can get information about all the indices (`/_stats`), one particular index (for example, `/library/_stats`), or several indices (for example, `/library,map/_stats`). If you've tried the examples shown previously in this book, you can check the status by using the following command:

```
curl localhost:9200/library,map/_stats?pretty
```

The response probably has almost 300 lines, so we only describe its structure. in addition to information about status and response time, we can see three objects named `primaries`, `total`, and `indices`. The `indices` object contains information about `library` and `map` indices. The `primaries` object contains information about all primary shards allocated on the current node, and the `total` object contains information about all the shards including replicas. All these objects have the same structure and contain objects such as `docs`, `store`, `indexing`, `get`, and `search`. Let's discuss the information stored in those objects.

Docs

These statistic shows information about indexed documents. For example:

```
"docs" : {
 "count" : 4,
 "deleted" : 0
}
```

The main information is the count value, indicating the number of documents in the described index. When we delete documents from the index, ElasticSearch doesn't remove these documents immediately and only marks them as deleted. Documents are physically deleted in the segment merge process. The number of documents marked as deleted is presented as the deleted attribute and should be 0 right after the merge.

> If you are not familiar with the Apache Lucene library, then you may not know what segment merge is. Lucene divides the index into parts called **segments**, which once written can't be changed. After some time the number of segments grows, and when Lucene decides that the index is built of too many segments, it starts the process of segment merging. Lucene creates a new, larger segment with the information from the smaller ones and deletes the small indices.

Store

The next statistics, as you can guess, are connected with storage. The following is an example:

```
"store" : {
 "size" : "7.6kb",
 "size_in_bytes" : 7867,
 "throttle_time" : "0s",
 "throttle_time_in_millis" : 0
}
```

The main information is about the size of the index (or indices). We can also look at throttling statistics. This information is useful when the system has problems with I/O performance and has configured limits on the internal operation during segment merge.

Indexing, get, and search

The next three statistics are information about data manipulation: indexing with delete operations, using real-time get, and searching. Let's look at the following example:

```
"indexing" : {
 "index_total" : 11501,
 "index_time" : "4.5s",
 "index_time_in_millis" : 4574,
 "index_current" : 0,
 "delete_total" : 0,
 "delete_time" : "0s",
 "delete_time_in_millis" : 0,
 "delete_current" : 0
},
"get" : {
 "total" : 3,
 "time" : "0s",
 "time_in_millis" : 0,
 "exists_total" : 2,
 "exists_time" : "0s",
 "exists_time_in_millis" : 0,
 "missing_total" : 1,
 "missing_time" : "0s",
 "missing_time_in_millis" : 0,
 "current" : 0
},
"search" : {
 "query_total" : 0,
 "query_time" : "0s",
 "query_time_in_millis" : 0,
 "query_current" : 0,
 "fetch_total" : 0,
 "fetch_time" : "0s",
 "fetch_time_in_millis" : 0,
 "fetch_current" : 0
}
```

As we can see, all of these statistics have a similar structure. We can read the total time spent in various request types (in human-readable form and in milliseconds) and the number of requests (which, with total time, allows us to calculate the average time of one query). In the case of get requests, valuable information is the number of fetches that were unsuccessful (missing documents).

The mentioned `docs`, `store`, `indexing`, `get`, and `search` are returned by default. The indices stats API can also provide additional information about the merge process, flush, and refresh. You can add this information to the reply using appropriate parameters. For example:

```
curl 'localhost:9200/_stats?merge&flush&refresh&pretty'
```

The status API

There is a second way of obtaining information about indices: the `/_status` endpoint. The available information describes the available shards (and information about which of them is currently considered primary), information about the transaction log and merge process. Adding additional parameters such as `recovery` and `snapshot` adds additional information about the shard recovery status and the snapshot status. You can review this information but most of it is connected with the usage of the Lucene library or is very low-level and is beyond the scope of this book.

The nodes info API

The next source of information about the cluster is the nodes info API available at the `/_cluster/nodes` or the `/_nodes` REST endpoints. This API can be used to fetch information about particular nodes or a node using the following:

- The node name (for example, `/_nodes/Pulse`)
- The identifier (for example, `/_nodes/ny4hftjNQtuKMyEvpUdQWg`)
- The address (for example, `/_nodes/192.168.1.103`)
- The parameters from the ElasticSearch configuration (for example, `/_nodes/rack:2`)

This API also allows us to get information about several nodes at once by:

- Using patterns (for example, `/_nodes/192.168.1.*` or `/_nodes/P*`)
- Using enumerations (for example, `/_nodes/Pulse,Slab`)
- Using both patterns and enumerations (for example, `/_nodes/P*,S*`)

By default, this query returns the basic information about a node such as the name, identifier, and address. But by adding additional Boolean parameters, we can obtain many other items of information. The available parameters are as follows:

- `settings`: To get the ElasticSearch configuration
- `os`: To get information about the server, such as processor, RAM, and swap space
- `process`: To get the process identifier and the available file descriptors
- `jvm`: To get information about the Java virtual machine, such as the memory limits
- `thread_pool`: To get the configuration of thread pools for various operations
- `network`: To get the network interface name and addresses
- `transport`: To get listen addresses for transport
- `http`: To get listen addresses for HTTP
- `all`: To get all the previously mentioned information

A sample usage of the previously mentioned API can be seen by using the following command:

```
curl 'localhost:9200/_nodes/Pulse?os&jvm&pretty'
```

This `curl` invocation returns information about the machine and the Java virtual machine on a node named `Pulse`.

The nodes stats API

This API is similar to the nodes info API previously described. The main difference is that the previous API provides information about the environment, and the one we are talking about now tells us about what happens with the cluster during its work. The nodes stats API is available under `_cluster/nodes/stats` and `/_nodes/stats`. Similar to the nodes info API, we can obtain information from selected nodes (for example, `/_nodes/Pulse/stats`). The available flags for returned statistics are as follows:

- `indices`: To get information similar to the information from the indices stats API and information about cache usage
- `os`: To get information about server uptime, load, memory, and swap usage
- `process`: To get information about the memory and CPU used by the process
- `jvm`: To get information about the memory and garbage collector statistics for a Java virtual machine

- `network`: To get TCP-level information
- `transport`: To get information about the data sent and received by the transport module
- `http`: To get information about the HTTP connections
- `fs`: To get information about the available disk space and I/O operations statistics
- `thread_pool`: To get information about the state of the threads assigned to various operations
- `all`: To get all the above information

An example usage can look like the following command:

```
curl 'localhost:9200/_nodes/Pulse/stats?os&jvm&pretty'
```

The cluster state API

The `/_cluster/state` endpoint provides basic information about nodes, state, settings, aliases, and the mappings of the indices. In addition to that information, you can find information about shard assignment. There is the possibility to filter out unnecessary information using the following parameters: `filter_nodes`, `filter_routing_table`, `filter_metadata`, `filter_blocks`, and `filter_indices`. In the last filter, you can set a comma-separated list of indices that should be included in the response. The example usage is as follows:

```
curl 'localhost:9200/_cluster/state?filter_indices=library&pretty'
curl 'localhost:9200/_cluster/state?filter_nodes&pretty'
```

The indices segments API

The last API is available by using the `/_segments` endpoint. There is also the possibility to address only one or several indices (for example, by using the following REST endpoint: `/library,map/_segments`). This API not only provides information about shards and their placing but also information about segments connected with a physical index managed by the Lucene library.

Controlling shard and replica allocation

As we already discussed, indices that live inside your cluster can be built of many shards and each shard can have many replicas. With the ability to have multiple shards of a single index, we can deal with indices that are too large to fit on a single machine. The reasons may be different—from memory to storage ones. With the ability to have multiple replicas of each shard, we can handle a higher query load by spreading replicas over multiple servers. In order to shard and replicate, ElasticSearch has to figure out where in the cluster it should place the shards and replicas. It needs to figure out which server/node each shard or replica should be placed on.

Explicitly controlling allocation

Imagine that we have our cluster divided into two sections. We want one index, named shop, to be placed on some nodes and the second index called users to be placed on other nodes, and the last index called promotions to be placed on all the nodes that the users and shop indices were placed on. We do that because the third index is much smaller than the other ones and thus we can afford having it along with other indices. However, with the default ElasticSearch behavior we can't be sure where the shards and replicas will be placed. But luckily, ElasticSearch allows us to control that.

Specifying nodes' parameters

So let's divide our cluster into two zones. We say zones, but it can be any name you want; we just like "the zone". So, our nodes numbered 1 and 2 will be placed in a zone called zone_one and the nodes numbered 3 and 4 will be placed in a zone called zone_two.

Configuration

In order to do that, we add the following property to the elasticsearch.yml configuration file on nodes 1 and 2:

```
node.zone: zone_one
```

We add the following property to the elasticsearch.yml configuration file on nodes 3 and 4:

```
node.zone: zone_two
```

Index creation

Now let's create our indices. First let's create the `shop` index. We do that by running the following commands:

```
curl -XPOST 'localhost:9200/shop'
curl -XPUT 'localhost:9200/shop/_settings' -d '{
 "index.routing.allocation.include.zone" : "zone_one"
}'
```

You should be familiar with the first command, which creates our index. The second command is sent to the `_settings` REST endpoint to specify additional settings for that index. We set the `index.routing.allocation.include.zone` property to the `zone_one` value, which means that we want to place the `shop` index on the nodes that have the `node.zone` property set to `zone_one`.

We perform similar steps for the users' index:

```
curl -XPOST 'localhost:9200/users'
curl -XPUT 'localhost:9200/users/_settings' -d '{
 "index.routing.allocation.include.zone" : "zone_two"
}'
```

However, this time we've specified that we want the `users` index to be placed on the nodes with the `node.zone` property set to `zone_two`.

Finally, the `promotions` index should be placed on all the above nodes; so we use the following command to create and configure that index:

```
curl -XPOST 'localhost:9200/pictures'
curl -XPOST 'localhost:9200/promotions'
curl -XPUT 'localhost:9200/promotions/_settings' -d '{
 "index.routing.allocation.include.zone" : "zone_one,zone_two"
}'
```

Excluding nodes from allocation

In the same manner with which we specified on which nodes the index should be placed, we can also exclude nodes from index allocation. Referring to the previously shown example, if we would like the index called `pictures` not to be placed on nodes with the `node.zone` property set to `zone_one`, we would run the following command:

```
curl -XPUT 'localhost:9200/pictures/_settings' -d '{
 "index.routing.allocation.exclude.zone" : "zone_one"
}'
```

Notice that instead of the `index.routing.allocation.include.zone` property, we've used the `index.routing.allocation.exclude.zone` property.

Using IP addresses for shard allocation

Instead of adding a special parameter to the node's configuration, we are allowed to use IP addresses to specify which nodes we want to include or exclude from shard and replica allocation. In order to do that, instead of using the `zone` part of the `index.routing.allocation.include.zone` or `index.routing.allocation.exclude.zone` property, we should use the `_ip` part. For example, if we would like our `shop` index to be placed only on nodes with IP addresses `10.1.2.10` and `10.1.2.11`, we would run the following command:

```
curl -XPUT 'localhost:9200/shop/_settings' -d '{
 "index.routing.allocation.include._ip" : "10.1.2.10,10.1.2.11"
}'
```

Cluster-wide allocation

Instead of specifying allocation inclusion and exclusion on the index level (which we did till now), we can do that for all the indices in our cluster. For example, if we would like to place all the new indices on the nodes with IP addresses `10.1.2.10` and `10.1.2.11`, we would run the following command:

```
curl -XPUT 'localhost:9200/_cluster/settings' -d '{
 "transient" : {
  "cluster.routing.allocation.include._ip" : "10.1.2.10,10.1.2.11"
 }
}'
```

Notice that the command was sent to the `_cluster/settings` REST endpoint instead of the `INDEX_NAME/_settings` endpoint. Note that ElasticSearch will just process the command and will not return any response.

 Please note that the `transient` and `persistent` cluster properties are going to be discussed in *Controlling cluster rebalancing* in *Chapter 8, Dealing with Problems*.

Number of shards and replicas per node

In addition to specifying shard and replica allocation, we are also allowed to specify the maximum number of shards that should be placed on a single node for a single index. For example, if we would like our `shop` index to have only a single shard per node, we would run the following command:

```
curl -XPUT 'localhost:9200/shop/_settings' -d '{
 "index.routing.allocation.total_shards_per_node" : 1
}'
```

This property can be placed in a `elasticsearch.yml` file or can be updated on live indices using the preceding command. Please remember that your cluster can stay in the red state if ElasticSearch is unable to allocate all the primary shards.

Manually moving shards and replicas

The last thing we wanted to discuss is the ability to manually move shards between nodes. ElasticSearch exposes the `_cluster/reroute` REST endpoint, which allows us to control that. The following operations are available:

- Moving a shard from node to node
- Canceling shard allocation
- Forcing shard allocation

Now let's take a closer look at each of the previously mentioned operations.

Moving shards

Let's say we have two nodes called `es_node_one` and `es_node_two` and we have two shards of the `shop` index placed by ElasticSearch on the first node, and we would like to move the second shard to the second node. In order to do that we can run the following command:

```
curl -XPOST 'localhost:9200/_cluster/reroute' -d '{
 "commands" : [ {
  "move" : {
   "index" : "shop",
   "shard" : 1,
   "from_node" : "es_node_one",
   "to_node" : "es_node_two"
  }
 } ]
}'
```

We've specified the `move` command that allows us to move shards (and replicas) of the index specified by the `index` property. The `shard` property is the number of shards we want to move, and finally the `from_node` property specifies the name of the node we want to move the shard from, and the `to_node` property specifies the name of the node we want the shard to be placed on.

Canceling allocation

If we would like to cancel an on-going allocation process, we can run the `cancel` command and specify the index, node, and shard for which we want to cancel the allocation. For example:

```
curl -XPOST 'localhost:9200/_cluster/reroute' -d '{
 "commands" : [ {
  "cancel" : {
   "index" : "shop",
   "shard" : 0,
   "node" : "es_node_one"
  }
 } ]
}'
```

The preceding command would cancel the allocation of shard 0 of the shop index on the es_node_one node.

Allocating shards

In addition to canceling and moving shards and replicas, we are also allowed to allocate an unallocated shard to a specific node. For example, if we have an unallocated shard numbered 0 for the users index and we would like it to be allocated to es_node_two by ElasticSearch, we would run the following command:

```
curl -XPOST 'localhost:9200/_cluster/reroute' -d '{
 "commands" : [ {
  "allocate" : {
   "index" : "users",
   "shard" : 0,
   "node" : "es_node_two"
  }
 } ]
}'
```

Multiple commands per HTTP request

We can, of course, include multiple commands in a single HTTP request. For example:

```
curl -XPOST 'localhost:9200/_cluster/reroute' -d '{
 "commands" : [
  {"move" : {"index" : "shop", "shard" : 1, "from_node" : "es_node_one",
"to_node" : "es_node_two"}},
  {"cancel" : {"index" : "shop", "shard" : 0, "node" : "es_node_one"}}
 ]
}'
```

Tools for instance and cluster state diagnosis

As we saw in the previous chapter, ElasticSearch exposes a lot of information about both machines and search usage. This lets us build monitoring applications as well as applications that show usage or other available statistics. There are many tools we can use for monitoring our cluster state. In this chapter we will only slightly touch the top of the pile of information about such applications, but we strongly advise you to get familiar with some of them as they can make your everyday work with ElasticSearch easier.

The first three tools are available as ElasticSearch plugins and present various information from ElasticSearch using JavaScript and AJAX techniques. Data is fetched periodically from the cluster, prepared for visualization on the browser side, and shown to the user.

Bigdesk

This tool allows us to track statistics on a particular node. The browser can present information up to the last one hour. The following screenshot shows the graphical user interface from Bigdesk:

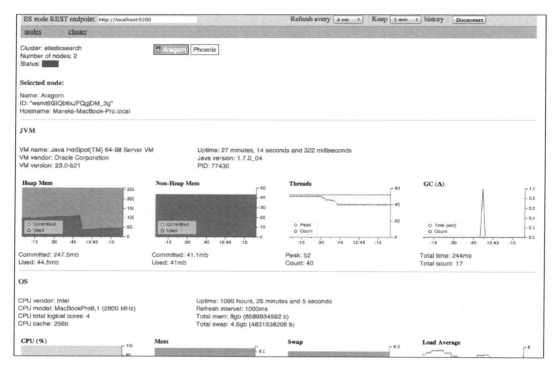

As you can see in the presented screenshot, we have information about the name of the cluster, number of nodes, and its health. We can also see which node we are looking at and some statistics about the node, which include the memory usage (both heap and non-heap), number of threads, Java virtual machine garbage collector work, and so on.

In order to install Bigdesk, one should just run the following command:

```
bin/plugin -install lukas-vlcek/bigdesk
```

After that, the GUI will be available at http://localhost:9200/_plugin/bigdesk/.

elasticsearch-head

This tool can show the shard placement for every index and node. In addition, it provides an index browser and a tool for building queries. You can also run several commands such as alias creation or deletion of indices. Many operations, using this tool in its current form, will only give you a raw JSON format response from the ElasticSearch server.

The following screenshot shows the graphical user interface of this tool:

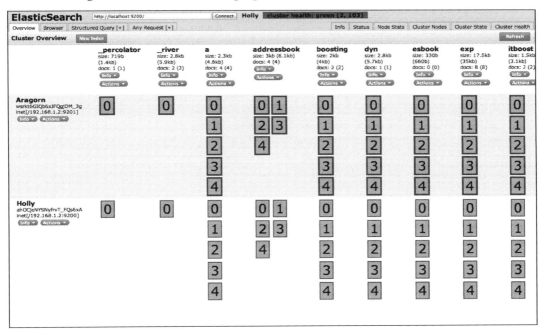

The main page of the elasticsearch-head gives us graphical information about the allocation of each of the index primary shards and replicas. We can also see some basic statistics for each index such as the size and number of the document. Also, the cluster health is visible.

In order to install elasticsearch-head, one should just run the following command:

```
bin/plugin -install mobz/elasticsearch-head
```

After that, the GUI will be available at http://localhost:9200/_plugin/head/.

elasticsearch-paramedic

elasticsearch-paramedic is another tool that lets us see up to 15 minutes of server statistics, cluster state information, and a clean view of the most important parameters as a chart. It also presents the information about shard placement.

The following screenshot shows the graphical user interface of elasticsearch-paramedic:

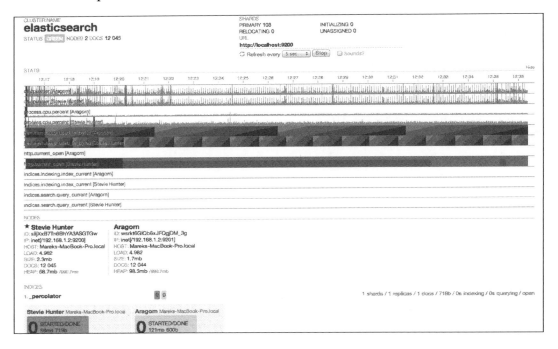

As you can see in the elasticsearch-paramedic screenshot, we have the information about all the shards, the cluster name, and health. In addition to that, the current CPU usage is shown, heap memory, opened HTTP connections, indexing, and querying statistics. You can also see information about each node, such as its identifier, IP address, host name, stored indices and many more things.

In order to install elasticsearch-paramedic, one should just run the following command:

```
bin/plugin -install karmi/elasticsearch-paramedic
```

After that, the GUI will be available at http://localhost:9200/_plugin/paramedic/index.html.

SPM for ElasticSearch

This tool presents a different approach than the previously mentioned tools. SPM is a **Software as a Service (SaaS)** solution created for monitoring ElasticSearch installations of any size and allows monitoring several clusters.

Information is sent by simple client software installed on the ElasticSearch machine to SPM servers. The main advantage is the possibility of storing information for a wider range of time and seeing what was happening in the past.

The following screenshot shows the dashboard of SPM for ElasticSearch:

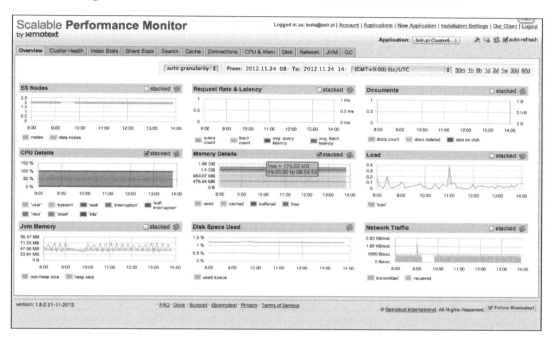

The dashboard shown in the screenshot provides information about cluster nodes, request rate and latency, number of documents in the indices, CPU usage, load, memory details, Java virtual machine memory, disk space usage, and finally network traffic. You can get detailed information about each of those elements by going into the tab dedicated to it.

You can find additional information about SPM installation and configuration available at `http://sematext.com/spm/index.html`.

Your ElasticSearch time machine

Apart from our indices and the data indexed inside them, ElasticSearch needs to hold the metadata, which can be of the type mappings, index-level settings, and all of that. All that information needs to be stored somewhere in order to be safe when the whole cluster restarts. It is due to these needs that ElasticSearch introduced the gateway module. You can think about it as a safe haven for your cluster data and metadata. Each time you start your cluster, all the needed data is read from the gateway, and when you make a change to your cluster it is persisted using the gateway module.

The gateway module

ElasticSearch allows us to use different gateway types, which we will discuss in a moment. In order to set the type of gateway we want to use, we need to add the `gateway.type` property to the `elasticsearch.yml` configuration file and set it to one of the following values:

- `local`: This specifies a local gateway
- `fs`: This specifies a shared filesystem gateway
- `hdfs`: This specifies the Hadoop distributed filesystem gateway
- `s3`: This specifies the Amazon s3 gateway

Local gateway

This default and recommended gateway type stores the indices and their metadata in the local filesystem. In order to use this type of gateway, one should set the `gateway.type` property to `local` in the `elasticsearch.yml` configuration file.

Compared to other gateways, the write operation to this gateway is not performed in an asynchronous way. So whenever a write succeeds, you can be sure that the data was written into the gateway (basically indexed or stored into the transaction log).

Shared filesystem gateway

The shared filesystem gateway stores the information about indices and metadata in a shared, distributed filesystem that is accessible by all ElasticSearch nodes in the cluster. In order to use this type of gateway, one should set the `gateway.type` property to `fs` in the `elasticsearch.yml` configuration file. In addition to that, we need to set the `gateway.fs.location` property, which will inform ElasticSearch where the shared filesystem is located. ElasticSearch will append the cluster name to the value provided by the `gateway.fs.location` property.

The following example uses the shared filesystem gateway:

```
gateway.type: fs
gateway.fs.location: /shared/elasticsearch/gateway/
```

In addition to the required properties one can also change the `gateway.`
`fs.concurrent_streams` property (which defaults to 5), which controls how
many concurrent streams are used in order to perform the **snapshotting** operation.
Snapshotting is a process of writing changes that need to be applied with the gateway
(such as metadata changes). If you want to have your cluster recover faster from the
gateway, increase the value of that property (however, you have to remember that it
will add more pressure on the CPU and I/O). If you want to reduce the pressure on
the nodes during recovery, decrease the value of this property.

Hadoop distributed filesystem gateway

The Hadoop distributed filesystem gateway type stores all the needed information
in the HDFS filesystem. In order to use this type of gateway, one should set the
`gateway.type` property to `hdfs` in the `elasticsearch.yml` configuration file. In
addition to that, we need to set the following properties:

- `gateway.hdfs.uri`: This is the URI of the Hadoop cluster
- `gateway.hdfs.path`: This is the path where the data will be stored in HDFS

For example, if we have our Hadoop cluster available at `hfds://10.1.2.1:8022`
and we want to store the data in `/elasticsearch`, we would need to place the
following configuration entries in `elasticsearch.yml`:

```
gateway.type: hdfs
gateway.hdfs.uri: hdfs://10.1.2.1:8022
gateway.hdfs.path: /elasticsearch
```

In addition to the required properties, one can also change the `gateway.hdfs.`
`concurrent_streams` property (which defaults to 5) that controls how many
concurrent streams are used in order to perform the snapshotting operation.

Plugin needed

In order to use the `hdfs` gateway type, one needs to install an appropriate
plugin—the `elasticsearch-hadoop` plugin. You can learn more about
installing plugins in the *Installing plugins* topic at the end of the current chapter.

Amazon s3 gateway

The Amazon s3 gateway type stores all the needed information in the Amazon s3 filesystem. In order to use this type of gateway, one should set the `gateway.type` property to `s3` in the `elasticsearch.yml` configuration file. In addition to that we can set the following properties:

- `gateway.s3.bucket`: This is the name of the s3 bucket
- `gateway.s3.chunk_size`: This is the size of a file chunk (defaults to `100m`)

We also need to add information about the **Amazon Web Services (AWS)** authentication and region. In order to do that one should add the following properties:

- `cloud.aws.access_key`: The AWS access key
- `cloud.aws.secret_key`: The secret key to your AWS
- `cloud.aws.region`: The region (the available values are: `us-east-1`, `us-west-1`, `ap-southeast-1`, and `eu-west-1`)

This is how the full configuration could look (this should be placed in the `elasticsearch.yml` configuration file):

```
gateway.type: s3
gatewat.type.s3.bucket: elasticsearch-cluster-bucket
cloud.aws.access_key: JDSHcnzjhydASDI
cloud.aws.secret_key: NcxnbdJHDSY/r/sdda8273=+_SAD
cloud.aws.region: eu-west-1
```

In addition to the mandatory properties, one can also change the `gateway.s3.concurrent_streams` property (which defaults to `5`) that controls how many concurrent streams are used in order to perform the snapshotting operation.

Plugin needed

In order to use the `s3` gateway type, one needs to install an appropriate plugin — the `cloud-aws` plugin. You can learn more about installing plugins in the *Installing plugins* section at the end of this chapter.

 Please note that from ElasticSearch 0.20, all gateway types, except the local one, are deprecated, which means that they will be removed in the future. ElasticSearch creators plan to introduce a proper backup and restore API that should be available in the near future.

Recovery control

In addition to choosing the gateway type and configuring type-specific properties, ElasticSearch lets us configure when to start the initial recovery process. The recovery is a process of initializing all the shards and replicas, reading all the data from the transaction log, and applying it on the shards. Basically it's a process needed to start ElasticSearch.

For example, let's imagine that we have a cluster that consists of 10 ElasticSearch nodes. We should inform ElasticSearch about the number of nodes by setting the `gateway.expected_nodes` to that value: 10 in our case. We inform ElasticSearch about the number of expected nodes that are eligible to hold the data and be selected as a master. ElasticSearch will start the recovery process immediately if the number of nodes in the cluster is equal to that property.

We would also like to start the recovery after eight nodes for the cluster. In order to do that, we should set the `gateway.recover_after_nodes` property to 8. We could set the value to any value we like. However, we should set it to a value that ensures that the newest version of the cluster state snapshot will be available, which usually means that you should start recovery when most of your nodes are available.

However, there is also one thing—we would like the gateway recovery process to start 10 minutes after the cluster was formed, so we set the `gateway.recover_after_time` property to `10m`. This property tells the gateway module how long to wait with the recovery after the number of nodes specified by the `gateway.recover_after_nodes` property have formed the cluster. We may want to do that because we know that our network is quite slow and we want the nodes' communication to be stable.

The previously mentioned property's values should be set in the `elasticsearch.yml` configuration file. If we wanted to have this value in the mentioned file, we would end up with the following section in the file:

```
gateway.recover_after_nodes: 8
gateway.recover_after_time: 10m
gateway.expected_nodes: 10
```

Node discovery

When you start your ElasticSearch nodes, one of the first things ElasticSearch does is it looks for a master node that has the same cluster name and is visible to them. If a master is found, the node gets joined into an already formed cluster. If no master is found then the node itself is selected as a master. The process of forming a cluster and finding nodes is called **discovery**. The module responsible for discovery has two main purposes—electing a master and discovering new nodes within a cluster. In this section we will discuss how we can configure and tune the discovery module.

Discovery types

By default, without installing additional plugins, ElasticSearch allows us to use **zen discovery**, which provides us with **multicast** and **unicast** discovery. In computer networking terminology, multicast is the delivery of messages to a group of computers in a single transmission. On the other hand we have unicast, which is the transmission of a single message over the network to all possible hosts.

When choosing multicast or unicast, you should be aware if your network can handle multicast messages. If it can, use multicast. If not, use a unicast type of discovery.

 If you are using the Linux operating system and want to check if your network supports multicast, please use the `ifconfig` command for your network interface (usually it will be eth0). If your network supports multicast, you'll see the `MULTICAST` property in response to the above command.

Master node

As we already mentioned, one of the main purposes of discovery is to choose a master node that will be used as a node that will oversee the cluster. The master node is the one that checks all the other nodes to see if they are responsive (the other nodes ping the master too). The master node will also accept new nodes that want to join the cluster. If the master is somehow disconnected from the cluster, the remaining nodes will select a new master from themselves. All these processes are done automatically on the basis of the configuration values we provide.

Configuring master and data nodes

By default, ElasticSearch allows every node to be a master node and a data node. However, in certain situations you may want to have worker nodes, which will only hold the data and the master nodes that will only be used to process requests and manage the cluster.

In order to set the node to only hold data, we need to tell ElasticSearch that we don't want such a node to be a master node. In order to do that, we add the following properties to the `elasticsearch.yml` configuration file:

```
node.master: false
node.data: true
```

In order to set the node not to hold data but only to be a master node, we need to tell ElasticSearch that we don't want such a node to hold data. In order to do that we add the following properties to the `elasticsearch.yml` configuration file:

```
node.master: true
node.data: false
```

Please note that the `node.master` and `node.data` properties are set to `true` by default, but we tend to include them for the sake of configuration clarity.

Master election configuration

Imagine that you have a cluster that is built of 10 nodes. Everything is working fine until one day when your network fails and three of your nodes are disconnected from the cluster, but they still see each other. Because of the zen discovery and master election process, the nodes that got disconnected elect a new master and you end up with two clusters with the same name, with two master nodes. Such a situation is called a **split-brain** and you want to avoid it as much as possible, because you may end up with two clusters that won't join each other after the network (or any other) problems are fixed.

In order to prevent split-brain situations, ElasticSearch provides a `discovery.zen.minimum_master_nodes` property. This property defines a minimum number of master-eligible nodes that should be connected to each other in order to form a cluster. So now let's get back to our cluster; if we were to set the `discovery.zen.minimum_master_nodes` property to 50 percent of the total nodes available plus 1 (which is 6 in our case), we would end up with a single cluster. Why is that? Before the network failure we would have 10 nodes, which is more than six nodes and those nodes would form a cluster. After the disconnection of the three nodes, we would still have the first cluster up and running, but as three is less than six, those three nodes wouldn't be allowed to elect a new master and they would wait for reconnection with the original cluster.

Setting the cluster name

If we don't set the `cluster.name` property in our `elasticsearch.yml` file, ElasticSearch will, by default, use `elasticsearch` as its value. This is not always a good thing and because of that we suggest setting the `cluster.name` property to some other value of your choice. Setting a different `cluster.name` property is also needed if you want to run multiple clusters inside a single network. Otherwise you would end up with nodes belonging to different clusters joining together.

Configuring multicast

Multicast is the default zen discovery method. Apart for the common settings, which we will discuss in a second, there are four properties we can control. They are as follows:

- `discovery.zen.ping.multicast.group`: This is the group address to use for the multicast requests. It defaults to `224.2.2.4`.

- `discovery.zen.ping.multicast.port`: This is the port used for multicast communication. It defaults to `54328`.

- `discovery.zen.ping.multicast.ttl`: This specifies the number of hops for which the multicast request will be considered valid. It defaults to `3` hops.

- `discovery.zen.ping.multicast.address`: This is the address ElasticSearch should bind to. It defaults to the `null` value, which means that ElasticSearch will try to bind to all network interfaces available.

In order to disable multicast, one should add the `multicast.enabled` property to the `elasticsearch.yml` file and set its value to `false`.

Configuring unicast

Going by how unicast works, we need to specify at least a single host that the unicast message should be sent to. In order to do that we should add the `discovery.zen.ping.unicast.hosts` property in our `elasticsearch.yml` configuration file. Basically, we should specify all the hosts that form the cluster in the `discovery.zen.ping.unicast.hosts` property. For example, if we want the hosts `192.168.2.1`, `192.168.2.2` and `192.168.2.3`, for our host we should specify the preceding property in the following way:

```
discovery.zen.ping.unicast.hosts: 192.168.2.1:9300, 192.168.2.2:9300,
192.168.2.3:9300
```

Please note that the hosts are separated with the comma character, and we've specified the port on which we expect unicast messages.

Nodes ping settings

In addition to the settings discussed previously, we can control or alter the default ping configuration. **Ping** is a signal sent between nodes to check if they are running and responsive. The master node pings all the other nodes in the cluster and each one of the other nodes in the cluster pings the master node. The following properties can be set:

- `discovery.zen.fd.ping_interval`: This defaults to `1s` (one second) and specifies how often nodes ping each other
- `discovery.zen.fd.ping_timeout`: This defaults to `30s` (30 seconds) and defines how long a node will wait for the response to its ping message before considering a node as unresponsive
- `discovery.zen.fd.ping_retries`: This defaults to `3` and specifies how many retries should be taken before considering a node as not working

If you experience some problems with your network or you know that your nodes need more time to see the ping response, you can adjust the previously mentioned values to the ones that are good for your deployment.

ElasticSearch plugins

In various places in this book we have used ElasticSearch plugins. You probably remember the additional programming languages used in scripts or rivers and their support for attachments to documents. Let's see how plugins work and how to install them.

ElasticSearch plugins are located in their own subdirectory in the `plugins` directory. If you downloaded a new plugin from a site, you can just create a new directory with the plugin name and unpack that plugin archive to that directory. There is also a more convenient way to install plugins — by using the plugin script. We have used it several times in this book so this is the time to describe this tool.

Installing plugins

By default, plugins are fetched from the `download.elasticsearch.org` site. If the plugin is not available in this location, Maven Central (`http://search.maven.org/`) and Maven Sonatype (`https://repository.sonatype.org/`) repositories are checked. The plugin tool assumes that the given plugin address contains the organization's name followed by the plugin name and version number. Look at the following example:

```
bin/plugin -install elasticsearch/elasticsearch-lang-javascript/1.1.0
```

We want to install an additional language for scripting functionality. We chose version `1.1.0` of this plugin. We can also omit version number, that is, in this case ElasticSearch will try to find a version that equals the version of ElasticSearch or the latest (master) version. This is an example result of this command:

```
-> Installing elasticsearch/elasticsearch-lang-javascript/1.1.0...
Trying http://download.elasticsearch.org/elasticsearch/elasticsearch-
lang-javascript/elasticsearch-lang-javascript-1.1.0.zip...
Downloading ................................................................
.................................................................
.................................................................
.................................................................
.................................................................
.................................................................
.................................................................
.................................................................
.................................................................
.................................................................
............DONE
Installed lang-javascript
```

If you write your own plugin and have no access to the previously mentioned sites, there is no problem. The plugin tool also provides a `-url` option that allows us to set any location for plugins including the local filesystem (using the `file://` prefix).

Removing plugins

Removing a plugin just means removing its directory. You can also do this using the plugin tool; for example:

```
bin/plugin -remove river-mongodb
-> Removing river-mongodb
```

Plugin types

ElasticSearch has two main types of plugins based on their contents: Java plugins and site plugins. ElasticSearch treats site plugins as a file set that should be served by a built-in HTTP server under the `/_plugin/plugin_name/` URL (for example, `/_plugin/bigdesk/`). In addition to that, every plugin without Java content is automatically treated as a site plugin. That's all. From ElasticSearch's point of view, a site plugin doesn't change anything in the ElasticSearch behavior.

Java plugins usually contain JAR files that are scanned for the `es-plugin.properties` file. This file contains information about the main class that should be used by ElasticSearch as an entry point to configure plugins and allow them to extend the ElasticSearch functionality. The Java plugins can contain a site part that will be used by the built-in HTTP server (just like with the site plugins). This part of the plugin needs to be placed in the `_site` directory.

Summary

In this chapter we've looked at cluster health and state monitoring both by using the ElasticSearch API and by using various tools. In addition to that we've learned how to control shard and replica allocation. We've also seen how to use the gateway module to store indices and their metadata, and we've learned what a discovery module is responsible for and how to configure it. Finally we've seen how to install third-party plugins for ElasticSearch. In the next chapter, we will discuss how some common problems can be overcome; for example, we'll see how to scroll through a large number of search results, how to validate your queries, and how to use the query warm up functionality. We'll also see how to control cluster rebalancing.

8

Dealing with Problems

In the previous chapter, we looked at cluster health and state monitoring possibilities by using ElasticSearch API as well as third-party tools. We learned what the discovery module is and how to configure it. In addition to that, we learned how to control shard and replica allocation and how to install additional plugins to our ElasticSearch instances. We also saw what each gateway module is responsible for and which configuration options we can use.

In this chapter, we will take a look at how to efficiently fetch a large amount of data from ElasticSearch. We will discuss the ability to control cluster shard rebalancing and how to validate our ElasticSearch queries. In addition to that, we will see how to use the new warming up functionality to improve the performance of our queries. By the end of this chapter, you will have learned the following:

- How to use scrolling for fetching a large number of results efficiently
- How to control cluster rebalancing
- How to validate your queries
- How to use the warming up functionality

Why is the result on later pages slow

Let's imagine that we have an index with several millions of documents. We already know how to build our query, when to use filters, and so on. But looking at query logs, we see that particular kinds of queries are significantly slower than the other ones. These queries may be using paging. The `from` parameter indicates that the offsets have large values. From the application side, this can mean that users go through an enormous number of results. Often this doesn't make sense—if a user doesn't find desirable results on first few pages, he/she gives up. Because this particular activity can mean something bad (possible data theft), many applications limit paging to dozens of pages. In our case, we assume that this is a different scenario and we have to provide this functionality.

What is the problem?

When ElasticSearch generates a response, it must determine the order of documents forming the result. If we are on the first page, this is not a big problem. ElasticSearch just finds the set of documents and collects the first ones, let's say 20 documents. But if we are on the tenth page, ElasticSearch has to take all the documents for pages 1 to 10 and then discard the ones that are on pages 1 to 9. The problem is not ElasticSearch-specific; a similar situation can be found in database systems, for example.

Scrolling to the rescue

The solution is simple. Since ElasticSearch has to do some operation (determine documents for previous pages) for each request, we can ask it to store this information for the subsequent queries. The drawback is that we cannot store this information forever due to limited resources. ElasticSearch assumes that we can declare how long we need this information to be available. Let's see how it works in practice. First of all, we query ElasticSearch as we usually do, but in addition to all the usual parameters, we add one more—the parameter with information for which we want to use scrolling and how long we suggest that ElasticSearch should keep the information about results:

```
curl 'localhost:9200/library/_search?pretty&scroll=5m' -d @query.json
```

The content of this query is irrelevant. The important thing is how ElasticSearch modifies the reply. Look at the first few lines of the response returned by ElasticSearch:

```
{
  "_scroll_id" :
  "cXVlcnlUaGVuRmV0Y2g7NTsxMDI6dklNMlkzTG1RTDJ2b25oTDNENmJzZzsxMD
  U6dklNMlkzTG1RTDJ2b25oTDNENmJzZzsxMDQ6dklNMlkzTG1RTDJ2b25oTDNEN
  mJzZzsxMDE6dklNMlkzTG1RTDJ2b25oTDNENmJzZzsxMDM6dklNMlkzTG1RTDJ
  2b25oTDNENmJzZzswOw==",
  "took" : 9,
  "timed_out" : false,
  "_shards" : {
    "total" : 5,
    "successful" : 5,
    "failed" : 0
  },
  "hits" : {
    "total" : 1341211,
    ...
```

The new part is `_scroll_id`. This is a handle that we will use in the next queries. ElasticSearch has a special endpoint for this. Let's look at the following example:

```
curl -XGET 'localhost:9200/_search/scroll?scroll=5m&pretty&scroll_
id=cXVlcnlUaGVuRmV0Y2g7NTsxMjg6dklNlkzTG1RTDJ2b25oTDNENmJzZZsxMjk6
dklNMlkzTG1RTDJ2b25oTDNENmJzZZsxMzA6dklNMlkzTG1RTDJ2b25oTDNENmJzZ
zsxMjc6dklNMlkzTG1RTDJ2b25oTDNENmJzZZsxMjY6dklNMlkzTG1RTDJ2b25oT
DNENmJzZZswOw=='
```

Now, every call to this endpoint with `scroll_id` returns the next page of results. Remember that this handle is only valid until the defined time-out. After this time, you can see an error response similar to the following:

```
{
  "_scroll_id" :
  "cXVlcnlUaGVuRmV0Y2g7NTsxMjg6dklNMlkzTG1RTDJ2b25oTDNENmJzZZsxMj
  k6dklNMlkzTG1RTDJ2b25oTDNENmJzZZsxMzA6dklNMlkzTG1RTDJ2b25oTDNEN
  mJzZZsxMjc6dklNMlkzTG1RTDJ2b25oTDNENmJzZZsxMjY6dklNMlkzTG1RTDJ2
  b25oTDNENmJzZZswOw==",
  "took" : 3,
  "timed_out" : false,
  "_shards" : {
    "total" : 5,
    "successful" : 0,
    "failed" : 5,
    "failures" : [ {
      "status" : 500,
      "reason" : "SearchContextMissingException[No search context
      found for id [128]]"
    }, {
      "status" : 500,
      "reason" : "SearchContextMissingException[No search context
      found for id [126]]"
    }, {
      "status" : 500,
      "reason" : "SearchContextMissingException[No search context
      found for id [127]]"
    }, {
      "status" : 500,
      "reason" : "SearchContextMissingException[No search context
      found for id [130]]"
    }, {
```

```
        "status" : 500,
        "reason" : "SearchContextMissingException[No search context
        found for id [129]]"
      } ]
    },
    "hits" : {
      "total" : 0,
      "max_score" : 0.0,
      "hits" : [ ]
    }
  }
}
```

As you may think, this solution is not ideal and it is not suited when there are many requests to random pages of various results or time between requests is difficult to determine. But you can use this with success, for example, when implementing data transfer between several systems.

Controlling cluster rebalancing

By default, ElasticSearch tries to keep the shards and their replicas evenly balanced across the cluster. Such behavior is good in most cases, but there are times where we want to control that behavior. In *Chapter 7, Administrating Your Cluster*, we discussed how to take total control over how shards and replicas are distributed. In this section, we will look at how to avoid cluster rebalance and how to control the behavior of this process in depth.

Imagine a situation where you know that your network can handle a very high amount of traffic or the opposite to that—your network is used extensively and you want to avoid too much stress on it. The other example is that you may want to decrease the pressure that is put on your I/O subsystem after a full-cluster restart and you want to have less shards and replicas being initialized at the same time. These are only two examples where rebalance control may be handy.

What is rebalancing?

Rebalancing is the process of moving shards between different nodes in our cluster. As we have already mentioned, it's fine in most situations, but sometimes you may want to completely avoid that. For example, if we define how our shards are placed and we want to keep it that way, we want to avoid rebalancing. However, ElasticSearch, by default, will try to rebalance the cluster whenever the cluster state changes and ElasticSearch thinks rebalancing is needed. This may happen, for example, after each full-cluster restart that can happen during upgrade, plugin installation, or after node failure.

When is the cluster ready?

We already know that our indices can be built of shards and replicas. Primary shards or just shards are the ones that are used when new documents are indexed, there is an update, or there is a delete—or just in case of any index change. We also have replicas, which get the data from the primary shards.

You can think of the cluster as being ready to use when all primary shards are assigned to their nodes in your cluster—as soon as the yellow health state is achieved. However, ElasticSearch may still initialize other shards—the replicas. But you can use your cluster and be sure that you can search your whole data set and you can send index change commands. Then those will be processed properly.

The cluster rebalancing settings

ElasticSearch lets us control the rebalancing process with the use of a few properties that can be set in the `elasticsearch.yml` file or by using ElasticSearch REST API. Since the first method is very simple, let's skip discussing it and look at the second method—the one using the REST API.

In order to set one of the properties described later, we need to use the HTTP PUT method and send a proper request to the `_cluster/settings` URI. However, we have two options—transient and permanent property settings.

The first one—the transient—will set the property only till the first restart. In order to do that, we send the following command:

```
curl -XPUT 'localhost:9200/_cluster/settings' -d '{
  "transient" : {
    "PROPERTY_NAME" : "PROPERTY_VALUE"
  }
}'
```

As you can see, in the preceding command, we used the object named `transient` and we added our property definition there. This means that the property will be valid only until the next restart.

If we want our property setting to persist between restarts, instead of using the object named `transient`, we will use one named `persistent`. So, the sample command will be as follows:

```
curl -XPUT 'localho  :9200/_cluster/settings' -d '{
  "persistent" : {
    "PROPERTY_NAME" : "PROPERTY_VALUE"
  }
}'
```

And now let's look at what ElasticSearch allows us to control.

Controlling when rebalancing will start

`cluster.routing.allocation.allow_rebalance` allows us to specify when rebalancing will start. This property can take the following values:

- `always`: Rebalancing will be started as soon as it's needed
- `indices_primaries_active`: Rebalancing will be started when all primary shards are initialized
- `indices_all_active`: The default one, rebalancing will be started when all shards and replicas are initialized

Please note that the described property can't be changed during runtime, so you need to set it in the configuration file.

Controlling the number of shards being moved between nodes concurrently

`cluster.routing.allocation.cluster_concurrent_rebalance` allows us to specify how many shards can be moved between nodes at once in the whole cluster. If you have cluster that is built of many nodes, you can increase this value. This value defaults to 2.

Controlling the number of shards initialized concurrently on a single node

The `cluster.routing.allocation.node_concurrent_recoveries` property lets us set how many shards ElasticSearch may initialize on a single node at once. Please note that the shard recovery process is very I/O intensive, so you'll probably want to avoid too many shards being recovered concurrently. This value defaults to the same value as the previous one, 2.

Controlling the number of primary shards initialized concurrently on a single node

The `cluster.routing.allocation.node_initial_primaries_recoveries` property lets us control how many primary shards are allowed to be concurrently initialized on a node.

Disabling the allocation of shards and replicas

When the `cluster.routing.allocation.disable_allocation` property is set to `true`, it totally disables the allocation of primary shards and replicas. This setting only makes sense when using the REST API, because you probably don't want to start ElasticSearch and do not have shards assigned to nodes.

Disabling the allocation of replicas

When the `cluster.routing.allocation.disable_replica_allocation` property is set to `true`, it totally disables the allocation of shards and replicas. This can come in handy in situations where you want to operate only on primary shards and don't want ElasticSearch to allocate replicas to nodes.

> If you seek more information about shard allocation and the initial shard allocation process, please refer to the *Your ElasticSearch time machine* and *Controlling shard and replica allocation* sections in *Chapter 7, Administrating Your Cluster.*

Validating your queries

Do you remember our example with the percolator in *Chapter 6, Beyond Searching*? The assumption was that the user could generate a query, probably by using some kind of wizard, which was stored in ElasticSearch and used for matching documents. You already know that ElasticSearch has many possibilities and many kinds of queries, and sometimes it is difficult to tell if a query is correct or not. To help with this, ElasticSearch exposes the Validate API.

How to use the Validate API

The Validate API is simple. Instead of sending the query to the _search endpoint, we send it to the _validate/query endpoint. And that's it. Let's look again at a query that we are already familiar with:

```
{
  "bool" : {
    "must" : {
      "term" : {
        "title" : "crime"
      }
    },
    "should" : {
      "range : {
        "year" : {
          "from" : 1900,
          "to" : 2000
        }
      }
    },
    "must_not" : {
      "term" : {
        "otitle" : "nothing"
      }
    }
  }
}
```

This query was used twice in this book. Note that for validation we have omitted the query attribute and sent only the enclosed object. We know that everything is right with the query, but let's check it with the following command:

```
curl -XGET 'localhost:9200/library/_validate/query?pretty' -d @query.json
```

And of course, everything should be fine. So, let's look at the response from ElasticSearch:

```
{
  "valid" : false,
  "_shards" : {
    "total" : 1,
    "successful" : 1,
    "failed" : 0
  }
}
```

Look at the `valid` attribute. It is set to `false`. Something went wrong. Let's execute the query validation once again with the `explain` parameter added in the query:

```
curl -XGET 'localhost:9200/library/_validate/query?pretty&explain'
--data-binary @query.json
```

Now the result returned from ElasticSearch is more verbose:

```
{
  "valid" : false,
  "_shards" : {
    "total" : 1,
    "successful" : 1,
    "failed" : 0
  },
  "explanations" : [ {
    "index" : "library",
    "valid" : false,
    "error" : "org.elasticsearch.index.query.QueryParsingException:
[library] Failed to parse; org.elasticsearch.common.jackson.core.
JsonParseException: Illegal unquoted character ((CTRL-CHAR, code 10)):
has to be escaped using backslash to be included in name\n at [Source:
[B@61e918c2; line: 9, column: 16]"
  } ]
}
```

Now everything is clear. In our example, we have improperly quoted the `range` attribute.

 You may be wondering why in our URL query we used the `--data-binary` parameter. This parameter properly preserves the new line character when sending a query to ElasticSearch. This means that the line and column number will be intact and it's easier to find errors. In the other cases, the `-d` parameter is more convenient, because it's shorter.

The Validate API can also detect other errors, for example, incorrect format of a number or other mapping-related issues. Unfortunately, for our application, it is not easy to detect what the problem is because of lack of structure in the error messages.

Warming up

Sometimes, there may be a need to prepare ElasticSearch to handle your queries. Maybe it's because you rely heavily on the field data cache and you want it to be loaded before your production queries arrive or maybe you want to warm up your operating system's I/O cache. Whatever the reason is, ElasticSearch allows us to define the warming queries for our types and indices.

Defining a new warming query

A warming query is nothing more than the usual query stored in a special index in ElasticSearch called `_warmer`. Let's assume we have the following query that we want to use for warming up:

```
{
  "query" : {
    "match_all" : {}
  },
  "facets" : {
    "warming_facet" : {
      "terms" : {
        "field" : "tags"
      }
    }
  }
}
```

In order to store the preceding query as a warming query for our `library` index, we will run the following command:

```
curl -XPUT 'localhost:9200/library/_warmer/tags_warming_query' -d '{
  "query" : {
    "match_all" : {}
  },
  "facets" : {
    "warming_facet" : {
      "terms" : {
        "field" : "tags"
      }
    }
  }
}'
```

The preceding command will register our query as a warming query with the name `tags_warming_query`. You can have multiple warming queries for your index, but each of those queries needs to have a unique name.

We can also define warming queries not only for the whole index, but also for the specific types in it. For example, if we want to store our previously shown query as the warming query only for the `book` type in the `library` index, we will run the preceding command not to the `/library/_warmer` URI, but to the `/library/book/_warmer` one, so the whole command will be as follows:

```
curl -XPUT 'localhost:9200/library/book/_warmer/tags_warming_query' -d '{
  "query" : {
    "match_all" : {}
  },
  "facets" : {
    "warming_facet" : {
      "terms" : {
        "field" : "tags"
      }
    }
  }
}'
```

After adding a warming query, before ElasticSearch allows a new segment to be searched on, it will be warmed up by running the defined warming queries on that segment. This allows ElasticSearch and the operating system to cache data and thus speed up searching.

> If you are not familiar with the Apache Lucene library, you may not know what a segment is. Lucene divides the index into parts called `segments`, which once written can't be changed. Every new commit operation creates a new segment (which is eventually merged if the number of segments is too high), which Lucene uses for search.

Retrieving defined warming queries

In order to get a specific warming query for our index, we just need to know its name. For example, if we want to get the warming query named `tags_warming_query` for our `library` index, we will run the following command:

```
curl -XGET 'localhost:9200/library/_warmer/tags_warming_query?pretty=true'
```

And the result returned by ElasticSearch will be as follows (note that we've used the `pretty=true` parameter to make the response easier to read):

```
{
    "library" : {
        "warmers" : {
            "tags_warming_query" : {
                "types" : [ ],
                "source" : {
                    "query" : {
                        "match_all" : { }
                    },
                    "facets" : {
                        "warming_facet" : {
                            "terms" : {
                                "field" : "tags"
                            }
                        }
                    }
                }
            }
        }
    }
}
```

We can also get all the warming queries for the index and type by using the following command:

```
curl -XGET 'localhost:9200/library/_warmer'
```

We can also get all the warming queries for a specific type—for example, if we want to get all the warming queries for the `library` index and the `book` type, we will run the following query:

```
curl -XGET 'localhost:9200/library/book/_warmer'
```

And finally, we can also get all the warming queries that start with a given prefix. For example, if we want to get all the warming queries for the `library` index that start with the `tags` prefix, we will run the following command:

```
curl -XGET 'localhost:9200/library/_warmer/tags*'
```

Deleting a warming query

Deleting a warming query is very similar to getting one, but we just need to use the DELETE HTTP method. Let's look at how to delete a warming query.

In order to delete a specific warming query from our index, we just need to know its name. For example, if we want to delete the warming query named `tags_warming_query` for our `library` index, we will run the following command:

```
curl -XDELETE 'localhost:9200/library/_warmer/tags_warming_query'
```

We can also delete all the warming queries for the index by using the following command:

```
curl -XDELETE 'localhost:9200/library/_warmer'
```

And finally, we can also remove all the warming queries that start with a given prefix. For example, if we want to remove all the warming queries for the `library` index that start with the `tags` prefix, we will run the following command:

```
curl -XDELETE 'localhost:9200/library/_warmer/tags*'
```

Disabling the warming up functionality

In order to disable the warming queries totally, but save them in the `_warmer` index, one should set the `index.warmer.enabled` configuration property to `false` (setting this property to `true` will result in enabling the warming up functionality). This setting can be either put into the `elasticsearch.yml` file or just set using the REST API on a live cluster.

For example, if we want to disable the warming up functionality for the `library` index, we will run the following command:

```
curl -XPUT 'http://localhost:9200/library/_settings' -d '{
  "index.warmer.enabled" : false
}'
```

Which queries to choose

You may ask which queries should be used as the warming queries—typically, you'll want to choose the ones that are expensive to execute and ones that require caches to be populated—so you'll probably want to choose the queries that include faceting and sorting, based on the fields in your index. Those are the usual candidates. However, you may also choose other queries by looking at the logs and finding where your performance is not as great as you want it to be. Such queries may also be perfect candidates for warming up.

For example, let's say that we have the following logging configuration set in the `elasticsearch.yml` file:

```
index.search.slowlog.threshold.query.warn: 10s
index.search.slowlog.threshold.query.info: 5s
index.search.slowlog.threshold.query.debug: 2s
index.search.slowlog.threshold.query.trace: 1s
```

And we have the following logging level set in the `logging.yml` configuration file:

```
logger:
  index.search.slowlog: TRACE, index_search_slow_log_file
```

Notice that the `index.search.slowlog.threshold.query.trace` property is set to `1s` and the `index.search.slowlog` logging level is set to `TRACE`. That means whenever a query is executed for more than one second (on a shard, not in total), it will be logged into the slow log file (the name of which is specified by the `index_search_slow_log_file` configuration section of the `logging.yml` configuration file). For example, the following can be found in a slow log file:

```
[2013-01-24 13:33:05,518][TRACE][index.search.slowlog.query] [Local
test] [library][1] took[1400.7ms], took_millis[1400], search_
type[QUERY_THEN_FETCH], total_shards[32], source[{"query":{"match_
all":{}}}], extra_source[]
```

As you can see, in the preceding log line, we have the query time, search type, and the query source itself, which shows us the executed query.

Of course, the values can be different in your configuration, but the slow log can be a valuable source of queries that are running too long and may need to have some warm up defined—maybe those are parent-child queries and need some identifiers fetched to perform better or maybe you are using a filter that is expensive when executing for the first time?

There is one thing you should remember; don't overload your ElasticSearch cluster with too many warming queries, because you may end up spending too much time warming up instead of processing your production queries.

Summary

In this chapter, we looked at the scrolling functionality and how it can help to go through many pages of query results efficiently. We also learned how to control cluster rebalancing and how to validate our queries before they are executed. In addition to that we learned how we can use the warming up functionality and how it can help us.

So, now you have reached the end of the book. We hope that it was a nice reading experience and that you found the book interesting. We also hope that you have learned something from this book and now you will find it easier to use ElasticSearch every day. As the authors of this book, but also ElasticSearch users, we tried to bring you, our readers, the best reading experience we could. In addition to that, ElasticSearch is not only user friendly, but also provides a large number of configuration options, querying possibilities, and so on. Due to that, we had to choose which functionality to describe in greater details, which should be only mentioned, and which would have to be totally skipped. We hope that our choice was good.

One last thing—please remember that ElasticSearch is constantly evolving. When writing this book, the latest stable release was the 0.20.x one; however, even back then we knew that new features are coming, such as the new Suggest API. Be sure to check www.elasticsearch.org periodically for the release notes for new versions of ElasticSearch, if you want to be up to date with the new features being added.

Index

Symbols

A

B

default sorting 105
dynamic criteria 108
missing fields behavior, specifying 107
required fields, selecting 106, 107
date histogram 225
directory structure
about 10
bin 10
config 10
lib 10
discovery 264
discovery.zen.ping.unicast.hosts property 266
document 8
document search
about 157
example data 234
field, analyzing 158, 159
query 160, 161
similar documents, finding 235, 236
document type 9
dynamic mappings
about 35, 38
pattern, defining 38, 39
type determining mechanism 35-37

E

ElasticSearch
about 7, 8
cluster 9
configuring 11
data, storing 16
document 8
document type 9
index 8
installing 10
node 9
querying 56
replica 9
running 12-14
running, as system service 15
shard 9
shutting down 14
span queries 184
elasticsearch-head 257

elasticsearch-paramedic 258
ElasticSearch plugins
about 267
installing 268
removing 268
types 269
ElasticSearch querying
about 56
fields, selecting 61, 62
paging 59
partial fields 63
preference request parameter, setting 67
result size 59
right search type, choosing 66
score, limiting 60, 61
scripts fields, using 63
simple query 57, 58
version, returning 59
enabled property 129
equivalent synonyms 176
exist filter 90
explicit synonyms 176

F

faceting
about 215
aggregated data, calculating 224
calculation scope 230
document structure 216
filter 219
histogram 224
query 218
range 222, 223
results, filtering 230
returned results 216, 217
spatial 229
statistical 226, 227
terms 220, 221
terms_stats faceting 227, 228
faceting calculation
memory consideration 234
on nested documents 231
on query matched nested documents 232
scope 230
field data cache 234

index_routing property 50
index structure
  _all field 125
  _boost field 127, 128
  extending, additional internal information
      used 123
  identifier field 123, 124
  _index field 128
  modifying, update API used 196
  _size field 128
  _source field 126
  _timestamp field 129
  _ttl field 130, 131
  _type field 125
index structure modification update API
      used
  about 196
  fields, modifying 197, 198
  mapping 196
  new field, adding 196, 197
index-time boosting
  boosting, defining in mapping 173
  document boosting, defining 173
  field boosting, defining 172
  using 172
indices query 101
indices segments API 249
indices stats API
  about 244
  data manipulation 246
  docs 245
  store 245
in_order parameter 188

J

JavaScript Object Notation (JSON) 13

L

Language Detection 179
limit filter 92
local gateway 260
Logstash 47
lucene query syntax 74

M

manual index creation
  document types 21
  index 21
  index, manipulating 21, 22
  schema mapping 22
mappings
  about 54, 55, 119, 120
  data 56
  final mappings 120
  sending, to ElasticSearch 121, 122
master node
  about 264
  configuring 264, 265
  master election configuration 265
match all query 81
match phrase prefix query 71
match query
  about 69
  Boolean match query 70
  match phrase prefix query 71
  multi match query 72
  phrase match query 71
max_gram tokenizer 142
min_gram tokenizer 142
missing filter 90
more like this field query 84
more like this query
  about 84
  parameters 83
multivalued 8
MVEL 110

N

named filter 95-97
nested objects
  using 198-201
newScript() method 113
node 9
node discovery
  about 264
  cluster name, setting 266
  master node 264
  multicast, configuring 266

result delay
   about 271
   issue 272
   issue, solving 272-274
river
   about 207
   configuring 207-210
   data, fetching from 207
   installing 207-210
routing
   about 41, 44
   fields 45, 46
   indexing 42
   parameters 45
   searching 42, 43
routing parameter 46
run() method 113

S

SaaS 259
schema mapping
   analyzers, using 29
   core types 24
   document source, storing 33
   fields 24, 34
   multi fields 28
   type definition 23, 24
score modification
   constant score query 165
   custom boost factor query 166
   custom filters score query 168-172
   custom score query 167, 168
   query, boosting 166
script filter 91
scripts
   about 109
   library 111
   MVEL 110
   native code 112, 113, 114
   objects 109
   other languages 111
scripts fields
   about 63, 64
   parameters, passing to 65

searching 54
search_routing attribute 51
search_routing property 50
segments 245
shards
   about 242, 9
   allocating 254
   allocation, canceling 254
   count 253
   moving manually 253
   multiple commands, including in HTTP
      request 255
   replicas per node 253
shared filesystem gateway 260, 261
Software as a Service. *See* SaaS
span 185
span first query 185, 186, 187
span near query 188, 189
span not query 191, 192
span or query 189, 190
span queries
   about 184, 185
   span first query 186, 187
   span near query 188, 189
   span not query 191, 192
   span or query 189, 190
   span term query 185, 186
split-brain 265
SPM for ElasticSearch
   about 259
   dashboard 259
statistical faceting 226, 227
status API 247
string-based fields 26
synonym filter 174
synonym rules
   Apache Solr synonyms, using 176
   WordNet synonyms, using 177
synonyms
   about 174
   in files 175
   in mapping 175
synonyms_path property 175

Thank you for buying
ElasticSearch Server

About Packt Publishing

Packt, pronounced 'packed', published its first book "*Mastering phpMyAdmin for Effective MySQL Management*" in April 2004 and subsequently continued to specialize in publishing highly focused books on specific technologies and solutions.

Our books and publications share the experiences of your fellow IT professionals in adapting and customizing today's systems, applications, and frameworks. Our solution based books give you the knowledge and power to customize the software and technologies you're using to get the job done. Packt books are more specific and less general than the IT books you have seen in the past. Our unique business model allows us to bring you more focused information, giving you more of what you need to know, and less of what you don't.

Packt is a modern, yet unique publishing company, which focuses on producing quality, cutting-edge books for communities of developers, administrators, and newbies alike. For more information, please visit our website: www.packtpub.com.

About Packt Open Source

In 2010, Packt launched two new brands, Packt Open Source and Packt Enterprise, in order to continue its focus on specialization. This book is part of the Packt Open Source brand, home to books published on software built around Open Source licences, and offering information to anybody from advanced developers to budding web designers. The Open Source brand also runs Packt's Open Source Royalty Scheme, by which Packt gives a royalty to each Open Source project about whose software a book is sold.

Writing for Packt

We welcome all inquiries from people who are interested in authoring. Book proposals should be sent to author@packtpub.com. If your book idea is still at an early stage and you would like to discuss it first before writing a formal book proposal, contact us; one of our commissioning editors will get in touch with you.

We're not just looking for published authors; if you have strong technical skills but no writing experience, our experienced editors can help you develop a writing career, or simply get some additional reward for your expertise.

Apache Solr 4 Cookbook

ISBN: 978-1-782161-32-5   Paperback: 328 pages

Over 100 recipes to make Apache Solr faster, more reliable, and return better results

1. Learn how to make Apache Solr search faster, more complete, and comprehensively scalable

2. Solve performance, setup, configuration, analysis, and query problems in no time

3. Get to grips with, and master, the new exciting features of Apache Solr 4

Apache Solr 3 Enterprise Search Server

ISBN: 978-1-849516-06-8   Paperback: 418 pages

Enhance your search with faceted navigation, result highlighting, relevancy ranked sorting, and more

1. Comprehensive information on Apache Solr 3 with examples and tips so you can focus on the important parts

2. Integration examples with databases, web-crawlers, XSLT, Java & embedded-Solr, PHP & Drupal, JavaScript, Ruby frameworks

3. Advice on data modeling, deployment considerations to include security, logging, and monitoring, and advice on scaling Solr and measuring performance

Please check **www.PacktPub.com** for information on our titles

Hadoop Real World Solutions Cookbook

ISBN: 978-1-849519-12-0   Paperback: 325 pages

Realistic, simple code examples to solve problems at scale with Hadoop and related technologies

1. Solutions to common problems when working in the Hadoop environment

2. Recipes for (un)loading data, analytics, and troubleshooting

3. In depth code examples demonstrating various analytic models, analytic solutions, and common best practices

Cassandra High Performance Cookbook

ISBN: 978-1-849515-12-2   Paperback: 310 pages

Over 150 recipes to design and optimize large-scale Apache Cassandra deployments

1. Get the best out of Cassandra using this efficient recipe bank

2. Configure and tune Cassandra components to enhance performance

3. Deploy Cassandra in various environments and monitor its performance

Printed in Great Britain
by Amazon.co.uk, Ltd.,
Marston Gate.